Australian Patriography

Anthem Australian Humanities Research Series

The **Anthem Australian Humanities Research Series** incorporates a broad range of titles on the past, present and future of Australia, comprising an excellent collection of interdisciplinary academic texts. The series aims to promote the most challenging and original work being undertaken in the field by both Australian and non-Australian scholars on Australian culture, society, politics, history and literature. Some of the most innovative research in both the traditional and new humanities today is being done by scholars in the Australian humanities, including literature, history, book history, print culture, cinema, new media and digital cultures, gender studies, cultural studies and indigenous studies.

Series Editor

Robert Dixon – University of Sydney, Australia

Editorial Board

Alison Bashford – University of Sydney, Australia
Jill Bennett – University of New South Wales, Australia
Nicholas Birns – Eugene Lang College of the New School, USA
Frances Bonner – University of Queensland, Australia
David Carter – University of Queensland, Australia
Barbara Creed – University of Melbourne, Australia
Martin Crotty – University of Queensland, Australia
Paul Eggert – University of New South Wales, Australia
John Frow – University of Melbourne, Australia
Ken Gelder – University of Melbourne, Australia
Helen Gilbert – Royal Holloway, University of London, UK
Gerard Goggin – University of Sydney, Australia
Bridget Griffen-Foley – Macquarie University, Australia
Ian Henderson – King's College London, UK
Jeanette Hoorn – University of Melbourne, Australia
Graham Huggan – University of Leeds, UK
Catharine Lumby – Macquarie University, Australia
Martyn Lyons – University of New South Wales, Australia
Andrew L. McCann – Dartmouth College, USA
Ian McLean – University of Wollongong, Australia
Philip Mead – University of Western Australia, Australia
Meaghan Morris – University of Sydney, Australia
Stephen Muecke – University of New South Wales, Australia
Deb Verhoeven – Deakin University, Australia
Gillian Whitlock – University of Queensland, Australia

Australian Patriography

How Sons Write Fathers in Contemporary Life Writing

Stephen Mansfield

ANTHEM PRESS
LONDON · NEW YORK · DELHI

Anthem Press
An imprint of Wimbledon Publishing Company
www.anthempress.com

This edition first published in UK and USA 2014
by ANTHEM PRESS
75–76 Blackfriars Road, London SE1 8HA, UK
or PO Box 9779, London SW19 7ZG, UK
and
244 Madison Ave. #116, New York, NY 10016, USA

First published in hardback by Anthem Press in 2013

Copyright © Stephen Mansfield 2014

The author asserts the moral right to be identified as the author of this work.

All rights reserved. Without limiting the rights under copyright reserved above, no part of this publication may be reproduced, stored or introduced into a retrieval system, or transmitted, in any form or by any means (electronic, mechanical, photocopying, recording or otherwise), without the prior written permission of both the copyright owner and the above publisher of this book.

British Library Cataloguing-in-Publication Data
A catalogue record for this book is available from the British Library.

Library of Congress Cataloging-in-Publication Data
The Library of Congress has catalogued the hardcover edition as follows:
Mansfield, Stephen, 1977–
Australian patriography : how sons write fathers in contemporary life writing / Stephen Mansfield.
   pages cm
Includes bibliographical references and index.
ISBN 978-0-85728-330-6 (hardback : alk. paper)
1. Australian literature–History and criticism. 2. Fathers in literature. 3. Fathers and sons–Australia. 4. Autobiography–Authorship. I. Title.
PR9605.5.F38M36 2013
820.9'994–dc23
2013009373

ISBN-13: 978 1 78308 338 1 (Pbk)
ISBN-10: 1 78308 338 7 (Pbk)

This title is also available as an ebook.

CONTENTS

Acknowledgements   vii

List of Illustrations   ix

Introduction   Writing Patrimony: The Son's Book of the Father as a Sub-genre   1

Part I: Challenging Authority

Chapter One   'The Paradigm Case': Contesting the Father in Edmund Gosse's *Father and Son: A Study of Two Temperaments*   17

Chapter Two   'An Indubitable Australian': Renouncing the Father in Hal Porter's *The Watcher on the Cast-Iron Balcony*   39

Part II: Memorialising Self-Denial

Chapter Three   'Words to Keep Fully Amongst Us': Honouring the Father in Raimond Gaita's *Romulus, My Father*   61

Chapter Four   'I Really Was the Son of Such a Man': Replacing the Father in Richard Freadman's *Shadow of Doubt: My Father and Myself*   87

Part III: Performing Masculinity

Chapter Five   A Speaking Subject/A Watching Object: Addressing the Father in Peter Rose's *Rose Boys*   115

Chapter Six   Choosing Patrimony: Performing for the Father in John Hughes's *The Idea of Home*   139

Chapter Seven   'Neither to Vindicate nor to Vilify': Becoming the Father in Robert Gray's *The Land I Came Through Last*   161

Conclusion   The Turn to the Father in Autobiography   191

Bibliography   201

Index   209

ACKNOWLEDGEMENTS

No one is ever able absolutely to erase himself from his criticism, but in researching autobiography the posture of critical distance seems especially fraught, particularly for one examining family memoirs. This book is not ficto-critical, nor will the critic's life story intrude upon his examination of the lives of others. Nevertheless, I am a son and, in the course of writing this book, have become a father.

Therefore I wish to acknowledge my mother and father, Helen and David Mansfield, and my sisters, Jenny Franke and Kimberly Reid, for shaping my understanding of what it means to be a son and a brother. My daughter Patience was born early in my research, and her demand for care and reflexive love have given me a glimpse of the joy and anxiety of being a father. My twin sons Asher and Lucas were born towards the end of this project, amplifying this joy and anxiety in equal measure, and causing a friend to remark, 'that will teach you for writing a book about patrimony'.

Most importantly, my wife Julia Shearsby commands my immense gratitude for the innumerable ways she has supported me. Her encouragement led me to take on this project and to see it to its conclusion. And she has almost finished Robert Gray's autobiography.

Bernadette Brennan has contributed much to this book, both during our many hours of discussion and in her insightful critique of my writing. Most of all, she has been encouragement itself, and without her I do not think this book would exist. Discussions with Noel Rowe when I was just starting out also contributed much to my desire to research autobiography.

My colleague Jacinta van den Berg served as a wonderful sounding board during the planning stage of my book, as well as providing much needed advice during the final hours. Greg McLaren offered helpful feedback on an early draft of Chapter Seven. Alex Segal did likewise with Chapter Three. I thank them for their insights. John Hughes and Peter Rose were extremely generous with their time. Their willingness to be interviewed has contributed much to my analysis of their writing.

Earlier versions of two chapters have appeared elsewhere: Chapter Five in *Life Writing* 9.12 (2012), and Chapter Six in *Antipodes* 26.2 (2012).

LIST OF ILLUSTRATIONS

1.	The author, with his father David Mansfield and grandfather Alfred Mansfield, 1992.	vi
2.	Paul Freadman, circa 1935.	106
3.	Bob Rose and Robert Rose, circa 1954.	117

All images reproduced with permission.

Introduction

WRITING PATRIMONY: THE SON'S BOOK OF THE FATHER AS A SUB-GENRE

There was once a father and a son. A son is like a mirror in which the father beholds himself, and for the son the father too is like a mirror in which he beholds himself in the time to come. [...] And the father believed that he was to blame for the son's melancholy, and the son believed that he was the occasion of the father's sorrow – but they never exchanged a word on the subject.

   Then the father died, and the son saw much, experienced much, and was tried in manifold temptations; but infinitely inventive as love is, longing and the sense of loss taught him, not indeed to wrest from the silence of eternity a communication, but to imitate the father's voice so perfectly that he was content with the likeness. So he did not look at himself in the mirror [...] for the mirror was no longer there; but in loneliness he comforted himself by hearing the father's voice [...] For the father was the only one who had understood him, and yet he did not know in fact whether he had understood him.

—Søren Kierkegaard, *The Parables of Kierkegaard*

A Modern Parable

A man has a son. Overjoyed at his son's arrival, this father goes to work as usual. This is Australia in the 1950s, after all, before the era of shared care and involved dads. Maternity wards were not places for men.

   As his son grows, this father goes about his business. He works hard, comes home to eat and sleep, to snore most likely, and rises to do it all again. He leaves early and arrives home late. And on the weekend there is golf or some other manly pursuit that keeps him out of the house, and then drinking with the other men at the pub. To his young family he is an itinerant. They remember strong arms and moments of tenderness, but mostly a father who was half there, his focus and intent on the world outside.

And the father? He worries for his son; he occasionally feels mildly embarrassed about some aspect of his young boy's demeanour, and tries to teach him what he can about staying out of trouble in the world of men. Even more occasionally he is knocked sideways by a gesture or a minor achievement of his progeny: a mixture of simple pride and something like self-recognition – though he would never call it that. In his weaker moments he is unnecessarily stern, competitive. Perhaps he envies his son his place in his mother's heart. But for the most part he is a good father; as good a father as anyone expects him to be.

Then this father gets old and frail, and eventually he dies. If they were on speaking terms before his death, this son delivers the eulogy at his father's funeral. Describing a man he realises he hardly knew, the son uses broad brush strokes, tries to avoid platitudes, manages to not cry in public. Then the father is buried, and the son, according to Freud, experiences an existential crisis both quiet and disassembling: he is the next in line; he is one step from the grave.

This is where most fathers' stories end. But not the fathers detailed in this book. For the sons of these fathers grew up to be writers. More importantly, they grew up to write a book of Australian patrimony. Whether one should consider such fathers fortunate or unfortunate for being immortalised in literature is in part the focus of this study.

Australian Patrimony as a Sub-genre

This book explores representations of patrimony by male authors in Australian memoir and autobiography. More specifically, this book will analyse an author's construction of a masculine self in life writing through his formulation of various modes of paternal inheritance. The central focus will be how sons portray fathers, though as we will discover, these writers cast wide their nets in attempting to account for what has been passed down to them.

What kinds of texts are these books of Australian patrimony, and what should we call this sub-genre? They are undoubtedly a form of life writing, though this umbrella term has been broadened to include so many disparate forms of artistic self-representation that we need to be more exact. In their dual focus on the self and other, these texts fall somewhere between biography and autobiography, although they tend towards the latter's awareness of subjectivity – hence the usefulness of the term auto/biography.[1] The currency

---

[1] The term auto/biography itself has a short but complex history. Susanna Egan and Gabrielle Helms emphasise the fluidity of the genre, the slash signaling 'the broad continuum of life writing discourses that range from writing about the self (auto) to writing about another (biography)' and may include 'the collaborative work or the family memoir, the art installation, the film, or the web site that combine performance

of this compound term in literature studies today is part of a major shift in autobiographical theory and its conception of identity formation over the past 25 years: the turn towards relational approaches to life writing. Broadly speaking, this mode complicates notions of self-representation in autobiography by challenging the genre's claims of autonomy by giving precedence to intersubjectivity over individuality, foregrounding the self's contingency on others.

Crucially, the shift has its origins in feminist approaches to autobiography: the term 'relational autobiography' was first used by Susan Stanford Friedman to define the notion of the self in women's autobiography as being a 'sense of shared identity with other women, an aspect of identification that exists in tension with a sense of their own uniqueness' (in Benstock 44). Similar but more radically demarcated is Domna C. Stanton's mode of 'autogynography', claimed as the alternative for 'autobiographical writing by women' (5) and linked the splitting of a woman's subjectivity to her 'different status in the symbolic order' (15). In Australia, Joy Hooton's *Stories of Herself When Young: Autobiographies of Childhood by Australian Women* (1990) highlighted the way female autobiographers, as opposed to their male counterparts, have eschewed notions of an autonomous self and often written life stories that are also the stories of communities of women.[2] As she asserts: 'in the language of criticism there is no name for the female autobiography [...] it refuses to be defined by male standards' (102). Hooton's important study, along with Gillian Whitlock's *Intimate Empire: Reading Women's Autobiography* (1999) has contributed much to our understanding of female autobiography in Australia. However, there has to date been no study of Australian relational autobiography that has focussed exclusively on male writing – this study seeks to redress this gap.

For John Paul Eakin has countered such demarcations, claiming, 'the criterion of relationality applies equally *if not identically* to male experience' (*Our Lives* 50, emphasis in the original). Nancy K. Miller supports Eakin's assertion, showing how a number of male-authored texts exhibit 'precisely the structure of self-portrayal through the relation to a privileged other that

---

of identity with sophisticated levels of irony and full consciousness of theoretical implications' (6–7). When my discussion is relevant to the broader field of 'life writing' I will use this umbrella term or 'autobiography'. When within the narrow focus of autobiographical texts that focus on a significant other, I will use 'auto/biography'.

2 Hooton emphasises that the father in women's autobiography in Australia is a 'weak' or failed paternal figure (135–98): he is represented as either 'the austere, distantly severe father' who fails his daughter emotionally (136), or 'fathers are exposed as weak in that they are improvident, uncertain providers, failures in their chosen way of life' (141). For women's autobiography focussed on mothers, see also Barbara Johnson's *A World of Difference*.

characterizes most female-authored autobiography' (3). For Eakin, the male and female autobiographical 'I' is 'truly plural in its origins and subsequent formulation' and modern autobiography's dominant mode demonstrates 'the extent to which the self is defined by – and lives in terms of – its relations with others' (43), primarily what he terms the 'proximate other' (86). This most common of relational life narratives tells 'the self's story […] through the lens of its relation with some other key person, sometimes a sibling, friend or lover; but *most often a parent*' (86, emphasis added). In such instances, claims Eakin, the originary power-relationship is inverted, and the parent is placed at the mercy of the child turned adult-narrator (181).

The criterion for relationality, however, extends beyond an attempted focus on others. Some authors may write within an explicitly relational frame, yet their construction of selfhood and a simultaneous retreat to the language of autodidacticism constantly undercuts their claim to relational identity formation. This paradoxical construction of selfhood would seem a characteristic unique to the sub-genre discussed here – life narratives by sons writing about fathers – and seems to challenge the notion that relationality applies equally to the male experience. This book will explore the distinctive conception of relational identity within the particularly masculine frame of patrimonial life narrative. Further, this study recognises and illustrates the way recent theorising about this sub-genre – undertaken almost exclusively by male critics – exists in an uneasy tension with the (unacknowledged?) debt it owes to feminist theories about relationality, autobiography and 'writing the body'.[3]

Recent Theorising of Patrimony

Relational life writing about fathers has indeed received a great deal of attention in the past decade, predominantly from male critics, though there is no general agreement on the name of the form. David Parker introduces the term 'intergenerational auto/biography' ('Narratives of Autonomy' 140)

---

3   Of particular relevance is the way feminist theorising has forced into the open an exploration of the male body in literature. Eve Sedgwick's work on homosocial relations (1985) and Judith Butler's on gender as a performative act (1990) has helped to render masculinity 'visible' as a gender construction. Building on such work, Peter Schwenger observes: 'The maleness of experience, at a primary level, must mean the infusion of a particular sense of the body into the attitudes and encounters of a life' (102). This desire to 'make visible' continues to exist in conflict with a discomfort about writing the male body, or of men writing at all. In *Male Matters*, for example, Calvin Thomas explores 'the social construction of masculinity, the representation of the male body that is necessary to that construction, and the way that writing – as a corporal and material process, a way of putting the body on the line – can disturb or subvert that repression' (2).

for narratives of parents by children, while G. Thomas Couser argues for his term 'narratives of filiation', insisting that 'filiation' takes on a double meaning in this context:

> First, it refers to 'the condition or fact of being the child (not necessarily the son, though the root is the Latin *filus*, son) of a particular parent' (not necessarily a father); second, in law, it refers to 'judicial determination of paternity' […] By calling the texts in question narratives of filiation, rather than merely memoirs of fathers, I seek to highlight their relationality, their rootedness in a sense of entitlement and their intent to enact some kind of engagement with the father, whether living or dead. ('Genre Matters' 635)

Couser's second point is aptly expressed, for the books examined here typically display a dynamic relationality, an engagement often manifesting as a struggle with the father, and even in some cases, as an address *to* the father. Couser has more recently revised his terminology, coining the terms patriography for memoirs of the father by sons and daughters and matriography for books of the mother ('My Father's Closet', 891). While the stylistic simplicity of these terms will most likely see them emerge in the critical lexicon (thanks in part to the title of this book), their limitation for the present discussion is that they do not designate the gender of the author who constructs him or herself in relation to the parent.

For male-authored texts of patrimony, C. Martin Redman has introduced the term son–father auto/biographies, insisting that 'the hybridity that is implicit in the compound term "auto/biography" is an essential component of this form of life writing' (129). Redman sees his sub-genre as broadly conforming to Lejeune's oft-cited definition for autobiography as 'a retrospective prose narrative written by a real person concerning his own existence, where the focus is his individual life, in particular the story of his personality' (Lejeune 4), but observes, 'Publishers' lists and library catalogues generally categorise [son–father auto/biographies] as "memoir", presumably because of the sub-genre's dual focus whereby the author, narrator and co-protagonist are one and the same person and because the son is as much a focus as the father' (129–30). This 'mis-categorisation', according to Redman, is 'a response to the fact that though these volumes contain a quasi-biography of the father they are too personal and too much given to authorial self-revelation to be designated "biography"' (130). In fact, memoir would seem to me equally valid a categorisation as autobiography for son–father auto/biographies, having more to do with the scope of the lives narrated than the balance between self and other, and when discussing texts described by their authors as memoir, I will employ this term.

While the present discussion will not be overly involved with the semantics of generic markers, my study will argue for the term 'patrimonial life narratives' as a further alternative for categorising the texts I explore in this book. Importantly, my term focuses attention on the narratological components of this form, whilst broadening the 'father' frame to encompass males within or beyond the family structure who may act as surrogate figures for the writer-son of the text. While the term implies a patrilineal conception of heritage, this is not always necessarily so. As we will discover in Chapter Four, the 'afterlife' of Richard Freadman's text has included his daughter's acknowledgement of her part in a patrimonial line, suggesting that the concerns of patrimonial life narrative do not necessarily entail (or provoke in a reader) gender exclusivity.

This leads me to acknowledge and introduce the critic and his term that were the inspirations and initial reference guide for the present study. The Son's Book of the Father was coined in 2003 by Freadman in his memoir *Shadow of Doubt: My Father and Myself*. Freadman traces the sub-genre at least as far back as the late nineteenth to early twentieth century. Pointing towards precedents for his memoir, the author quotes from John Stuart Mill's *Autobiography* (1873) and Edmund Gosse's *Father and Son* (1907), but singles out the latter as 'the paradigm case of the sort of book I'm trying to write: the Son's Book of the Father' (*Shadow of Doubt* 177). Within the narrative, he expands on his conception of the sub-genre, stating:

> It is hardly surprising that such patterns [of the father's centrality] should be so widely occurring: after all, they reflect common aspects of male identity formation and parenting in patriarchal cultures, not least those of British origin. In fact, so many men have followed Gosse's example that the Son's Book of the Father now constitutes a substantial sub-genre of life-writing. (86–7)

Freadman outlines modern British and American examples of the Son's Book, such as J. A. Ackerley's *My Father and Myself* and Philip Roth's *Patrimony*, before turning his attention to the situation in Australia: 'In the current narrative I'm trying to relate my father's life, and the meaning of that life, to its Australian cultural context. As has often been noted, the figure of the father looms large in life-writing by Australian men' (287). This study examines some texts Freadman lists as examples, such as Raimond Gaita's *Romulus, My Father*, Peter Rose's *Rose Boys* and of course his own Son's Book. In addition, I incorporate works that post-date Freadman's. I also follow Freadman's lead in placing these texts simultaneously in relation to their literary forebear of *Father and Son* and in their uniquely Australian cultural context in order to make observations about fathers, sons and masculinities in this country.

At first glance, not all of the works discussed here could be categorised as Sons' Books of the Father. Bernard Smith's *The Boy Adeodatus*, for example, features an absent father who abandoned his family when the author was young. Hal Porter's *The Watcher on the Cast-Iron Balcony* portrays a father who remained but is for the most part absent in other ways – a shadowy, indistinct, ineffectual presence who is denounced by his more feminine, artistic son as a mere stereotype; a cardboard cut-out of a man who taught his son little of any real value. However, as we will discover, the figure of the 'absent-present' father in Australia is surprisingly common and enacts a powerful authority over the author-son. A recurring pattern in works discussed is the author's struggle to adequately depict the father in life writing: to give him 'voice' or 'presence' in literature – an especially remarkable phenomenon in those texts where the father is the ostensible focus of the narrative. The father of the Australian Son's Book is for the most part reticent, laconic, indistinct. The fact that this figure occurs so frequently raises important questions about the difficulties of representing certain versions of Australian masculinity in life writing. This problem is largely a literary one, revolving around the demands of autobiographical narrative modes, but is informed also by sociological notions of masculinity, particularly that of hegemonic masculinity. This study therefore engages at various points with theorists from the burgeoning field of masculinity studies, notably R. W. Connell, Michael S. Kimmel and David Buchbinder.[4]

'The Child is the Father of Man'

Writing about and even 'back to' the father is intrinsically linked to notions of authority[5]: of acknowledging, challenging or even denying the paternal

---

[4] A related but not necessarily allied development in popular literature is the so-called men's movement, which has caused a revision, and in some cases a reassertion, of traditional or essentialist notions of masculinity. In North America the origins of this movement are typically traced back to Robert Bly's *Iron John: A Book About Men* (1990). A more understated influence in the Australian context can be traced through Steve Biddulph's popular works on masculinity, such as *Manhood: A Book About Setting Men Free* (1994). Within evangelical Christianity and even (pop) psychology, this movement has fostered notions of the 'father wound'. Gordon Dalbey writes for the man 'who has been wounded by his father […] who has dared to consider his dad's human limitations and has begun to sense that neither Dad nor any other man can now fulfill his deep and persistent father-longing […] who is ready to […] surrender his wound at last to the Father God who defines and shapes all men' (xxi).

[5] As Roger Porter describes of his 'Childs' Books of Parental Deception', 'we could regard them as akin to the discourse of formally colonized figures in the empire who "write back" against the power and threat of nullification, insisting on the right of self-representation and regained authority' (*Bureau* 6–7).

influence. Redman describes the task of the son–father auto/biographer in the following way:

> In writing the life of his father, the son cannot but write his own self. Indeed, it may be argued that it is in part through the writing of his father that the son forms his own identity. However, in locating himself in relation to his father, the son in effect gives textual birth to the parent – a rather neat literalizing of Wordsworth's 'The Child is the father of Man'. Of course, given that the father transmits to the son his own understanding of maleness and fathering, the son's revision of his father is necessarily belated: it always looks back, as it were, to the example of the Father. (129)

This dialogic (and dialectical) relationship between self and other captures well the way the writer-son must necessarily travel two ways simultaneously: from his father to himself, by demonstrating the extent to which he has taken on or rejected the masculine exemplar of the father; and, in the act of representation or literary creation, from himself (his worldview, his biases) to his father. However, the balance between the two – self from other, other from self – does not function equally in every book. As G. Rocio Davis notes, the direction one travels is largely guided by each author's autobiographical impulse: 'sons often write about their fathers in an attempt to discover or learn about a person who was either largely physically or psychologically absent or whose presence was so overwhelming that the autobiographical act becomes an attempt to control the influence of that person on the author's life' (231). This book seeks to plot these conflicting motivations along two spectra. In order to do this, we must come to some conclusion about how present (or absent) the self of the author-son and the other of the subject-father is in each text, as well as to what degree the self can be read as growing out of, or being contingent upon, the other.

At one end of the first spectrum stands the towering presence of the father, the 'fully realised' biographical subject of the text through whom the autobiographical self of the son is formed. The identity of the author is created out of his depiction of the father, even when, as in the case of *Father and Son*, it is drawn against or in opposition to the father. In such cases, the father is the enduring presence of the narrative and a reader may favour him over the son, regardless of the author's intentions. At the other end of that spectrum one encounters the dominant presence of the author-son, the more realised subject of the narrative through whom the author attempts to construct an image of the father. In many cases, even when the portrait is a sympathetic one, the device of foregrounding the autobiographical self seems to be adopted reluctantly, as perhaps the only way to give birth or shape to the reticent figure of the father. In Freadman's *Shadow of Doubt*, although the author sets out to describe his father's influence (both positive and negative) on him, the 'absent-presence' of his father in the text and his own fully realised autobiographical self become so pronounced that the son can be read as birthing the textual father, echoing the Wordsworthian adage.

Such talk of birthing may cause us to wonder: where is the mother in this paradigm? Can the maternal be expunged so easily, as if the last half-century of feminist theory never took place? The question of the presence (or at times the telling absence) of the mother in my texts will also be addressed in time. Yet since the focus of this book is father–son relationships, the key figure to be explored here is paternal. Most autobiographers who choose to write extensively about parents tend to represent only one at the expense of the other, though there are exceptions – *The Land I Came Through Last* and *The Idea of Home* being two that are discussed here.[6] I will return to the difficult question of imbalance in 'honouring' both mother and father in autobiography in my conclusion.

A second spectrum for plotting Sons' Books involves the manner in which the father is represented – the extent to which the son's portrait is primarily positive or negative. This may be termed the eulogy-denouncement continuum, and according to Redman encompasses 'texts that range from nostalgic eulogies for loved "Dads", at one end of the spectrum, to bitter denunciations of the monstrous "toxic" Father, at the other' (130). Our discussion will cover the full spectrum of modes in the Australian context, from elegiac to denunciatory, in order to come to some conclusions about which is the dominant mode in the Australian Son's Book over the past 15 years.

The Ethical Turn in Life Writing

In reading my texts within the genre of 'relational autobiography' and assessing my authors' conceptions of relationality, I am already situated within an approach to literature that has been termed 'the ethical turn'. Gathering momentum in the 1990s as a reaction against the dominant theory paradigms of postmodernism and its so-called 'constructivist antihumanism' (Freadman and Miller 194), the turn to ethics in literary studies is defined in part by 'a systematic approach, grounded not in Theory as it is normally understood in literary studies, but in moral philosophy' (Parker, *The Self* 3). Whilst an 'ethics of autobiography' can be glimpsed within the burgeoning field of autobiographical theory written in

---

6   Rarer still is the author who writes a book of the father and a book of the mother. A notable exception is British author Blake Morrison, who followed up *And When Did You Last See Your Father?* with *Things My Mother Never Told Me* nearly ten years later. In the Australian context, Gabrielle Carey has written memoirs of both parents – *In My Father's House* and *Waiting Room*. It is worth noting that in both cases the impulse to write the father precedes the impulse to write the mother, making the secondary act seem somewhat belated.

the latter half of the twentieth century, particularly from the 1980s onward, and while it is implied in Lejeune's conception of the 'autobiographical pact' to 'tell the truth, the whole truth, and nothing but the truth' (22), it is essentially in the last decade and a half that the turn to ethics in life writing has progressed apace. The questions Wayne Booth asked of fiction in *The Company We Keep* (1988) – 'What are the Author's Responsibilities to Others Whose Lives Are used as "Material?"' (130) and 'What are the Responsibilities of the Author to Truth?' (132) – have since been applied, perhaps even more stringently, by critics of autobiography. It is, arguably, not until *How Our Lives Become Stories* (1999) that Eakin began explicitly engaging with the ethics of the autobiographical act, bringing interdisciplinary approaches from neurology and developmental psychology to bear on questions of truth in life writing, and focussing on the consumption of autobiography in the marketplace to ask serious questions about notions of privacy and representing others. Likewise, Couser's *Recovering Bodies* (1997) and especially *Vulnerable Subjects* (2004) saw a shift in his approach from an earlier engagement with post-structuralist questions of subjectivity to ethical questions of representing illness and disability in life writing. Other important studies that mark this new focus on ethics, and specifically on agency, include John Barbour's *The Conscience of the Autobiographer* (1992), Freadman's *Threads of Life* (2001), and Parker's *The Self in Moral Space* (2007). Each of these critics, along with other important figures such as Nancy Miller, contributed to the collection of essays *The Ethics of Life Writing* (2004), in which editor and colloquium convener Eakin proclaimed that 'ethics [is] the deep subject of autobiographical discourse' (6). Though wide ranging in their approaches and interests, these theorists all engage with the ethical in autobiography, with what Parker calls 'the question of what it is right for a life writer to do' (*The Self* 2).

In posing Parker's query to son–father auto/biographers an important subset of questions emerge, for example:

- How does one decide what an ethical representation of the father is? As Barbour finds, 'When we are troubled by or take issue with the memoir writer, it is usually for ethical reasons that focus on whether their judgements are fair, that is, consistently made' ('Judging' 96–7).
- What are some of the ethical complexities that must be negotiated when representing the reticent-laconic father in auto/biography?
- How does the desire to judge or not to judge the father, to condemn or to celebrate, complicate the act of representation? In making a judgement of the father, as Barbour finds, 'the writer may reflect on the limits of moral agency in another person, integrating moral judgements of a parent and interpretation oriented toward understanding the determining influences that made the parent who he or she was' ('Judging' 91).

- If the father is deceased (as is the case in the majority of the texts discussed in this book), how do notions of regret or debt affect the task at hand? How does the father's death impact upon a reader's judgement of whether an author's representation is ethical? As Eakin observed (and sought to rectify), 'The other's right to privacy is frequently assumed to terminate at death' (*Our Lives* 182).

Such questions form the basis of my exploration.

Focal Texts

The focal texts of this study are Richard Freadman's *Shadow of Doubt* (2003), Raimond Gaita's *Romulus, My Father* (1998), Robert Gray's *The Land I Came Through Last* (2008), John Hughes's *The Idea of Home* (2004) and Peter Rose's *Rose Boys* (2001). These five texts represent the full spectrum of the Son's Book, from the elegiac mode of *Romulus, My Father* to ambivalent representations such as Hughes's, to the denunciatory mode of *The Land I Came Through Last*. The close readings of these texts are designated as 'case studies' of this sub-genre, though neither the fathers nor sons of these texts are offered as 'representative' or 'exemplary' Australian lives. I will argue that, for the sons at least, the very act of writing often disqualifies these sons from being 'exemplary' males.

It should be noted from the outset that not all fathers explored here are of Australian origin. Smith's and Gaita's fathers grew up in Europe, for example, with Raimond Gaita arriving in Australia as a 4-year-old boy. While Freadman's father was born in Australia, *Shadow of Doubt* demonstrates that he retained a strong connection to his Jewish ancestry. As a consequence of this, and more generally as an increasingly common feature of the Australian condition, the authors here do not often conceive of purely Australian heritages, but rather lay claim to and explore diverse (though admittedly largely 'White' European[7]) cultural ancestries, including Jewish, British,

---

7   I do not discuss Australian indigenous autobiography in this study, as I believe attempting to also cover this tradition in one book would be impossible and result in a tokenistic representation at best. Two examples of aboriginal patriography are Rosemary van den Berg's *No Options, no Choice: The Moore River Experience, Thomas Corbett, an Aboriginal half-caste* (1994) and Bill Cohen's *To My Delight: the Autobiography of Bill Cohen, a Grandson of the Gumbangarri* (1987). Besides this omission, the relative hegemony of the 'White' European-Australian authors detailed in this study can be in part explained by my focus on the baby boomer generation of auto/biographers, who have largely taken up the project of writing the father as they have reached middle age during the past 20 years. These authors are the sons of pre-World War I or inter-war migrants, who for the most part emigrated from Europe. In my conclusion I will speculate on how this picture may change with the next wave of Australian patriography.

German Romanian, Irish, and Welsh Ukrainian.[8] However, all writer-sons engage with notions of Australian masculinity in their representations of patrimony, allowing us to draw some wider conclusions about men in contemporary Australia.

I have chosen to focus almost exclusively on patrimonial life narratives by writers who are authors by profession. While studies of autobiography are typically egalitarian, analysing literary works alongside 'trade' publications and even self-published family memoirs, I have restricted myself to Son's Books by professional writers for two reasons. First, as one key focus is questions about what is enabled and disabled by generic frameworks in patrimonial life narratives, I wish to critique authors who are (or should be) attentive to such concerns. Secondly and more importantly, I want to consider writing as a masculine pursuit in this country. Is there a place within the Australian conception of idealised masculinity for the heroic writer?

This book is a study of *contemporary* Son's Books of the Father: therefore, the chosen focus texts were all published in the past 15 years. However, portions of my analysis, particularly in Chapter Two, will engage with works published before 1998 that are relevant to the current discussion. These texts include David Malouf's *12 Edmondstone Street* (1986), Alan Marshall's *I Can Jump Puddles* (1955), Hal Porter's *The Watcher on the Cast-Iron Balcony* (1963) and Bernard Smith's *The Boy Adeodatus* (1984). Besides the Marshall classic, none of these works could be categorised as Sons' Books of the Father, yet their representations of largely absent fathers set important precedents for the later works discussed, and also help to frame the discussion of the reticent-laconic Australian father and other versions of Australian masculinity.

Chapter One will focus on *Father and Son* as the 'paradigm case' for son–father auto/biographies, investigating how it can be read as a model for many later Sons' Books. I engage with the significant body of contemporary criticism on Gosse's autobiography before briefly examining the most explicit engagements with *Father and Son* in Australian literature generally. Chapter Two will read Porter's *The Watcher on the Cast-Iron Balcony* and other 'classic' Australian texts back to *Father and Son*, arguing for them as examples of 'deconversion narratives' in the Gossian mode, and exploring their representations of early- to mid-twentieth-century 'absent' Australian fathers.

Chapters Three to Seven present close examinations of five contemporary Sons' Books. These texts are ordered in two ways. First, they are placed in

---

8   Based on the few studies of patriography internationally, the sub-genre is by no means confined to a 'White' European demographic. See for example David L. Dudley's *My Father's Shadow: Intergenerational Conflict in African American Men's Autobiography* (1991), and Davis' 'Writing Fathers: Auto/biography and Unfulfilled Vocation in Sara Suleri Goodyear's *Boys Will be Boys* and Hanif Kureishi's *My Ear and his Heart* (2009).

approximate chronology of publication, providing a passage through this sub-genre over the past 15 years. Secondly, my analysis moves from more positive or elegiac accounts, through ambivalent portrayals, to a denunciatory or 'supremely ambivalent' representation. Chapter Three offers a reading of *Romulus, My Father* and the contentious criticism it has inspired, revealing how paying tribute to the father is not without its pitfalls. My own examination will focus on the problems of representing the virtue of self-denial in autobiography. Chapter Four continues this examination of the difficulties of celebrating self-denial in *Shadow of Doubt*. I will argue that Freadman enacts an inversion of the father–son relationship in order to bring his father textually into being.

Chapter Five examines *Rose Boys* as an instance of a unique sub-branch of son–father auto/biography: the Brothers' Book of the Father. Though the text is sole authored, I will argue that Peter Rose attempts to speak *for* his brother, and I will contend that the text is a performance of sonship for the father, who is also the addressee of the text. Chapter Six analyses John Hughes's performance of masculinity in *The Idea of Home*, contending that the author must choose between competing patrimonial performances in his act of self-writing. Chapter Seven develops the theory that son–father auto/biographies often embody this act of choosing one's patrimony, examining Robert Gray's portrayal of numerous father figures in *The Land I Came Through Last* alongside the 'toxic' father of his text. I will argue that Gray's objective 'neither to vindicate nor vilify' leads the author to enact a textual becoming of his father. Gray's auto/biography also returns us in some surprising ways to *Father and Son*, demonstrating how erecting a textual 'monument' to the father is very often a supremely ambivalent autobiographical act.

Part I

CHALLENGING AUTHORITY

Chapter One

'THE PARADIGM CASE': CONTESTING THE FATHER IN EDMUND GOSSE'S *FATHER AND SON: A STUDY OF TWO TEMPERAMENTS*

> A son cannot speak adequately about his father. There is a certain impiety in formulating sentences about the author of our being and the moulder of our character.
>
> —John Addington Symonds, *Memoirs*

> FATHER! – to God himself we cannot give
> A holier name! then lightly do not bear
> Both names conjoined.
>
> —William Wordsworth, 'Ecclesiastical Sketches'

> The author of this book has no doubt settled it with his conscience how far in the interests of popular edification or amusement it is legitimate to expose the weaknesses and inconsistencies of a good man who was also one's father.
>
> —*Times Literary Supplement* review of *Father and Son*

A little over one hundred years ago the British author Edmund Gosse published *Father and Son: A Study of Two Temperaments*. It detailed the author's memories of his austere upbringing in London and the Devonshire coast, his mother's tragic death while he was still a young boy, his religious education under his father's strict yet loving hand, and his eventual break with his father at the age of 18. Lauded both by critics and prominent fellow writers upon its release in 1907, it also caused somewhat of a stir for its candid and at times unflattering depiction of the author's father, the eminent naturalist Philip Henry Gosse. Rudyard Kipling called it 'extraordinarily interesting – more interesting than *David Copperfield* because it's true', while one review remarked that 'This is an excellent book, though we hardly like the anatomisation of one's father' (cited in Thwaite, *Literary Landscape* 435–6). Andre Maurois declared that it 'contains a proof, and a very rare proof, that an unfettered examination of one's self is possible' (cited in Marcus 110).

Yet, one hundred years after its first appearance, *Father and Son* stands as somewhat of an anomaly within the canon: a book published six years after the end of what is commonly termed the Victorian period and written by a once-eminent man of letters who came to represent the worst of high Victorianism, which self-importantly valued 'graciousness of style' at the expense of good scholarship (Orel 179). David Callahan has noted the irony of how Gosse's only enduring work is that which explores 'his production of the space and authority necessary for him to be able to challenge his father. The clearing of the space has become Gosse's one insertion into the authority structure of remembered literature; the work he was able to do in the space cleared has been cleared away itself as shallow and false' (25). As Alexis Harley argues, if Edmund Gosse had not penned *Father and Son* he would now be long forgotten, 'interred in a field of […] lapsed literary notables' (180).

Exactly what kind of book is Gosse's one contribution to remembered literature? Despite the author's claim that 'this is not an autobiography' (151), *Father and Son* is now entrenched in critical literature as one of the masterpieces of the genre. Yet early studies of Victorian biography fail to agree upon what kind of book *Father and Son* is: Edgar Johnson called it a 'mingling of biography and autobiography' (212), while Harold Nicholson saw it as neither (146). Some later critics have attempted to read the work as fiction, dismissing its historical claims in favour of its sharply conceived scenes and fictive elements. The central argument of the following chapter is that *Father and Son* is in fact the first relational auto/biography of a father by a son; in its conception of patrimony it is the paradigmatic text of the subgenre the Son's Book of the Father.[1]

What I would like to propose from the outset is that the shadow of this important work falls heavily upon the contemporary Son's Book of the Father in Australia. As a model of 'the struggle for self-identity' through a challenge to paternal and divine authority, and as a son's depiction of a complex father–son relationship, Gosse's classic of European autobiography is an instructive text for much contemporary life writing. Although it is by no means the case that all the subsequent writers in this study are familiar with Gosse, there is a convincing argument that *Father and Son*, and before that, Augustine's *Confessions*,

---

1   John Stuart Mill's *Autobiography* and John Ruskin's *Praeterita* are the two other European 'classics' that might qualify for this honour, yet the patrimonial oppression Mill struggled against is not the primary focus of his text, and the gradual weakening of Ruskin's belief in his father is not sufficiently conceived of within a relational frame.

are paradigmatic and grasp the emotional and psychological dynamics of this relation in ways that are indicative and formative. By reading a series of Australian works back to *Father and Son* one begins to see the still pertinent need for an autobiographer to face the question of divine-paternal authority in establishing an authorial identity. In its conflation of biological father and Heavenly Father, *Father and Son* usefully reminds us that the term patrimony originally denoted the estate or endowment of the Church, bestowed by ancient right.[2]

In this chapter I will first engage in some detail with recent critical scholarship on *Father and Son* and outline a series of key tropes in Gosse's autobiography that recur in my Australian examples. The latter portion of Chapter One will investigate the more explicit re-occurrences of *Father and Son* in Australian literature, particularly Peter Carey's *Oscar and Lucinda*. While not autobiography, Carey's novel is the most overt example of Gosse's presence in Australian literature and is important as an illustration of how father–son dynamics pattern Australia's relationship to our literary ancestry. The Australian autobiographies to be covered in Chapter Two, most notably *The Boy Adeodatus* and *The Watcher on the Cast-Iron Balcony*, are not strictly patriographies, but both resonate with *Father and Son* in important ways. Smith's narrative of deconversion engages with the tradition of spiritual autobiography and, like Gosse, he struggles against 'the Fathers' of the genre, while Porter's renunciation of both God and a father's model of masculinity highlights the importance of the Gossian model in an Australian context.

Re-framing Edmund Gosse

James Hepburn, in his introduction to the 1974 Oxford University Press edition of *Father and Son*, remarked:

> It is in fact astonishing how little criticism of any sort has ever been levelled against the book. The revolt against certain Victorian beliefs and practices has been so thorough that from 1907 to the present day the viewpoint of the author has seemed to be merely the truth. (xiii)

This paucity of criticism has since been redressed. Victorian scholarship has seen a re-emerging interest in *Father and Son* over the past 30 years, producing a

---

2   In its earliest usage, the 'patrimony of Saint Peter' was 'the property belonging to the Church', and subsequently 'the territory held by the Pope in the city of Rome', *Oxford English Dictionary*, 2nd ed. (Oxford: Oxford University Press, 1989): accessed online 8 July 2010, http://www.oed.com

number of divergent re-readings and re-imaginings of the author's intentions and achievements in the text. It is worth remarking however that most modern critics continue to approach *Father and Son* with a marked respectfulness, at least for the aesthetic and affective qualities of the work. The opening lines of Avrom Fleishman's examination are typical. He states that the author might be 'open to the charge of exploitativeness and artificiality were it not for the palpable emotion with which he writes' (300). That *Father and Son* is a unique and enduring literary achievement does not seem to be in doubt. What the text actually achieves is very much open to debate.

According to Michael Newton, the text has not been out of print since its publication, largely due to the relevance of its subject matter. Centrally, this revolves around the narrative of 'a conflict that makes Gosse's story one of the most significant of the nineteenth century. And not just of the nineteenth century: Gosse's struggle resonates in our culture too, in ways that may yet surprise us' (ix). In his introduction to the 2004 Oxford University Press edition of the text, Newton identifies a central paradox in the internal logic of the book:

> In his consideration of vocation, the question Gosse poses for himself and for us is whether identity derives from our parents, our past, or is it made by the individual in refutation of that past. Gosse claims the latter, while the autobiographical mode in which he writes, with its commitment to memory and to the very idea of 'formative experiences' and parental influence, argue for the other. This is a very self-divided book. It chooses freedom while placing the origins of the self within the circumscription that the self rejects. The very title of the book shows that the self is a self in so far as it is in relatedness, as one of a pair, father and son […] Young Edmund exists in this contradiction. To declare independence is an act of rejection that still yearns towards that which one claims independence from. (xxv–vi)

This articulates well the tension inherent in the Gossian mode of patriography: a conflict between claiming and disclaiming his past; between celebrating and denouncing his father; between recognising 'formative experiences' and parental influence and writing as a 'self-made-man' – a modern apostate and aesthete, a child of literature and nature in the best Romantic tradition. It also cuts to the heart of the problematic question of genre.

Clinton Machann has addressed the problematic question of genre, arguing against critics who would posit the work as a novel, despite its utilisation of 'some of the common attributes of fiction' and its 'novelistic neatness' (135–6). He likewise resists other interpretations (including

Gosse's own assessment) that the work is biography or memoir, contending that despite the author's attempt in his epilogue to place the father 'in the foreground of the piece' (Gosse 162), it is the son, and particularly his self-development, internal life and identity, who is the focus of the narrative: 'In spite of Gosse's limiting thesis and his focus on the father–son relationship, it is clear that the son's very essence of selfhood, not just some part of it, is in question here' (137).[3]

Using Lejeune's model of autobiographer as author, narrator and main character, Machann goes on to analyse the devices used to create distance between past and present, and between the narrator and protagonist – a distance necessary for the pronouncements the adult Gosse makes about his childhood self 'fluttering in the net-work of my father's will, and incapable of the smallest independent action' (Gosse 163). The result of this distance is to create for both writer and reader an 'historical perspective' that allows us to look back from our 'relatively enlightened' age that has been 'released from the grip of a benighted religious tradition' (Machann 143). In this way, Machann reads Gosse's narrative as an exemplary tale of the Edwardian age, a self-history that is 'a particularly extreme individual example of a general development within English history', a development into 'consciousness and enlightenment' (143).

Machann identifies an important feature of the Child's Book of the Parent, the relational frame of which must by necessity make an account of changes or continuity across generations. A major trope of the Child's Book of the Parent is the narrative of progress or enlightenment – the writing self's conception of how she has moved away from the values and worldview of her parents to become her own person, and in so doing has moved with the progress of history. Rarely is the portrayal of the struggle as violent or the declaration of liberty as absolute as the one represented by Gosse, though Robert Gray's narrative of progress discussed in Chapter Seven shares some uncanny similarities with the Gossian model. A more common pattern, as we will discover, is for the child to continue the progression towards enlightenment begun by the parent.

However, Machann's reading of *Father and Son* feels ultimately too simplistic, attributing more weight of certainty to Gosse's vision than the text can sustain. Is Gosse's break from his father and religion as conclusive as he claims? Is his progress from religious darkness to secular light as unequivocal as Mahann suggests? My reading of *Father and Son* seeks to resist the temptation towards absolute binaries – between past/present, unenlightened/enlightened and so forth – and argues for a more nuanced reading that foregrounds the ambiguities

---

3 All in text references to Gosse's *Father and Son*, unless otherwise stated, are to the 1974 Oxford University Press edition of the text.

of the text. This is turn will be reflected in the ambiguities identified in the works discussed as 'descendants' of *Father and Son*.

Other critics posit Gosse's text at the forefront of a new form of literary autobiography which emerged at the turn of the twentieth century; wilfully self-conscious, and bearing a novelistic sophistication that re-writes traditional autobiography by turning the standard elements of the genre back on itself in the form of literary parody. Fleishman identifies *spiritual* autobiography as the main object of this parody, not only due to the particular circumstances of an oppressive religion from which Gosse struggles to emerge but also because of the author's participation in the late Victorian project of de-authorising the Bible in favour of the secular text (301). His specific targets are the pre-eminent spiritual autobiographers such as John Bunyan, and ultimately 'the central text of autobiographical tradition, Augustine's *Confessions*' (308). In this way one may figure the capitalised Father of *Father and Son* not only as Edmund's biological father Philip Henry Gosse (hereafter Henry Gosse), but also as the Father(s) of the genre.

This de-authorising, according to Fleishman, 'is conducted by a precise inversion of the figures employed in that tradition', such as the tropes of Eden, the Fall, Dedication and especially Conversion (301). Linda Peterson concurs, asserting that Gosse's 'sophisticated' parody works by imitating the language and formal generic patterns of spiritual autobiography but 'with a displacement of meaning' (173). Thus the Edenesque beauty of the Devon seacoast chronologically follows the Fall – in this case the father's fall in the son's eyes from the status of Deity – leading the son to test God and commit idolatry by bowing down to a wooden chair (Gosse 30). But while Peterson's Gosse is a clever parodist interested in wordplay and generic disruption, Heather Henderson contends that there is far more at stake here for this autobiographer: 'it is only by working *through* the terms of biblical typology that Gosse can define his own identity' (120, emphasis in the original). This identity is that of an idolater who turns to secular narrative for meaning, casting himself against his father's intended biblical models.

For it is where Edmund looks for salvation from this bondage of biblical typology that the conversion narrative of spiritual autobiography is most profoundly subverted. Gosse turns to literature to save him from religion; as Henderson puts it, 'his miracles are secular, aesthetic and literary' (137). Henderson focuses on the language used to describe Edmund's early discoveries of Virgil, Greek sculpture and Shakespeare in religious terms, as revelatory and metaphysical. It is here, rather than in scripture, that the son finds a model for selfhood: characters to empathise with, beauty to be inspired by, and most importantly a language to express himself. 'The terms of the conflict have now been clearly set out', claims Henderson, 'Religion represents bondage from which only literature can provide salvation' (139). This prototype of a narrative of deconversion through literature, which Henderson traces through Ruskin's *Praeterita* to *Father and Son*, will be important when we turn our attention to works by Smith, Porter and Gray, where the world of aesthetics offers salvation from a paternal bind, but with important divergences from the Gossian model. For it is not primarily a question of religion but of authority, and a father's model of masculinity, that is 'thrown off' in our contemporary texts.

Other critics concur with Henderson, identifying *Father and Son* as a kind of allegory of enlightenment, of salvation through art. 'The values espoused by *Father and Son* are entirely those of the literary system', writes Laura Marcus, 'and it is central to the autobiographical canon in part because it so emphatically endorses the claims of the literary life' (111). According to Marcus, it is this aspect of Gosse's only enduring work that accounts for its longevity:

> The success of the text results from its control over the discourses and dichotomies it incorporates or ironises: autobiography/biography, literature/science, Calvinism/Enlightenment, tragedy/comedy, past/present. In ironic contrast, Henry Gosse, at least in his son's account, 'dies' to history in large part as a result of his absurd attempt to reconcile his religion and his science. (111)

Like Machann, Marcus's use of dichotomies to describe the tensions inherent in *Father and Son* feels altogether too precise. While Gosse's hyperbolic claim that the work 'is the record of a struggle between two temperaments, two consciences and almost two epochs' (5) may support this reading, the attribution of binaries to father and to son gives too much weight to the polemical aspects of the book at the expense of the nuances and uncertainties that run through it. Rather than controlling these dichotomies, Gosse vacillates between them, is enmeshed in their fluidity, and in fact mimics the father by attempting to reconcile such binaries.

Cynthia Northcutt Malone takes the discussion of *Father and Son*'s dichotomous nature in an instructive direction, claiming it as an example of what Bakhtin calls 'polemically coloured autobiography'. In a narrative exhibiting Bakhtin's 'hidden polemic':

> the argument or point of view of another is, so to speak, submerged in the text; only the author's answer or refutation is visible [...] even when Henry Gosse's voice is not itself produced, it is merely implied, those implied words shape the structure of the narrative. (Malone 16)

According to Malone, this Bakhtinian notion usefully shifts the discussion from generic categorisation to 'the engagement of the autobiographical "I" in debate' (17). While foregrounding the movement from familial unity to separation in the text and the various ways Gosse casts his own journey as 'a movement forward, as progress, and the father's trajectory as a movement backward, as regression' (18), Malone also demonstrates the way this narrative is destabilised by the father's 'hidden polemic', which continually recasts the son's story of progress. In placing his father's letter to his son as the epilogue of the text, which both 'ends the dialogue, for the rupture is absolute' and returns us to the author's polemical opening as 'the temporal point from which retrospective narration begins' (29), Gosse's narrative becomes encircled by his father's, and his own argument threatens to be consumed by the one it contests. Hemmed in by the father's dominating presence, Edmund's anti-clerical (read authoritarian) polemic risks being drowned out by the Henry anti-secular (read libertarian) one.

This argument is one way of accounting for an unusual reader-response to *Father and Son*: the prospect of the biographical (other of the) father emerging as a stronger, more sympathetic, or more fully realised literary presence than the protagonist-son. Jerome Buckley writes, 'The unintended irony of the book – its strength as well as its weakness – lies in the possibility that our sympathy may ultimately shift from the son to the father' (107). Despite the author's attempts to frame himself as the hero of the narrative, and his journey as positive and progressive, readers frequently respond by favouring the father:

> Whatever his narrowness of view, his literalism, his fear of art and artifice, his misplaced ingenuity in the attempt to forestall the heresies of Darwin, the father remains a strong character, a man of impeachable integrity, loyal though mistaken in some of his loyalties, sincerely committed to his faith. His survives the son's weighted descriptions against him [...] The son, by comparison is disingenuous and evasive [...] for all his declared devotion to Truth, [he] cares most for his own comfort and his final escape from the burden of 'dedication'. (Buckley 107)

As we will discover, patriographies cause judgements to be made about father *and* son in ways that are not typically easy to control. A patriography that denounces its subject may often cause us to favour the father's 'strength of character' over the son's. Paradoxically, a Son's Book written in tribute to the father often finds him an elusive study, causing the textual presence of the son to overshadow his patrimony.

Yet as Newton notes of *Father and Son*, perhaps this 'common reaction for readers to prefer the father to the son' is deliberate (xvi). Gosse's first biographer Evan E. Charteris declares it to have been one of Gosse's intended aims, quoting as evidence a letter in which the author wrote, 'The book is a monument to my father, an extraordinary man' (307). At the very least, Gosse's claims regarding his intentions must cause us to examine the ambiguities and contradictions of *Father and Son* more closely as a key for understanding the broader field of patriographies. As a 'monument' to the father, the Son's Book is typically a supremely ambivalent autobiographical act.

Peter Allen has highlighted these uncertainties, stressing 'the disparity between the attitudes professed by the narrator and those unconsciously or indirectly revealed' (501). He points to Virginia Woolf's famous criticism that Gosse would have been a better writer 'if only his pagan and sensual joy had not been dashed by perpetual caution' (cited in Allen 500), and while Allen does not agree with Woolf's assessment of the writing's value, he does find ample evidence of 'reticence and indirection' in *Father and Son*. This stems in part, Allen argues, from Gosse's conflicting loyalties: to his father and himself, to genteel Victorianism and an emerging Edwardianism, even to his father's religious beliefs and those with which he chooses to replace them (497–501). Jerome Buckley concurs about the inconclusiveness of the text and the divided nature of author and narrator, wondering about Gosse's ability to ultimately throw off 'the yoke of his dedication' to 'fashion his inner life for himself' (Gosse 178). He writes: 'Of the child's secret resistance, we have indeed some distinct notion. Of the sincerity and strength of the selfhood to be shaped by the liberated adult, we have no such clear assurance' (Buckley 107–8).

But as Henderson notes, in writing about this process of self-discovery in autobiography, Gosse also makes some significant claims about his own authority as author, and more generally about the lines of authority between autobiographers, their fathers and God:

> In effect, by choosing his own language and his own plot, Gosse becomes the author of his own life […] In doing so, he wrests authority not only from his father, but also from God. His parents have destined him to be the Son (the Lamb), but by rebelling against his father, he usurps his role. And later on he becomes, like every autobiographer, his own father through the act of self-authorship. (144)

It is a process we shall see repeated, to varying degrees, in a number of contemporary Australian works, and highlights the vital importance a challenge to paternal-divine authority plays in establishing authorial authority in autobiography.

Harley draws on Henderson and Peterson's work on biblical typology while resisting the diametric models of inversion and reversal discussed above to argue for a much more complex picture of Gosse the apostate. Harley casts his various intentions and allegiances in *Father and Son* as vacillating and paradoxical, befitting an author 'slung awkwardly across two generations: those of high Victorianism and late Victorian and Edwardian Aestheticism' (185). This 'Study of Two Temperaments' enacts Matthew Arnold's binary between 'the Hebraic father (who) is austere, cerebral, pious', who in Arnold's terms follows 'not our own will, but the will of God', and the 'Hellenic son obsessed with the sensuous and the beautiful', who according to Arnold 'see(s) things as they really are, and by seeing them as they are see(s) them in their beauty' (cited in Harley 182). Harley attributes the Arnoldian bias towards the latter to Edmund, but sees him pulled at times in both directions, wavering between 'the notion of literature as secular scripture and literature as a secular thing of beauty, between the priorities of truth and art' (185). This picture is complicated further by conflicting representations of the father, which Harley ascribes to 'the oedipal bind which has *Father and Son* both honouring and denouncing the father' (185). It is Gosse's ambivalence towards his father that seems most often missed by critics who use Gosse as a shorthand for the familial narrative of denouncement, but one that, as we shall see, makes *Father and Son* so appropriate as a rubric for understanding representations of fathers in contemporary auto/biography.

Edmund's struggle against his father is also placed within the historical moment of religion and science's great battle regarding the origins of life. Henry Gosse's most controversial work *Omphalos*, in which he attempted to reconcile his religious beliefs with his scientific knowledge to 'untie the geological knot', was published in 1857, around the time his contemporary Charles Darwin was formulating his theories to be published in *On the Origin of Species* (1859). Edmund Gosse not only records (with barely repressed glee) the scientific and wider community's derisive response to *Omphalos*, but also provides his own commentary on what it revealed about his father. *Omphalos* is described as a wilfully self-deceptive text in which the father 'closed the doors upon himself forever' (61). According to Harley, in his choice of language Edmund deliberately aligns himself with Darwin in opposition to his father:

> [*Father and Son*] adopts the grandest of all Victorian metaphors for struggle: Darwinism. Edmund Gosse recognises that both Darwin and himself find themselves common adversaries against Henry Gosse's orthodoxy and he implicitly invokes Darwinian tropes – of struggle and natural selection, extinction and evolution – in the way he addresses the contention between father and son. (191)

In so doing, Edmund categorises his father as a separate and dying species, offering his text as 'a *document*, as a record of educational and religious conditions which, having passed away, will never return' (Gosse, 3, emphasis in the original). Yet as we shall discover, this pronouncement of extinction is refuted by the striking similarities Gosse's 'document' shares with records of familial and religious struggles in the contemporary Australian context, even involving, in Robert Gray's case, the invocation of Darwin's *On the Origin of Species*.

Harley's investigation of *Father and Son*'s construction of authority, authorship and interiority is also instructive. Delineating between his father's and mother's notions of a divine authority which authorises 'their own authority-as-author's'[4] and Gosse's own, which gains authority through a process of de-authorising both his parents and God, Harley demonstrates 'the Victorian movement to adulate literature over God' (236) in action. Yet Gosse's literary antecedents in this pursuit are far from straightforward. Harley highlights Gosse's claim as a true devotee who worships literature and makes it 'quite as much as religion' (in Charteris 186). She shows how Gosse's appropriation of Wordsworth is a major key to formulating his Romantic 'radical individuality' and the authority of his authorship. Yet in tracing Gosse's formulation of an inner self back through the Romantics to Augustine, Harley highlights the deceptive neatness of literary-critical models such as those of Fleishman, Peterson and Henderson. To say that Gosse merely inverts the Augustinian model of biblical typology is too simplistic, Harley seems to imply, and ignores the continuities and divergences that co-exist in *Father and Son*. Despite the author's own claim that his 'record of a struggle between […] two epochs […] ended, as was inevitable, in disruption' (Gosse 5), there is as much connectedness to be found here as there is rupture from both the father and the history of autobiography. Retracing and expanding on these continuities and divergences through the lens of contemporary Australian autobiography back to Gosse, and from Gosse through the Romantics to Augustine, will be part of the focus of the following chapter.

A recent alternative reading of *Father and Son* from within the 'ethical turn' in life-writing studies sees David Parker (perhaps surprisingly) argue for the rights of the writing self over those of the written other. Parker resists criticism of the narrative's polemics, arguing that it is unfair to demand a polyphonic voice in texts such as this: 'Authorial neutrality over the matter of an autobiography's ultimate language(s) is not an available option' ('Life Writing', 60). According to Parker, it is important to recognise Gosse's narrative not simply as a record of the author's opinions about the truth and value of literature and

---

4   As *Father and Son* records, both of Edmund's parents were published authors – his mother of popular religious tracts; his father both theology and books of natural history. Their work, whatever the subject, was written under the authority of God (Harley 225).

modernity over 'a dying Puritanism' (Gosse 3), but as a story of how these opinions came to be formed, of how the child became the adult narrator. Elsewhere Parker has cited *Father and Son* as typifying 'the intergenerational narrative of autonomy', which is in contrast to the dominant contemporary mode of 'narratives of relationality': 'whereas Gosse's narrative terminates in an act of moral dis-identification with his father, the recent texts typically discover significant sources of self in the figures of parents and grandparents' ('Narratives of Autonomy', 212). While Parker's description of Gosse's dis-identification seems largely apt, such a conception is ultimately too simplistic. As with Gosse's text, my contemporary examples of patrimonial life narrative often demonstrate a simultaneous desire for autonomy from and relationality with the father.

Parker seeks to correct a bias in recent life-writing studies towards the rights of the 'other' in auto/biography. 'The claims of other persons can become vehicles of oppression', Parker reminds us, specifically when they 'afford no moral weight to the claims of the self, particularity, or difference. Such claims can only be regarded as immoral, amoral, or merely sub-moral, and so they are rhetorically disempowered before other regarding considerations' ('Life Writing' 65). In the case of Gosse and his parents, it is not simply a matter of the author choosing what he prefers (literature, beauty, scientific truth) but of adopting what Parker calls a 'language of authenticity':

> What happens at the end of the narrative is that, faced with the father's potentially overwhelming reminders of his obligations to both his parents and to God, the young man is empowered by discovering authenticity specifically as a *moral* language that can provide not only an adequate counterweight to the Puritan LMD [moral language] of the father but also an armoury of terms in which to mount a critique of it. (65, emphasis in the original)

Interestingly, this 'language of authenticity' is again identified as coming from a Romantic sensibility, leading Parker back to Wordsworth. The repeated invocations of a Wordsworthian notion of the heroic writer greatly confuse the picture of maleness represented by Edmund Gosse. Just what kind of males are the father and son of *Father and Son*?

Gosse and Masculinity

A further complicating factor in Gosse's various allegiances is his ambiguous sexuality. As well as highlighting Gosse's suggestive appreciation and promotion of the work of such figures as Wilde, Whitman and Symonds (whose *Memoirs* bear a striking resemblance to *Father and Son* and act as another autobiography of apostasy), Harley draws on Ann Thwaite's scholarship to argue for a homoerotic reading of *Father and Son* which interprets Gosse's admiration of beauty and literature as working against 'the mid-Victorian cult of manliness' (212).[5] In Gosse's 'fascination with masculinities distinct from the paternal, authoritative one displayed in his father' (212), and his embracing of 'decadent Aestheticism' (217), we again find fertile ground for comparison with the Australian context. Hal Porter, wilfully sexually ambiguous and anomalous with the ethos of Australian maleness embodied by his father, will be the first of many Australian auto/biographers explored in this book who define themselves in contrast to the paternal model, who write both 'as a son and a different kind of male' (*The Watcher* 94).

In *Father and Son*, the author's conception of his sexuality and masculinity is constructed in opposition to that defined by the father:

> The protagonist's struggle with his father and his father's religion broadens into a struggle with the ideology that more generally authorises fathers, so that Gosse's riposte to his father's version of Christianity becomes a riposte also to the version of upright Christian masculinity he attributes to his father. (Harley 195)

What exactly is this version of masculinity represented by Henry Gosse? Harley calls it 'muscular Christianity' (212). Certainly Gosse's choice of language, especially in relation to his father's religious beliefs, is tellingly aggressive – questions of faith are posed 'with menacing finger' (Gosse 68), while in the pulpit Henry Gosse was capable of 'fire-and-brimstone' sermons: 'It was a dark and rainy winter morning when he made this terrible address, which frightened the congregation extremely' (109–10). Occasions such as this,

---

5 Thwaite investigates the question of Edmund Gosse's sexuality, reading into much of his correspondence with fellow writers and artists and his other writings an identifiable pattern of homoeroticism. Analysing a series of letters Gosse wrote to Siegfried Sassoon's uncle, the sculptor Hamo Thornycroft, Thwaite writes, 'This is lover's talk, of course. There is no doubt that Edmund behaved constantly as lovers do' (*Literary Landscape* 194). While Thwaite depicts Gosse's marriage to Nellie as an unusually close and intimate one, his devotion to her does not necessarily preclude the possibility of his homosexual desire. Quoting from a letter Gosse wrote to his wife in which he describes watching 'a mass of handsome ruddy strong-backed youths' playing tennis, Thwaite finds ample evidence 'that Nellie knew his feelings about male beauty and male friendship. He could persuade himself that his pleasure in the Cambridge boys was as much aesthetic as sexual, though he knew, and admitted (unusually for the period) in his biography of Patmore, "the enormous part that sex plays in the whole comity of man"' (*Literary Landscape* 305).

where a father's masculinity is performed in a public setting for an audience including the son, and is often constructed as a speech-act, will be repeated in later texts, particularly in John Hughes's *The Idea of Home*.

However, to be fair, Edmund also records moments of genuine tenderness between father and son, such as this shortly after his mother's death:

> Sometimes, when the early twilight descended upon us in the study [...] he would beckon me to him silently, and fold me closely in his arms. I used to turn my face up to his, patiently and wonderingly, while the large, unwilling tears gathered in the corners of his eyelids [...] we would stay so, without a word or a movement, until the darkness filled the room. And then, with my little hand in his, we would walk sedately downstairs. (49)

The yearning inherent in this scene (which is tellingly rewritten by Peter Carey in *Oscar and Lucinda*) is instructive for my Australian examples. Each contemporary author records a similar moment of awkward intimacy with the father, and explores more generally the often-fraught terrain of expressing love within this particularly masculine frame, reconstructing Gosse's simultaneous expression and containment of emotion.

There is further evidence in other biographies, including Edmund Gosse's far more sympathetic *The Life of Philip Henry Gosse F.R.S.*, that Henry was indeed a gentle and emotional man. Quoting a story from Edmund's biography of his father, in which Henry is told that his first manuscript has been accepted for publication and breaks down 'into hysterical sob upon sob', Thwaite notes, '[Henry] Gosse, like many Victorian men, cried easily at moments of great emotion and was not ashamed to admit to the fact' (*Glimpses* 102). Reading Gosse's biography of his father alongside his patriography, one would be forgiven for concluding either that they could not be from the same author or they could not possibly be about the same father, highlighting the unique disadvantage the father faces in being represented in relation to his son. Indeed, very few sons these days would ever set out to write an objective biography of the father; for better or worse, the patriography is the enduring contemporary form.

For, in *Father and Son* Henry Gosse is most often portrayed as aloof and dispassionate, beyond the bounds of the son's earthly thoughts and emotions. This picture is complicated by the young Edmund's conflation of his father with God and Henry Gosse's particularly misogynist version of Christianity. Douglas Brooks-Davies describes Henry Gosse's *Omphalos* as 'a totally male-oriented text written by a man convinced that the Creation was perpetrated by a male god and that Adam's navel (in the existence of which Henry Gosse was a fervent believer) is the sign and mark of god's paternity' (119), while Harley states that Edmund depicts the work as 'enshrining the divine sanction given to maternal absence' (195). As we develop our exploration of contemporary patriographies, we shall see that the question of maternal absence in such texts (and how this is justified or not addressed by their authors) emerges as a fascinatingly fraught one.

It is within this backdrop that Edmund comes to represent a very different kind of masculinity. The author describes himself as a weak, sickly and 'fragile' child who many believed was 'not long for this world' (Gosse 79–80). Alongside the moments of intimacy between father and child, there is also evidence of the son's hatred. Brooks-Davies reads the narrative from within the paradigm of the Oedipus complex (119), pointing to examples such as the young Edmund, after he has been caned, walking about 'the house for some days with a murderous hatred of my Father locked within my bosom' (Gosse 65). The son's desire to triumph over his father may even extend beyond the latter's death. Under the guise of championing her maternal pride, Gosse cannot help remarking early in his text that, 'My Mother […] would proceed so far as to declare that in future times [Henry Gosse] would chiefly be known as his son's father' (18). To be sure, this is typically the lot of the father memorialised in a Son's Book. However, the persistent desire to triumph over the dead father – to measure one's achievements advantageously against his – is repeated in Freadman's and Gray's auto/biographies.

It is through his identification with the feminine that Edmund most abruptly subverts the masculinity represented by his father: 'Gosse's stance against patriarchal authority is enacted both when he aligns himself with women and when he engages in a self-feminisation' (Harley 198). The women Gosse aligns himself with include the nameless nurse who saved his life at birth, his anti-religious paternal grandmother, his stepmother, and Mary Flaw who attempts to kidnap him from a Brethren church meeting. However, it is the author's feminisation of his younger self, by deploying 'comparisons with mythological, historical and fictional women to suggest both empathy and identification with a marginalised sex' (Harley 203), which is most telling. These figures include St Teresa of Avila, Princess Blanchefleur and Charles Perrault's Fatima. For some authors in this study, such as Porter and Rose, identification with the mother and a feminisation of their childhood selves will align with questions of sexuality, but more generally I will seek to track the way an author-son deals with the idea of being a less masculine man than his father, of being feminised in an Australian cultural setting in the very act of writing itself.

Ultimately, such self-feminisations in *Father and Son* are less useful for pronouncing on the author's sexuality than on his conception of masculinity. As Harley finds, 'Whether Gosse was, in Thwaite's phrase, "a secret homosexual" or not, he certainly exhibits a fascination with masculinities distinct from the paternal, authoritative one displayed in his father' (212). This has particular relevance for the way the author aligns himself with literature and the literary. By writing himself into a Romantic tradition (both in his sensibilities and explicit references to Wordsworth (57)), Gosse enters a domain where the heroic writer is already complexly gendered. While David Simpson declares that 'the literary is a generally feminised category, notwithstanding the efforts of the Hemingways and the Mailers to render it otherwise' (126), Harley emphasises the maleness of Romantic figures such as Wordsworth:

> The Romantic feminisation of the literary domain [...] had to contend with the fact that the bardic poet-prophet, Wordsworth's narrator in *The Prelude*, for instance, is distinctly male. The male, but feminised, authorial pose that Gosse strikes in *Father and Son* (as feminine protagonist, and male author) effects the reconciliation between a traditionally disparate sex and gender demanded by Romantic discourses of authorship. (206)

In this way Gosse junior's literary enterprise of reconciliation is much like his father's hope that his ill-fated *Omphalos* would resolve the conflict between religion and science. Does *Father and Son* succeed where *Omphalos* failed? Can a male writer, in the tradition of Edmund Gosse, be both masculine and a different kind of male to his father? This question pervades my entire study.

'Some Sort of Cousin': *The Gosses* in Australia

In her opening to the exclusively male-oriented family history *The Gosses: An Anglo-Australian Family*, Fayette Gosse demonstrates the way the dominant mode of Australian masculinity eschews the kind of 'feminine' male embodied by Edmund Gosse, even when the writer is part of one's heritage:

> As a schoolgirl I asked a schoolboy how he was related to his namesake, Edmund Gosse, whose poem I had just encountered in our set anthology *In Fealty to Apollo*. It was meant as a joke for the schoolboy (later my husband) was captain of football, stroke of the crew and head prefect but had no inkling of poetry. Yet Edmund was, it appeared, 'some sort of cousin'. Alas, I never met him, but years later, after marrying my Gosse and going with him to Cambridge in 1945, I met Edmund's only son Philip, then aged sixty-eight and Cambridge's oldest undergraduate. (1)

This famous poetry-writing 'some sort of cousin' is of little interest to the captain of football, though of sufficient interest to this schoolgirl who eventually marries into the Gosse family to undertake the writing of a history of the Gosses in Australia. It is Edmund's son Philip who persuades Fayette to 'hunt the Gosses' (9) and write this well-researched, if somewhat eccentric family history.[6] One of the motivating factors for Fayette's research is that 'The well-documented lives of Philip, Henry and Edmund is out of all proportion to the scattered shreds about other members of the family' (9). Fayette seeks to redress this imbalance, writing chapters on lesser-known Gosses such as 'Thomas-the-painter' and 'John-the-merchant'.

The Gosses is a fascinating document in its own right. It is evidence of the burgeoning interest in family history writing that began in the 1980s and has continued until today, composing a large part of the publications often grouped under the term 'the memoir boom'. It is a trend that has spawned countless 'how-to' manuals for writing family history, television series and even websites and interactive computer software for mapping one's family tree. *The Gosses* is a useful exemplar of this genre, exhibiting a strong impulse for origins: the desire many Australians share for ongoing links with the 'mother country'. As Fayette explains:

> Soon after marrying into the Gosse family I began to discern the intricate network of marriages that threaded together most of the well-known families of that part of Australia. My own parents were not family minded and I had never seen a family album before. Those opulent books fascinated me. (1)

Fayette draws heavily on these opulent books in retelling the narrative of the patriarchal line of Gosses, tracing them back as far as William Gosse, Edmund's great grandfather, who was born in Ringwood in 1714. Drawing on a range of archives, including parish records and journals, Fayette constructs a history of the Gosses in England, New Zealand and Australia. Her research is formidable and *The Gosses* is acknowledged by Thwaite as a useful source for her biography of Edmund (*Literary Landscape* 518). However, unlike Thwaite, Fayette does not seek to challenge Edmund's version of his upbringing. *Father and Son* is utilised extensively in Fayette's chapters on Henry and Edmund, but treated simply as another untainted archival source (56–7).

Crucially for the current discussion, *The Gosses* presents a model of the narrative of patrimony that typifies son–father auto/biographies. Though its author is female, Fayette constructs a patrilineal family tree that completely

---

6   Some fifteen years earlier Fayette Gosse had published a short study of William Gosse Hay, an Australian author of convict novels in the early 1900s who was also 'some sort of cousin' of Edmund's. Though according to Fayette, it was to his disadvantage that Gosse Hay did not exploit his family connections: 'Edmund Gosse, in particular, who had such a keen critical sense, might have proved very useful' (*Gosse Hay* 7).

eschews the women of the Gosse family. Even Edmund's mother Emily, who was an author in her own right, commands no more than a passing comment, and her influence is always sublimated to the paternal. The text's fly-leaf offers a stark visual representation of this construction of patrimony: pendant-shaped portraits of the male Gosses adorn the double page spread, interconnected by ornamental branches, illustrating the clear lineage from Henry and Edmund Gosse down to the author's three sons. Neither Emily, the author nor any other woman is represented. Though Fayette's biographical impulse is to record the lives of the lesser-known Gosses, evidently such a desire does not extend to the maternal family line.

Though none of the family histories explored in the following chapters are as starkly patriarchal as this, the Son's Book of the Father exists within just such a paternal frame. Most author-sons conceive of heritages that incorporate their mother's family in some way, though typically they operate by providing an alternative patrimonial inheritance to that offered by the father. The reasons for the absence of the maternal vary. In addressing his fear that his daughter may feel alienated by the patriarchal focus of his book, Freadman appeals to his mother's and wife's desire for privacy (*Shadow of Doubt* 160). Gaita has defended his treatment of his mother in his text, though, he has recently conceded that the genre of his Son's Book is not one in which she can appear 'fully individuated' (*After Romulus* 117). Therefore, part of the task of delineating the form and structure of the Son's Book will be to explore how they justify (or fail to justify) the elision of the maternal line.

'A Battle with the God of His Father': Re-writing *Father and Son* in *Oscar and Lucinda*

The most explicit manifestation of *Father and Son* in Australian literature is not in autobiography but in the postmodern historical fiction of Peter Carey's *Oscar and Lucinda*. As his prefatory acknowledgements make clear, Carey borrowed liberally from Gosse's childhood to construct the comically unsettling early life of his male protagonist, the narrator's great-grandfather Oscar Hopkins. More than this, however, Carey has arguably made Gosse the central cultural-historical counterpoint in his Booker Prize–winning work. The presence of this intertext operates within the novel on many levels, allowing the author to critique notions of history, truth, religion, writing and the status of literature. But of primary relevance here is the way Carey challenges Gosse's portrayal of both his father and his 'dying Puritanism' (Gosse 3) in *Father and Son*. *Oscar and Lucinda*, though fiction, becomes a process of writing back to Gosse's canonical autobiography and therefore must be placed alongside the Australian autobiographical works discussed in this book. What is it about Gosse that makes him such an attractive target for historical revision in Carey's fiction? How does Carey, who on the surface would seem to have much in common with the secular, literary figure of Gosse, find himself on the other side of the divide, challenging and revising the status of both the author and his major work of literature?

Extracts of Carey's early manuscripts published in *Making Stories* reveal much about the genesis of his interest in Edmund Gosse and particularly Edmund's relationship with the father:

> [Henry Gosse's] son was at once a rebel against him, but also an echo of [him ... Edmund] was racked with guilt that the things he enjoyed, the beauty of the country which he saw earlier than most, the drinking, dancing, song, women, everything filled him with guilt and his relationship with the almighty was in accord with all his other relationships – it was in the nature of a dangerous bet [...] what a passion for life he had, what a battle with the god of his father. (In Grenville and Woolfe 42)

This brief sketch of the character Carey develops into Oscar Hopkins demonstrates the supreme ambivalence he attributes to the figure of Edmund Gosse. It is this ambivalence, read against the grain of the text by Carey of the author's self-conception in *Father and Son*, which I believe makes Gosse such a contentious and illuminating autobiographical son.

While it would be difficult to push too far the similarities between Oscar Hopkins and Edmund Gosse as they exist in these texts, one can make a strong case for the figure of Henry Gosse in *Father and Son* aligning with the character of Oscar's father Theophilus Hopkins. Both lead a Plymouth Brethren congregation in Devon in the 1850s. Both are naturalists of minor fame described as living through and even embodying the first great conflict between science and religion during the period when the theories of Darwin and Hooker were first challenging the authority of biblical scripture. Both are described as strict ascetics who pride themselves on having never read Shakespeare and forbid the reading of fiction in their households. Both are widowers whose wives died of breast cancer, and both lose their only sons in part due to their stubborn adherence to strict religious dogma. As David Callahan points out, Carey's mention in his acknowledgements of Henry Gosse never having read Shakespeare highlights the importance of this denial by the father of the 'great father' of western literature, a refutation which sets up the pattern of subversion: 'Of all the figures in the threatening English literary tradition, none is more powerful than Shakespeare; no act of defiance more defiant than not reading him' (24). As I will argue in Chapter Seven, not reading another's work can be an important act of refutation between father (figure) and son.

Such a conflation opens the way for Carey's defence of Henry Gosse. Through the character of Wardley-Fish, Carey makes the strongest challenge to Gosse's portrayal of his father, and to autobiography's claims to truth more generally. In stumbling upon Theophilus Hopkins' *Hennacombe Rambles* in a bookstore, Oscar's friend discovers a portrait of the father that sharply conflicts with the version he has been given:

> It was as if he had netted Oscar in his home pond and could see him properly for the first time […] he now realised – reading the book – that the pond was neither as he had seen it nor as Oscar had described it.
>
> Wardley-Fish had an impression of a killjoy, love-nothing […] a man who would snatch a little Christmas pudding from a young boy's mouth. But where he might have expected to find a stern and life-denying spirit, he found such a trembling and tender appreciation of hedgerow, moss, robin, and the tiniest of sea creatures that even Wardley-Fish […] was impressed and moved […] Wardley-Fish thought himself a man's man, steeped in brandy and good cigars […] he claimed to have no ear for poetry or music and yet he was moved – it nearly winded him – by the elder Hopkins's prose. (196–7)

It is the writing of Henry Gosse, quoted by Carey from *A Naturalist's Rambles on the Devonshire Coast* and attributed to the fictional Theophilus, which is used as evidence against Oscar's version of his father, but by association against Edmund Gosse's version of *his* father. It is as if Carey is encouraging his readers to go back to *Father and Son* and check the work against Henry Gosse's descriptions of the natural world to discover Gosse's misrepresentation of his father's nature. Henry Gosse could not have been that kind of father, Carey seems to suggest, because of how beautifully he wrote.

Elsewhere, Carey portrays the complex emotional landscape between father and son in his nuanced portrayal of Theophilus and Oscar's feelings towards him. Re-visioning some of the tension inherent in *Father and Son*'s descriptions of the rare moments of intimacy, Carey demonstrates how the 'softer' son may feel conflicted when faced with the tenderness of his characteristically stern father:

> Oscar looked up, but was embarrassed by something in his father's eyes. The look was soft and pleading. It did not belong in that hard, black-bearded face, did not suit the tone of voice […] You could not hold it, that soft and lovely centre of his father's feelings. (38)

A telling feature of the son–father auto/biographies discussed in this book is how the 'softer', more feminine or emotionally self-aware son seeks out, responds to, or fails to 'hold' the 'soft and lovely' centre of the father's emotional self.

The father/son dynamic established in *Oscar and Lucinda* can be extended to include Carey himself. A fascinating corollary of the writing-back project is the way Carey may be figured as the literary-provincial son writing back to the father of Victorian literature. David Callahan frames Gosse and Carey as literary father and son, and by extension British literature as the father to its Australian counterpart, using Gosse's model of a son 'dealing lovingly with his father rather than aggressively denying him' (25) as a metaphor for Carey's 'familiar' incorporation of the Victorian literary mode in *Oscar and Lucinda*. In so doing, Carey does not abandon an old heritage, but subsumes it playfully, 'with the ease of a family member' (26). Therefore, the 'Subversion of Subversion' referred to in the title of Callahan's article is the process of a novelist challenging 'the putative chain of aggression contained within the very notion of subversion and authority' and deconstructing 'the apparently butch cycle of authority replacing authority' (26). This formulation is very neat, but bases itself on a somewhat contentious reading of *Father and Son*. The extent to which Gosse's representation of his father is fair or ethical seems an open question amongst critics of the work, but it would be too much to claim that Gosse deals lovingly with his father rather than aggressively denying him.

Of course, such attempts to wrestle with authority figures of the past has relevance for the patriographical project. In his recent study of patriographies about fathers who led secret lives, Roger Porter reads his authors' autobiographical acts as akin to the post-colonial discourse of the 'writing back paradigm', where 'formally colonized figures in the empire [...] "write back" against power and the threat of nullification' (*Bureau* 6). Porter describes his sub-set of patriographies both as compensatory and emancipatory texts, and whilst no author discussed in this study (with the exception of Merv Lilley) seeks to expose a father's hidden life, the desire both for liberation from, and paradoxically, reconciliation with one's (paternal/literary) lineage is evident in the focus texts in this book.

This process of literary sonship and subversion is particularly relevant in light of the criticism regarding Gosse's subversion of spiritual autobiography. This notion, of writers writing back to their literary forebears, and in turn being written back to themselves, threads its way right throughout the current discussion. As we shall see, Carey is only the first Australian author of this book who will be figured as the son writing back to a literary father figure. Far from being merely incidental, *Father and Son*'s presence in *Oscar and Lucinda* creates a series of resonances between the two works, and between the two authors, that, while leaving open a number of ambiguities, usefully opens our discussion of

Father and Son in an Australian literary context. These complex negotiations, between authors and critics, biographers and readers, are especially prescient when we investigate how the father fared in what is arguably Australia's pre-eminent literary autobiography of the twentieth century, Hal Porter's *The Watcher on the Cast-Iron Balcony*.

Chapter Two

'AN INDUBITABLE AUSTRALIAN': RENOUNCING THE FATHER IN HAL PORTER'S *THE WATCHER ON THE CAST-IRON BALCONY*

You don't have to deserve your mother's love. You have to deserve your father's. He's more particular.
—Robert Frost, '*Paris Review* Interview'

We can never again speak of 'Australian Masculinity'; there are multiple masculinities on the continent.
—R. W. Connell, 'Australian Masculinities'

Determined thereto, perhaps by his father's ghost,
Permitting nothing to the evening's edge.
The father does not come to adorn the chant.
One father proclaims another, the patriarchs
Of truth…
—Wallace Stevens, 'The Role of the Idea in Poetry'

The Watcher on the Cast-Iron Balcony would seem to have little in common with the complex narrative of patrimony of *Father and Son*. Hal Porter's father, 'an unfurnished man' (93), remains a shadowy and indistinct presence for the entirety of Porter's early life story, while it is Porter's mother, and significantly her death, which provides the autobiography's narrative structure. She features so prominently in the text that Porter calls his autobiography 'my mother's biography' (62). It could equally be described as a matriography, and might have been fittingly called *Mother and Son*, though fortunately Porter left this title available for later use.[1] However, as with *Father and Son*, Porter's

---

1   *Mother and Son* aired on ABC television from 1984 to 1994 and is another example of the absent father in the Australian cultural imagination. World War II veteran Leo Beare, husband to Maggie and father to Arthur and Robert, had passed away before the beginning of the series.

text is centrally about the act of renouncing the father in order to assert an authorial identity. In this way, *The Watcher on the Cast-Iron Balcony* has much in common with another Son's Book of the Mother: Augustine's *Confessions*. Porter's construction of his father's masculinity, which he renounces utterly, accords with Augustine's and Gosse's discursive strategies of defining themselves in opposition to their fathers' masculine models. Further, Porter's renouncement of God demonstrates once again the importance of such manoeuvres in establishing an authorial identity. This chapter explores how Porter's tribute to the mother becomes a coincident denouncement of his paternal heritage, and how his attempt to define himself against this masculine model is in various ways thwarted by a simultaneous identification with the father, demonstrating the persistent influence of the writer-son's patrimonial inheritance. Porter's denouncement of a typical Australian father will be vitally important as we turn out attention to more recent manifestations of this masculine type.

Despite their seeming differences, Edmund Gosse's and Hal Porter's autobiographies bear some striking resemblances. For example, Porter's move at the age of six from Melbourne to Bairnsdale mirrors Gosse's geographical shift at a similar age from London to the Devonshire coast. Like Gosse, Porter tells the story of a rural and removed childhood in a small country town and appears to both the reader and the townsfolk as somewhat of an outsider. However, it is in the literary-historical spaces occupied by the two authors and the central works of their careers that bear the greatest comparison. Gosse and Porter wrote widely and extensively across a range of genres, including poetry, short stories and longer fiction, yet in each case their body of work has not enjoyed a critical or general readership beyond their lifetimes. Harley's assertion that if not for *Father and Son* Gosse would now be 'interred in a field of lapsed literary notables' could equally be applied to Porter and his one enduring work (Harley 180). Critics consider *The Watcher on the Cast-Iron Balcony* a pre-eminently successful and complex autobiography that has played a crucial role in changing the way Australian life writing has been written and read (Colmer 50; McCooey, *Artful Histories* 1). Like *Father and Son*, *The Watcher on the Cast-Iron Balcony* is highly literary and strongly endorses the literary life, being the story of a child's discovery of literature and the world 'against the odds'. Through both interview and autobiography Porter, like Gosse, constructs a mythology of himself as a 'self-made man', under-educated but highly literate, and wary of the assessment of the academy. Porter claims, for example, that, 'not having been scalped mentally by education, I am truly unaware of what is "good" or "bad" writing' (in Lord, *Hal Porter* 379).

Both authors also share the ignominy of becoming objects of parody in later life for being, as Peter Goldsworthy states of Porter, 'as baroquely mannered in person as he was in his prose' (77).² While John Gross once described Gosse as the 'one belletrist of his generation whose name still means something to the world at large' (cited in Thwaite, *Literary Landscape* 2), it is doubtful whether Porter's reputation has fared even this well; in Australia such a debatable honour would have to go to Porter's one-time rival Patrick White.

Porter and Gosse have also been subjects of highly controversial biographies that in part set about to re-write their autobiographies. Mary Lord's *Hal Porter: Man of Many Parts* and Thwaite's *Edmund Gosse: A Literary Landscape 1849– 1928* have functioned as literary exposé, outing their subjects' sexualities and so irrevocably altering their legacies and the way their autobiographies are read. As earlier noted, Thwaite's biography explores the possibility that Gosse was a 'secret' homosexual. Similarly, Porter's ambiguous sexuality is a common theme of much criticism about him (Goldsworthy 77). Yet it was the revelation in Lord's foreword, entitled 'A Declaration of Bias', that he had sexually abused her 10-year-old son that has irretrievably transformed Porter's reputation. Lord's controversial exposure of Porter's paedophilia has thus performed a similar function to Thwaite's 'outing' of Gosse, enacting a re-interpretation of much of Porter's work. Lord's justification for this revelation has since been called into question, most notably by Noel Rowe, who notes how the biographer's rationalisation of her actions comes to resemble Porter's rationalisation of his (195). As Rowe also notes, Porter's paedophilia is in fact owned up to in *The Watcher on the Cast-Iron Balcony*, albeit buried within a typically Porterian overabundance of information (Porter 126).

More relevant to the current discussion is Porter's other 'deceptions' in his autobiography. Lord details a number of inaccuracies in *The Watcher on the Cast-Iron Balcony*, including the author's disingenuous account of his heritage. During her research, Lord admits, 'it was extremely disconcerting' to find that Porter's claims regarding his family background 'were, in parts, invented' (*Many Parts* 174). She lists a series of discrepancies between the autobiography's claims to truth and her research, including Porter changing the date of his mother's death so it would fall fatalistically on her wedding anniversary, inventing a 'middle-class boyhood' and education for his father, fabricating an aristocratic heritage for his maternal grandmother, and omitting his father's occupation as an engine driver (175–7).

In *Edmund Gosse*, Ann Thwaite uncovers a number of comparable fabrications in Gosse's account of his family background, including a French ancestry on his

---

2   For his part, Porter did nothing to disavow such a reputation. In his essay 'Answers to a Funny, Kind Man', he quotes Voltaire in French, Sophocles in Greek and patronises everyone, including 'illiterate Saturday journalists, and semi-literate academics, and highly unintelligent intellectuals', and even the 'funny, kind man' who was foolish enough to approach him to write the essay (in Lord, *Hal Porter* 382).

father's side (8), an arduous servant's life for his mother (14) and an unremittingly austere childhood for himself in London prior to his mother's death (23). Similarly, Lord believes that in attempting to claim a noble heritage for his mother,

> Porter utterly abandons fact for fantasy [...] perhaps it was an attempt to shore up his mother's pretensions to gentility, presuming that she had any. Or Porter's pretensions on her behalf. Whatever the cause, the background with which Porter invested his mother's mother could hardly be more at odds with actuality. (*Many Parts* 183)

Revelations of dishonesty in autobiography are not new, and perhaps the genre's claims to truth are no longer bound by historical accuracy. Though the 'facts' an autobiographer might invent about his heritage may reveal something of his pretensions, they would seem no longer a hanging offence. Yet when liberty with the truth bears directly upon the representation (and particularly the harsh judgement) of a parent, it may be worth asking more serious questions. The revelation that Alan Marshall was dishonest about his father's occupation in *I Can Jump Puddles*, for example, is important because so much of the son's nostalgic portrayal of his father's character is bound up in his identity as a simple but wise horse-breaker. For Porter, omissions regarding his father's occupation are employed for opposite ends: to elevate his family up the social ladder in order to denounce his father. Does it matter that Porter elides his father's occupation as an engine driver? Perhaps not, but the invention of a middle-class boyhood for his father does matter, for one of Porter's chief complaints is that, 'Brought up middle class, he *chooses* to become lower middle class' (*The Watcher* 93, emphasis in the original).

A key impulse of Lord's and Thwaite's revisionist histories is a defence of the father against his misrepresentation and denouncement by the son. In a strident vindication of the 'inhuman actor' portrayed in *The Watcher on the Cast-Iron Balcony*, Lord writes:

> 'Harry' Porter fed, clothed and educated his son until he was able to leave school at fifteen, thus giving him the same start in life as he himself had enjoyed, and his father before him, and his father before that. It is unlikely that any other course suggested itself to him or he would have pursued it, if it had. Porter Senior was a good father and husband, an excellent golfer, cricketer and Mason. He was a much liked and well-respected citizen of Bairnsdale. On the day he retired from the railways [...] the local papers carried articles on his retirement headed 'Harry Signs Off' and 'Popular Engine driver Farewelled.' The family had every reason to be proud of him and most of them were. (*Many Parts* 180)

Similarly, while Thwaite intended her biography of Edmund Gosse 'to be read alongside *Father and Son*' (*Literary Landscape* 5), in part to highlight the son's misrepresentation of the father, the biographer was evidently not content with this, developing her revision of *Father and Son* in the comprehensive and sympathetic biography of the father, *Glimpses of the Wonderful: The Life of Philip Henry Gosse, 1810–1888*, published 17 years later. In the latter biography Thwaite expresses great disquiet that 'over and over again, subsequent writers refer to Philip Henry Gosse's "sombre and fanatical will", his "gloomy life"' (*Glimpses* xv). Describing her biographical impulse, Thwaite continues, 'When I finished trying to do justice to the son, I then saw I needed to do further justice to the father. Edmund's portrait is so distorted that it needs to be corrected' (xvii).

The desire to exonerate the father who has been mistreated in autobiography is evidently a strong one. As noted earlier, a common response to *Father and Son* is to read against the text's polemic and favour the father over the son, though few have gone to such lengths as Thwaite. Henry Gosse is of course an unusual case – no other father explored here is likely to have justice done with his own biography (except perhaps Bob Rose). Furthermore, Porter is the only Australian author discussed here who has to date been the subject of biography, so exposing his claims to historical scrutiny. Therefore, the work of this book will be a textual analysis of the authors' treatment of their fathers. Nevertheless, Thwaite's desire to 'do justice' is acknowledged as a component of the present book. As the discussion progresses I will attempt to account for this compulsion to side with the father over the son.

A Son's Book of the Mother

For earlier critics of Porter, such a compulsion is by no means universal. D. R. Burns finds nothing particularly noteworthy in Porter's depiction of a 'typically enthusiastic, all managing mother and typically little interested father, in the lower-middle-class flatlands of largely provincial Australia, from 1910 to 1928', believing that 'this experience is in no way remarkable, as social fact, and accords completely with the limited possibilities of that time and place' (359). Yet if one compares it to Marshall's *I Can Jump Puddles*, an autobiography which preceded Porter's by nearly ten years but which covers a similar historical period and socio-cultural milieu, one finds a much more sympathetic rendering of a simple but strong paternal figure. Marshall's father makes another compelling counterpoint to Gosse's, with the conflation of father and God working in somewhat the opposite direction. As Marshall explains: 'Whenever father mentioned God he criticised Him, but I liked father's attitude as it established him as someone upon whom I could rely if God failed me [...] Men like father, I thought, were stronger than any God' (17). While Marshall's and Porter's fathers seem to have been similar kinds of men – simple, practical, unreflective – their depictions by their sons could scarcely be more different. Porter's less-than-flattering portrayal of his paternal legacy clearly warrants further analysis.

However, while *The Watcher on the Cast-Iron Balcony* is viewed by most critics as the first and central literary autobiography in Australian life writing, there has been almost no discussion of Porter's portrayal of his father in the text, though Harry Heseltine notes that 'the paternal presence is, in its own way, just as pervasive in all that follows' as the author's mother (152). In *Artful Histories*, McCooey discusses Porter more than any other autobiographer, yet the father barely rates a mention beyond the assertion that the work 'is the narrative of the mother's death and the elision of his father' (73). In fact, Porter's tremendously ambivalent representation of his father is enormously significant, not only for its portrayal of a 'typically little interested' Australian dad, but also as the object against which the autobiographical self defines himself. Porter's may be a Book of the Mother, but the father is the central figure in his discursive construction of an identity. In reading *The Watcher on the Cast-Iron Balcony* back through *Father and Son* to Augustine's *Confessions*, one may again interpret Porter's as a narrative of deconversion, leading ultimately to the author's rejection of his father and God.

Of course, despite the fact that it is addressed to God the Father, Augustine's *Confessions* is itself a Book of the Mother. Peter Brown contends that 'the relationship between mother and son that weaves in and out of the *Confessions*, forms the thread for which the book is justly famous' (29), while Hawkins states that 'it seems impossible to overstate the significance of the relationship' (63).[3] Hawkins views the maternal nexus in the *Confessions* as central but complexly nuanced: the conflation of Augustine's mother Monica and his concubine into the 'erotic mother' and the depiction of the Heavenly City as an apotheosized mother – 'Jerusalem my Mother' – works to elevate the maternal so that, 'It is the archetypal mother who is the dominant figure in Augustine's religious imagination – an archetype symbolising both the goal of our redemptive longings and also the hunger that drives us in search of that goal' (58). As we will discover, the same could be applied to Porter's mother, though with less spiritual overtones. Importantly, Augustine's narrative of conversion is driven by the figure of Monica. It is her visions that foretell her

---

3   While this has led to many Freudian readings of the *Confessions* as being guided by an unresolved Oedipus complex (see for example Charles Kligerman's 'A Psychoanalytic study of the *Confessions* of St. Augustine'), I find Hawkins's application of Jungian archetypes far more convincing, particularly in relation to Augustine's depiction of his parents, and I will continue to draw on Hawkins's model here.

son's future, her prayers and supplications to which Augustine attributes his salvation, and the saint's ultimate conversion is cast as a double conversion as it transforms 'her mourning into rejoicing' (Augustine 467). As Hawkins contends, Augustine's 'knowledge of the Christian God is, quite literally, mediated by Monica' (64).

The most explicit manifestation of the *Confessions* in Australian autobiography is another matriography featuring an 'absent' father, where the mother acts as a kind of intermediary with the divine. Bernard Smith's *The Boy Adeodatus* details how his father Charlie abandoned his family when the author was an infant, leaving his Irish Catholic mother (and later his Plymouth Brethren adopted father) to guide him (via Augustine) towards God. According to John Colmer, Smith's title and his allusions to and quotations from Augustine 'establish a kind of mythic parallel between the twentieth-century Australian subject and the saint's illegitimate son Adeodatus, a parallel that unobtrusively distances the subject and bestows a degree of universality on the individual's struggle to reach the truth' (119–20). However, this manoeuvre carries other implications, particularly to do with authority and authorship. As Rosamund Dalziell states, 'By assuming the name of [...] Adeodatus, the writer appropriates the spiritual fatherhood of St Augustine and confers sonship on himself' (75). This assuming of sonship not only authorises the text but also positions Smith as an errant or prodigal son, perfectly placed to subvert the father of spiritual autobiography. Due to the absence of Smith's birth father in his life narrative, his identification with Adeodatus gives the author a literary father figure to struggle against.

As with Gosse's 'O Chair' incident or the thwarted Second Coming in *Father and Son*, Smith's famous epiphany in Wagga Park on Melbourne Cup Day is a major turning point in the narrative, a consciously canonical acting out of an Augustinian moment of revelation that comes to nothing. Interestingly, the moment is figured not as Smith's rejection of God but as God's rejection of him, and oddly linked to his biological father:

> It seemed that his spiritual father, if indeed he possessed one, was teasing him; that he did not really want him. Didn't care much what he did; hadn't put his name on the list. He knew that he'd been born outside the law anyway. But that old father of his flesh, the one that had taken off [...] he seemed at times to remain with him, almost inciting him. (220)

Smith's father (unlike Edmund's or Adeodatus's) was not 'a man of God', yet his abandonment of his son is conflated here with the notion of rejection by God. Smith's spiritual father is 'teasing him' and 'does not really want him', while his earthly father, 'the one that had taken off', nevertheless 'remained with him, almost inciting him'. This sense of rejection is echoed in an earlier scene, where the father is again linked to God's absence using a quote from the *Confessions*. Following three chance encounters with his abdicant father as a child, the author states, 'Then Ben's father took him back to Braeside and Ben never saw him again' (20), before quoting Augustine: '*He withdrew Himself from our eyes that we might return to our own heart and there find Him*'. Smith's ambivalent relationship with the paternal and divine, marked both by presence and absence, acceptance and rejection, demonstrates the way conversion and deconversion are held in tension in his text.

Likewise, according to Hawkins, 'Augustine's idea of God is shaped in part by his attitude toward his natural father' (67), largely in an oppositional sense, for 'the paternal archetype is organized around the two extremes of an imperfect but present father and a God who is perfect but transcendent' (69). Augustine's father is mentioned a mere handful of times in the *Confessions* and each time he is negatively represented, mostly for being inordinately proud of his son, or for attending to earthly things rather than heavenly ones. One significant admonishment is Augustine's recording of Patricius' delight at seeing 'how the signs of manhood began to bud in me' (73): Augustine concludes that the father has 'but vain conceits of me' (73). Most telling of all is the lack of emphasis Augustine places on his father's death, particularly in comparison to the keenly felt eulogies to others in the book. As Hawkins notes: 'Patricius dies when Augustine is seventeen: he mentions this fact only in passing and with no show of grief whatsoever, whereas he will soon experience the depths of sorrow in mourning the death of a friend' (68).

Harry Porter occupies a similar space in *The Watcher on the Cast-Iron Balcony*. Despite being referred to in the text's opening sentence, the death of Porter's father only rates one other mention. Following a long and stinging passage in which Porter details his father's many shortcomings, including choosing to become lower-middle-class, not whistling, not singing, not directly expressing opinions or collecting things (93), Porter travels briefly beyond the period covered in the book to give us this account of his father's passing:

> Years later, I spend some weeks fighting, with my own middle-aged obstinacy, his seventy-three-year-old stubbornness, which is taking the final form of starving himself to death in a posh hospital. From somewhere he dredges up his last mortal words, and gives them to me, using the long-unused nickname of my boyhood, 'Thank you Laddie, thank you for everything.' As a finale to a ludicrous death-bed scene, and a father–son relationship, and a life, it is, with its Yankee-Jewish-Metro-Goldwyn-Mayer sentimentality, a farewell both startling and mysterious. Irony? Cynicism? Pity for me, uselessly pitting my strength of will

against his in a battle to make him keep on living? Good sportsmanship? Charming manners, and being a nice man? His dead face, of course, was there to be seen. Dead faces, despite the novelists, despite even the poets, are nothing more than the faces of the dead which say nothing, nothing new, nothing worth recording or shedding tears for. (94–5)

Here we find Porter determined to point out just how little insight he has gained from such an experience – the indecipherable-ness (or meaninglessness) of his father's last words mirrored in his dead face, which 'says nothing, nothing new, nothing worth shedding tears for'. One must wonder at such points how this father came to deserve such memorialising. Particularly when contrasted with Porter's warm and sympathetic treatment of his mother, it is hard to maintain any sense of an equivalent 'objectivity' in relation to remembering his father. What could Porter's father have done to deserve such a portrayal? He blames him for a litany of things, including, possibly, even his mother's early death (239). But it is impossible to shake the feeling that some other vital piece of information is missing from Porter's account of the paternal other.[4]

At least one reviewer claimed this absence as the central weakness of Porter's autobiographical act. 'We do not expect an unpleasant character to be whitewashed simply because he is the writer's father', wrote R. G. Geering in *Southerly* in 1976, following the release of *The Extra*, 'but we do want to see justice done, or at least, appear to be done' (130). Geering had suspended his judgement until Porter had completed his autobiographical trilogy, believing the second and third volumes might provide 'sufficient evidence for the harsh judgement passed upon the father in the first'. However, he concludes, 'It must be said, now, that they do not', and believes that for 'lack of charity on the writer's part', Porter's treatment of his father 'would be hard to beat' (131). Indeed, Porter's last word on his father in *The Extra* seems staggeringly uncharitable. After his father's death, Porter describes finding newspaper clippings of his literary successes that 'trace my fleeting appearances in the spotlight' and even a book his father had labelled 'HIS FIRST COPY BOOK 1917' (64–5). Rather than taking them as proof of the father's 'sustained but never-expressed notice', Porter adopts a second person voice before addressing the father directly for the final patrimonial denouncement of his autobiographical trilogy: 'How simple and cynical of the man to preserve evidence of a concealed esteem in that one

---

4   In her biography, Lord claims that Porter himself found it 'difficult to explain' the 'grudge [he] held against his father […] giving different reasons for it on different occasions' (*Many Parts* 116). Ultimately, Lord speculates that 'he rationalized his antagonism towards his father as a failure on his father's part to give convincing signs […] that he truly cared for his son' (121).

small drawer. He foresaw that, as eldest son, you'd be the one most likely, some day, to turn the key. He foresaw too that you'd not get to do this until he was no longer there to face up to whatever expression discovery put into your eyes. None, father, none. Cynical! Knowing that refusal is possible, to beg without holding out a hand' (65). What might create a desire to memorialise a father so unsympathetically? Can we find something in Porter's discursive construction of self that may explain this?

The Sadistic Father

Whilst the Oedipal bind may have produced a number of unflattering depictions of fathers in patriography, in the Australian context nothing comes close to the monster of a father Merv Lilley portrays in *Gatton Man*. Though it was published in 1994, Lilley's book recounts a country upbringing in rural Queensland between the wars, making his father a contemporary of Porter's. William Lilley, a veteran of the Boer War, presides over what can only be described as a reign of terror on his farming family in Mount Morgan. Violent and abusive towards his wife and children, his influence on his sons is depicted as irredeemably destructive. Interestingly, Lilley claims to write in part to uncover a kind of hidden history of 'toxic' fathers in the Australian bush. Having recalled the story in the local paper of a daughter shooting her father 'in the best interests of the family' and wishing he had done something similar as a boy, the author states:

> What I'm saying about the sadistic life on dairy farms is not of an isolated nature in those times depending, I believe, on the nature of the head of the family, though not a lot has been written about it as yet. Writers are probably not coming from those areas, don't have the wish to put it down or someone up there in the publishing world is protecting the Australian image they want to endure and have nurtured in a literary fashion since the onset of colonisation. (15)

However, seemingly not content to merely recount the father's depravity against his family, Lilley's patriography becomes a detective story against his father, impugning him for the unsolved Gatton murders of 1898, in which the raped and bashed bodies of three children were found in a paddock in the Darling Downs. Though his evidence on this 'cold case' that took place some twenty years before he was born is at best circumstantial, Lilley mounts a compelling indictment against his long dead father. At the very least, by the conclusion of the harrowing *Gatton Man*, readers are unlikely to accuse this author of a lack of patrimonial charity.

Although Porter's attitude to his father's death is at best ambivalent, as he feels his own parents were to the death of Grandfather Porter (226), there are other deaths in *The Watcher on the Cast-Iron Balcony* that do 'say' something, and cause the autobiographer to ask more serious questions. Porter records for example the untimely death of one of his students, 'Wock Somebody'. Despite forgetting his name, Porter remembers him as 'a grubby boy with warty hands', who 'grins at my praise and grows younger', who is 'dear to my vanity', and whose death heralds another turning point (or countdown to zero) introduced by Porter as 'Avalanche on the move, Stage Two' (226). Porter posthumously records the comment '*Steadily Improving*' on this dead boy's last paper, which he frames as a kind of obituary, though he admits this is a 'prettied up lie' for the student's parents (229, emphasis in the original). This fitting schoolmaster's eulogy, in fact the very story itself, is offered not simply to give us insight into the making of Hal Porter, but it is offered as a testament to a life that has passed. As we will find in subsequent chapters, in elegiac autobiographies an author's mode of memorialisation is often best glimpsed by analysing their tributes-in-miniature. As with Augustine's numerous eulogies to friends, the memorialisation of such a peripheral figure merely intensifies Porter's glossing over of his father's death.

'The Living Feminine'

The Watcher on the Cast-Iron Balcony's central eulogy creates its dramatic climax. As noted, the death of Porter's mother is not only the work's primary narrative construct, but also its internal rubric. Porter measures every experience against his knowledge of this impending death. While the still somewhat innocent 11-year-old Harold states, 'I simply do not believe [...] for one moment in Mother's dying [...] she is too entangled in life' (80), the narrator peppers each moment leading up to the text's conclusion with running statistics that count backwards to zero: 'She bends to kiss me on the forehead for the fourth last time in life' (240). In this way the events of Porter's early life become a retrospective meditation upon the character of his mother as revealed by her endearing superstitions (82), or her singing (45). Even her weekly routine is inscribed with a weight of fond sentimentality:

> She is green-fingered Thursday, and happiest, dividing her violet and primrose plants [...] crushing a handful of lemon verbena leaves or eau-de-Cologne mint between her palms, and inhaling the scent of her hands which must smell also of earth and thyme and toil and happiness. (58)

It is an affecting passage of nostalgic memorialising, tinged with sexuality, and continues for a number of pages. It is following this sequence that Porter states, 'I am discovering as I write these words that my autobiography, at this period, is my mother's biography' (62). Some may find this assertion odd in an otherwise traditional, Rousseau-style autobiography, recalling Stanton's claim that 'relational autobiography' applies solely to 'women's stories'. However, due to the enduring presence of his mother's death even upon the story of her life, it might be more accurate to claim Porter's text not as biography but as an extended eulogy. Her impending and oft-foreshadowed death creates both for writer and reader the impetus to remember her life.

Jacques Derrida's self-division of the 'I' into father language (formal, scientific and dead)[5] and mother language (natural, embodied and living) sees him invest not only metaphorical significance into what he terms 'the living feminine' (*The Ear* 21), but, in 'Circumfession', also leads him to write his mother 'autobiographically'. As Linda Anderson observes, for Derrida 'the mother's death is unthinkable because it is she who underwrites his name with her body, who guarantees his name by providing him with his ground or being' (85), recalling Porter's own words that 'I simply do not believe for one moment […] in mother's dying' (80). Here, it is the mother who 'underwrites' the name that underwrites the autobiographical contract. Perhaps, then, it is unsurprising that, as for Porter, it is his mother's (impending) death that problematically creates Derrida's impetus to write autobiography:

> I am writing *for* my mother, perhaps even for a dead woman and so many ancient or recent analogies will come to the reader's mind even if no, they don't hold, those analogies, none of them, for if I were here writing for my mother, it would be for a living mother who does not recognize her son. ('Circumfession' 25, emphasis in the original)

One gets the same sense of the desire and anguish as Porter attempts to eulogise his mother, the longing to preserve her body within the physical body of his text. Echoing Derrida's distress at writing's lack and death's immutability, Porter famously concludes his mother's death-bed scene and the narrative with 'Mother is dead, God is dead, love is dead, all that I was dead' (254–5).

Even when Porter's story is forced to move away from a biographical account of his mother, when he leaves home at the age of 16, she remains an uncomfortable presence in his account of youth and early independence. While being seduced by his teaching colleague Miss Hart, a woman 'two and a half times' his own age (224), Porter observes: 'She is merely naked as life and pain and stupidity except for pink Celanese bloomers […] like Mother's' (223).

---

5   In the Australian context, as we will discover in subsequent chapters, Derrida's father-language is defined by its laconism, by the paucity of communication between father and son.

Despite his mother warning him in a letter that 'young men do not, and should never, accept presents from women' (221), Porter even suggests that she is somehow complicit in this seduction: 'Neither does she, as far as I know, write to Aunt Bona. Why? Because she knows that women, anyway, with their magnificently small aims, almost always get what they want' (221).

In *The Boy Adeodatus*, Smith's tribute to his mother is likewise complicated by the presence of the Oedipal, when for example Bernard's desire for his cousin Flo is linked to the maternal: 'It seemed a pity she was his cousin. So pretty. So like his mother' (227). Complexly however, such gestures seem as much to do with reclaiming the absent father as they are with the desire to take his place. Dalziell shows how Smith's 'old father of his flesh' remains with him in discomforting ways throughout the narrative. When Bernard loses his virginity to the sexually experienced housemaid Annie, Smith makes explicit comparisons between this union and the one that led to his conception. Roles are of course reversed. Smith, like his mother, is the sexually inexperienced, submissive one, while Annie, who uses contraception, is the less naïve female servant of the text. However, Dalziell reproves Smith for giving 'no attention to the broader social context' that his seducer Annie was situated within, and believes that 'he is distancing himself from the shameful thought that, in his sexual relationship with a housemaid, he is no better than his own father' (79). As we will discover again in Chapter Seven, an author often unconsciously demonstrates the extent to which he is his father's son.

'A Different Kind of Male'

Porter's identification with the mother is developed concurrently with a self-construction in direct contrast with his father. In another sustained passage of prose that continues for five pages, Porter sets out the frame of reference for his juxtaposition of father and son (91–5). The basis for Porter's 'precise and glass-clear' observations seems to run simultaneously in two ways: on the one hand Porter is 'able to sniff out many of my father's imperfections because he has passed them on to me from his own father' (92), yet on the other the author is, as he makes clear, 'a son and a different kind of male' (94), one who is bookish, intellectual and self-critical. This contrast manifests itself in one's attitude to sport. 'Nothing then, or now', Porter asserts, 'arouses me from a perfect disinterest in ball games' (90):

> My disinterest, openly expressed and lived up to, angers my father. It is a spurning of his hopes that I should equal, perhaps even surpass, his own skill for competently kicking, bowling, catching, or striking at balls of various sizes. [...] I first become aware that he is famous to himself

when he becomes aware (or has he been patiently waiting?) that I am old enough – no, big enough – to be taught some tricks with bat and ball. He is too late. I am not to be corrupted; and my precise and glass-clear and abominably priggish analysis of why I will not play with him, my own father, who buys my porridge and boots, begins a period of wry antagonism. [...] He is too late because I am born with some lack in or addition to my faculties which makes it impossible to pit myself against in games at the finish of which there are only two prizes, Winner or Loser, both meaning nothing, games that smell of wars conducted on gentleman's agreements, their sincerity hollow, their intentions cut-throat. (91–2)

Porter's narrative of deconversion from his paternal legacy is thus presented as a never-was-converted by his insistence that, 'I am not to be corrupted'. The artifice of Harry's 'performed' masculinity is (somewhat surprisingly for the theatrical Porter) anathema to the author. Earlier, Porter described his father as 'an inhuman actor', and he attempts to amend in himself the 'insulting indifference, a lack of imagination, self-satisfaction and bland selfishness' he has inherited from his father. In contrast:

Father, at thirty-six, merely conceals these flaws by a convincing pretence at hearty participation in the rites of public living – he is, for example, a Mason; he plays golf; he plays cricket; he plays masculinity and respectability and being a good husband, a good father and a nice man.
A form of wordless heroism? (92)

This is the model of a laconic (wordless) Australian masculinity which Porter, and, to a lesser extent the other authors discussed in this book, differentiate themselves from, embodied in part in their act of 'speaking' their masculinity onto the page. As Richard N. Coe notes, Porter's father 'appears to merely go through the motions of living, having "nothing of himself to give". These motions are geared to communal ideals of masculinity which the child savagely rejects' (175). Rather than the Victorian 'muscular Christianity' that the Edwardian Gosse flees from, the post-Edwardian Porter rejects a nominally Christian Australian-Edwardian masculinity (though, according to Lord, preserved many of his parents' Edwardian values and principles). Elsewhere Porter describes his father as 'an indubitable Australian' (13). Porter too identifies as 'an unmistakable Australian, albeit of the Awstralian rather than the Osstralian variety' (106), though his version of Australian masculinity clearly differs from his father's. The author's writerly affectation in person as well as in prose is a key facet of his identity, as Lord makes clear in her biography, and a major outworking of his self-construction against the father.[6] This performance is complicated further by Porter's ambivalent attitude to his (homo)sexuality, which, according to Lord, saw him 'radically reform his notions of dress' when he became aware of the impression his dandified self-image created as a younger man, so that 'the twenty-six-year-old Porter was soberly dressed in suit, collar and tie, with his hair shorn to the very short, shaved back-and-sides style worn by the manliest men in Australia' (*Many Parts* 297). This ambivalence regarding the 'indubitable' Australian male resurfaces in the Sons' Books to be discussed subsequently, particularly in *The Idea of Home*.

Two further Australian deconversion patriographies from the 1980s worth noting in this context are Roger Milliss's *Serpent's Tooth*[7] and James Murray's *The Paradise Tree*. As David McCooey has noted in his insightful reading of these texts (*Artful Histories* 70–90), both bear striking similarities to *Father and Son*, detailing a rupture in the father/son relationship that the autobiography both details and seeks to redeem or atone for. In Milliss's case, the fallout is over politics, while in Murray's it is religion. In a neat reversal of the Gossian narrative, Murray's father disavows him for wanting to become a man of God and join the priesthood. Yet whilst Murray details a litany of paternal failures, his text ultimately resists denouncing his patrimony, becoming, as McCooey describes 'a belated attempt at atonement, if not reconciliation' (88).

In contrast, Porter's father is further condemned for having no appreciation of beauty or knowledge as expressed in art: 'What he does not do makes another pattern for which I find no adjective. He does not whistle or sing or directly express an opinion or collect things or write letters or – until decades later, and then only the "relaxing" rubbish of Westerns and thrillers – read books' (93). While Henry Gosse repudiates secular art and literature in pursuit of beauty and knowledge only in the scriptures, in part leading to the son's rejection of 'the yoke of his dedication', Harry Porter embodies a kind of anti-intellectualism that has no higher cause. It is a particular brand of an Australian male ethos that Hal rejects so fervently, one he identifies as deceitful or fraudulent, one that 'chooses to become lower middle class [...] that class whose contribution to ethics is self-respect. The Australian form of self-respect, however rough-and-ready,

---

6 This affectation is clearly on display in the video recorded interview *Hal Porter*, filmed in 1975 when Porter was 63 years old. The author sips a glass of sherry throughout the interview and speaks with a pronounced Anglicised accent (Darlinghurst: Australia Council, AFI Distributors, 1987).

7 The cover of *Serpent's Tooth* demonstrates the way patriographies reframe the family narrative, typically eliding the mother and other siblings. It portrays the author as a child, framed by his father's arm around his shoulder, who stands above him smiling proudly. The back cover reproduces the original image, taken by a street photographer in Sydney's George Street during World War II. It is a shot of the whole family, with Roger's mother and brother walking beside them.

heart-of-gold, come-and-take-pot-luck-with-us, and matily extrovert is, essentially, ingrowing, self-pitying, vanilla-ice-cream hearted, its central fear a fear of the intellect' (93). Ultimately, the seeming authenticity of this form of masculinity is unmasked as both deceitful and destructive:

> by the age of ten I am dubious of the weight of his honesty and the safety of his simplicity […] From having observed my father, a man of mediocre intelligence, simple, honest and, ultimately, as destructive as cancer, I have learned to make out the signs of a blind wrecker. (92)

While convinced from an early age of being born 'with a lack or an addition to my faculties' which disqualifies the author from defining himself by 'kicking, bowling, catching, or striking at balls of various sizes', it is not until his discovery of poetry in high school that, in language again borrowed from spiritual autobiography, the true narrative of conversation is introduced. It is in the search for 'the *Something* that will empower me to say all I feel' (147, emphasis in the original) that the author is converted onto the path of becoming a writer:

> Next, suddenly, lightening suddenly, while I am still a child, a branch is lopped off my being, and a portion of my childhood ends for ever. I see what poets are.
> Long shafts of light pour from them through the galleries of the years, and cohere into a single greater shaft […] I see that the poet's possessions are everyone else's, and that he is saying what everyone else cannot say or read or even think clearly of. His skylark is the skylark I hear singing above the river flats; his daffodil is the daffodil that Mother grows; his ocean is the Southern Ocean I can now stand before at Seaspray or Lakes Entrance shouting as emotionally and vulgarly as Byron. (147–8)

Porter identifies Shelley's 'Ode to the West Wind' as the possible 'catalyst' for this sudden moment of conversion, and though he name-checks Byron, the figure he most resembles as he stands before the Southern Ocean is a young Edmund Gosse pretending to be Wordsworth as 'a little child': 'my own impregnation with the obscurely-defined but keenly-felt loveliness of the open sea dates from the first week of my ninth year' (Gosse 57). While Porter's epiphany brings pleasure, it also causes the anxiety of one who discovers that what he desires to say has already been said:

> What shocks me, then and now, is that, as a writer, I have been outraced before I begin to run and that, if I wish to outrace, I shall never be able to

stop running. Tranquillity and hope and conceit save me from chucking away my dream of communication, and taking up cricket. I can be said to set my mental jaw and set off for the foothills. (148)

Without such attributes as hope and conceit, Porter would like us to believe that he could indeed have followed in his father's footsteps and become an uncommunicative golfer and cricketer; that he too could have played 'masculinity and respectability and being a good husband, a good father and a nice man'. What saves him from such a fate is a love of words and a conversion to Literature. Once again, like Gosse, Porter's miracles are secular, aesthetic and literary. For the emblematic version of the Australian father represented here, the son's *Künstlerroman* narrative is simultaneously a renunciation of his model of masculinity.

Porter's declaration of the death of God, consciously placed at the conclusion of his narrative, impressionistically creates a link with Gosse's in *Father and Son*. As the young Edmund addressed the divine with the cry, 'Come now, Lord Jesus', before stating that 'The Lord has not come, the Lord will never come' (165), the young Hal Porter implores, 'Oh God, put me back on the balcony!' before concluding, 'There is no one to hear. God is dead' (*The Watcher* 254). Likewise, the mother's deathbed scene in *The Watcher on the Cast-Iron Balcony* recalls Emily's death in *Father and Son*, though in the former case it is artfully placed as the dramatic conclusion of the narrative. Following the devastating and much-celebrated scene from which Porter wrenches every last inch of pathos, the 18-year-old Hal exclaims, 'Mother is dead, God is dead, love is dead, all that I was is dead' (254–5). It is the moment Porter has been building towards since his mother's death is heralded in his opening paragraph, and while this event of loss gives his work its emotional structure, it is the death of God that retrospectively invests the narrator with such a compelling authority. According to Lord, it also made him 'free of moral and ethical restraint' (*Man of Many Parts* 46), as evinced in the opening pages of *The Paper Chase*.

Ultimately, the structure that binds the *Confessions*, *Father and Son* and *The Watcher on the Cast-Iron Balcony* together is the complex way the figures of father, mother and God intersect and diverge within the works. Patricius, Henry Gosse and Harry Porter are all ultimately rejected as the model of masculinity adopted by their sons. While Augustine's mother is valorised and credited with the saint's conversion to God, Gosse's mother dedicates her son to God on her deathbed. Though the author eventually threw off the yoke of his dedication, he does not renounce his mother, who is memorialised in *Father and Son* as 'the holiest and purest of women' (42). Likewise, the closing pages of *The Watcher on the Cast-Iron Balcony* describe how Porter, at his 'celebrated' mother's deathbed, throws off the yoke of the divine:

> Mother is dead, God is dead, love is dead, all that I was is dead. So I think, waiting for Father to make himself publicly possible, waiting to begin watching again those who are watching what they think is me, the dead one.
>
> I do not know that, not only have I not started to die, I have not started to live.
>
> I have not even helped Father across the road to the rectory. (254–5)

As almost every line of the harrowing final pages of *The Watcher on the Cast-Iron Balcony* could have served as its closing sentence, this brilliant finale is highly significant. While the death of God hands the author supreme authority to 'father' himself, Porter simultaneously replaces the biological father as the parent figure, reversing the earthly order as utterly as he has reversed the heavenly one. The aging and widowed father, bowed by grief and his own mortality, is rendered as helpless as a child who must be helped by his son across the road. In this way Porter rehearses a key reversal of the two Sons' Books to be explored in the subsequent chapter: the auto/biographical embodiment of the Wordsworthian 'the child is father of the man'.

Conclusion: Doing Justice

In the introduction to her biography of Henry Gosse, Thwaite retells a story from Edward Marsh's *A Number of People* in attempting to explain her motivations for writing successive books that strove first to reframe (and reclaim) a legacy for the maligned author-son of *Father and Son*, and then to vindicate the maligned father. According to Marsh, one of Edmund's harshest critics, 'the redoubtable Dr Furnivall' was eventually 'seized with remorse and told his victim that in the night the words JUSTICE TO GOSSE had appeared on the wall in letters of fire'. Thwaite concludes, 'I had no such Belshazzar-like visitation, but the message had seemed equally clear' (*Glimpses* xvii).

What does it mean to try to 'do justice' to a 'real' historical person who one believes has been misrepresented in literature (or criticism)? How does one carry out this attempt to do justice when the falsification has been perpetrated in auto/biography?[8] Thwaite marshalled the powers of biography to reframe

---

8   Gusdorf once claimed that 'No one can better do justice to himself than the interested party, and it is precisely in order to do away with misunderstandings, to restore an incomplete or deformed truth, that the autobiographer himself takes up the telling of his story' (in Olney 36). Such an assertion of the genre's veracity now seems somewhat spurious, but demonstrates how the process of doing justice extends to the auto/biographer as well.

both father and son. Carey used the postmodern novel, drawing on Henry's own writing to contest Edmund's portrayal of the father. The complex interplay between these various forms — autobiography, biography, fiction — and their interrelatedness[9] demonstrates the porousness of the borders between genres and the various truth-claims of each.

The subsequent readings rely neither on the verifiable historical sources of biography nor the playful subversive fictionalising of the postmodern novel, yet a key motivating factor of the textual analysis presented is to 'do justice' both to the writing sons and the written fathers of the Sons' Books discussed. Doing justice in this context means critiquing the textual veracity of each author's representations; or as Noel Rowe puts it, paying attention to a writer's 'ethico-textual manoeuvres' (196). Such a desire to, *pace* Geering, 'see justice done, or appear to be done', applies not only to negative representations, but may also apply equally to texts where the ostensible objective is to honour the father. It is to two such Sons' Books that we will now turn.

---

9   Carey read Thwaite's biography of Edmund before he read *Father and Son*, then Thwaite drew on Carey's novel in further explaining her motivations to do justice in her biography of Henry Gosse.

Part II

MEMORIALISING SELF-DENIAL

Chapter Three

'WORDS TO KEEP FULLY AMONGST US': HONOURING THE FATHER IN RAIMOND GAITA'S *ROMULUS, MY FATHER*

I say all this as his son, and because I say it at his funeral, I am conscious of the fact that many of you will believe that what I have said is, in the circumstances, an understandable and forgivable exaggeration. As God is my witness, I speak it as the truth about this singular man.

—Raimond Gaita, 'Romulus Gaita: Turnings of Attention'

It is only with Renunciation (*Entsagen*) that Life, properly speaking, can be said to begin.

—Thomas Carlyle, *Sartor Resartus*

POLUS. So you'd prefer to suffer injustice rather than do it?
SOCRATES. For myself I should prefer neither; but if it were necessary for me either to do or to suffer injustice, I should choose to suffer rather than do it.

—Plato, *Plato's Gorgias*

Raimond Gaita and Richard Freadman have been quite explicit about the reasons for writing patriographies. In the acknowledgements of *Romulus, My Father*, Gaita discloses how it originated from the eulogy he gave at his father's funeral, which was subsequently published in the journal *Quadrant*. The book's closing pages briefly recount the act of giving this eulogy, a task he performed because 'There was no one else who could do it' (207). Gaita quotes from the conclusion of his funeral speech, summing up what has been a major task of his work: to define his father's distinctive and admirable form of decency. Gaita writes, 'He was truly a man who would rather suffer evil than do it' (208). On his reasons for writing the book, Gaita has elsewhere stated that, 'I wrote it partly because I wanted to bear witness to, rather than merely record, or even celebrate, the values that defined my father's moral identity' ('From Book' viii). The closing pages of Richard Freadman's *Shadow of Doubt* bear some striking resemblances with Gaita's – following a harrowing and fully described death-bed vigil, the middle-aged author drives to his father's funeral, a man described as having embodied a peculiar strain of Australian decency that expressed itself through 'self-thwarting' and at times 'self-destructive' (81) self-denial. The text itself is offered 'In memoriam' of the father it depicts. In an essay about his memoir, Freadman addresses his dead father directly, stating that he wrote the book,

> to pay a kind of tribute to you. To say that even though you were disappointed in yourself, there was a lot to like about you and what you did with your life and that you gave me a lot as your son […] I guess too, that part of me wanted to spare you the indignity of oblivion. ('Decent' 140)

Exploring this impulse in literature, John Barbour asks, 'How does the son save the father?' When the father is dead, 'a reunion can come about only in symbolic form' ('Judging' 76).

This impulse for reunion through memorialisation raises a number of questions regarding the tribute mode of the Son's Book of the Father, which is the focus of the following two chapters. The first question relates to the text being required to in some way bear the weight of both the subject's life and the author's debt and mourning. Can a narrative carry out this work of reparation? The second relates to the author's sense of duty in carrying out this task, as the only person with access to the facts and memories who is willing to write. This perceived duty is sharpened by the knowledge that if he does not tell this story, it will remain untold, leading to more loss. Gaita's desire to 'bear witness to' the good of the father and Freadman's to spare his father 'the indignity of oblivion' gesture towards a belief in autobiography's unique capabilities: to represent and even resurrect a life, to preserve or even create a legacy. But are these desires and beliefs universal or exceptional? Most people live and die in relative anonymity, so the act of making public a father's life is a conscious choice that assumes such a process is innately valuable. It is not unfair to wonder whether the subject-father shares such an assumption. Finally, and central to the following discussion, these works are an exploration of a distinctive conundrum for the life writer – how does one render a subject in text who in various ways denied himself in life? How successfully or accurately can the characteristic of self-denial be represented within the confines of traditional autobiographical discourse, and what strategies can a writer employ to achieve this representation? Is it possible to 'bear witness to' this moral good in auto/biography, as Gaita intends his writing to do? Can a

Son's Book reverse (or make amends for) the kind of self-thwarting practiced by Freadman's father? Or does the self-denying subject present a paradox for the supremely 'referential art'? (Eakin, *Touching* 3).

Historically, the 'moral good' of self-denial – the renunciation or setting aside of one's own wishes, needs or interests – has not been universally valorised. In Western culture at least, it is constantly held in tension with the competing Aristotelian 'good' of self-concern and self-actualisation through achievement. As Mark Levon Byrne observes, 'the West has long worshipped figures who embody the heroic impulse "to strive, to seek, to find and not to yield", as Tennyson put it' (1). Self-denial is central to the Judeo-Christian tradition,[1] while in classical philosophy it dates back at least as far as Plato's *Gorgias* (32). Interestingly, however, in its earliest literary usage, the term is set against the notion of the self and described as 'her opposite'[2] and it is this secondary sense of renunciation as existing against the self, as an absence of self, that is also of central relevance here.

In the genre of autobiography, a male subject is traditionally defined by autonomy and achievement: he becomes self-actualised by action, by the pursuit and realisation of his desires and plans. I have in mind here the 'great man and his deeds' mode of autobiography as championed by the first theorists of the genre. Georg Misch, in his *History of Autobiography in Antiquity* (1907), as Smith and Watson describe, argued that 'the progressive unfolding of Western history can be read in the representative lives of the leaders who participated in its achievement of civilisation' (113). Fifty years after Misch, Georges Gusdorf, whilst permitting the inclusion of 'not so famous lives', claimed that 'Autobiography [...] requires a man to take a distance with regard to himself in order to constitute himself in the focus of his special unity and identity across time' (35). While relational auto/biography enacts a debunking of the 'myth' of autonomy and places less emphasis on the narrating of achievement, a text that seeks to tell 'male' stories must still engage with culturally dominant notions of what a masculine life should look like. In patrimonial life narrative two enmeshed male lives are represented, with the son's story extending out of his telling of his father's. The son 'comes from' the father, and the tribute mode is an acknowledgement of this debt. For Gaita and Freadman this is especially so, as their texts demonstrate their fathers' influence in the development of

---

1   Personified by the suffering servant of Isaiah 53 and embodied by Christ's act of washing the disciples' feet and, ultimately, in his sacrificial death. John Henry Newman proclaims, 'Let your very rising from your bed be a self-denial; let your meals be self-denials' (80).
2   'This notion of Selfe and her opposite Self-deniall'. Daniel Rogers, *Naaman the Syrian, his disease and cure* (cited in the *Oxford English Dictionary*, 2nd ed. (Oxford: Oxford University Press 1989): accessed online 19 September 2010: http://www.oed.com).

their professional interests and can be read alongside their academic writing: in Gaita's case, his works of moral philosophy; in Freadman's, his literary and autobiographical theory. Yet these sons' professional lives introduce a complicating factor, for they write as men who have achieved much and are well known for their achievements. Their lives fit the traditional male model of self-actualisation through accomplishment while the fathers' lives in many ways do not. A male subject who, constricted by self-doubt and depression, failed in his pursuit of success, as we will discover Paul Freadman did according to the text discussed in the next chapter, presents a particular kind of challenge for his son to render auto/biographically: 'I want to pay him a tribute that puts his honourable, interesting, sad life on record, but without falsifying that record' (*Shadow of Doubt* 12). A male subject like Romulus Gaita – who was disadvantaged by economic (and marital) circumstances and by mental illness, but who also is claimed to have embodied a different kind of ethic to that of 'the great man and his deeds' style of narrative life – is similarly difficult to portray. Gaita outlines the difference between these ethical constructs in the following way:

> Much of my philosophical work has been critical of an ethic that is defined by ideals of self-realisation or human flourishing, and by the virtues of courage, integrity, autonomy and nobility […] Justice and goodness are the focal concepts of a quite different conception of the ethical. The first is an ethic of assertion or at any rate an ethic of the relatively fortunate; the second is an ethic of renunciation. Only the latter, I believe, can find words to keep fully amongst us, to enable us to see the full humanity of those who suffer severe, ineradicable, and degrading affliction. ('Reply' 59–60)

Whilst expressing a clear preference for the ethic of renunciation over that of assertion, Gaita has encountered the difficulties of attempting to celebrate the former over the latter within the genre of autobiography.

Importantly, the notion of self-denial is itself often gendered. The masculine version most often celebrated is an active, 'heroic' self-denial; the self-sacrifice of war for example. Feminine self-denial, on the other hand, is typically passive, such as the martyrdom of the all-giving mother. The problems for these Sons' Books is how to render certain forms of masculinity when the lives being written about do not neatly follow such gendered patterns, but instead trouble culturally determined stereotypes and, relatedly, the conventions of autobiography. The major challenge for the authors here is to fully render their chosen subjects in writing while also representing the self-denial that is central to their fathers' natures, to demonstrate that the life they write about is not only a 'literary' one but also a sufficiently worthy *male* one. The work of the text then becomes one of restoring a self in text that denied itself in life, of revealing a male subject defined by abnegation, even whilst acknowledging the impossibility (and potential dubiousness) of such a venture.

'The Axe for the Frozen Sea'

Like the author of *Father and Son*, Raimond Gaita is his father's only child, allowing for an unusually intense identification with his patrimonial heritage. *Romulus My Father* is the only Australian Son's Book of this study that lays claim to a 'non-competitive' experience of patrimony, which may help to account for the absence of ambivalence in the narrative. Unlike the 'absent' fathers of Smith and Porter, Romulus is the major presence in Gaita's life; the primary care-giver throughout most (though not all) of his childhood, he is also credited as the central inspiration for, and influence on, Gaita's moral philosophy. While Gosse's claim that his Son's Book was 'a monument to my father, an extraordinary man' seemed somewhat spurious, in Gaita's case the description is remarkably apt. However, despite the centrality of the father, Romulus is constructed in comparison and contrast to at least three other key figures of Gaita's childhood: his mother Christine, and Mitru and Hora, who act as 'father figures' at various points in the narrative. The following discussion will examine how Gaita's representation of these secondary relational others of the auto/biography impacts upon his portrayal of the father.

What is most striking about Gaita's continuing relationship to his text over a decade after its publication is his willingness to engage in public debate about the way his memoir should be read and interpreted, culminating in the release of a collection of essays entitled *After Romulus* in 2011. What this repetition of the autobiographical act highlights is a kind of textual absence, an impossibility built in to the generic framework of the memoir itself, despite Richard Flanagan's assertion that 'Romulus fills every page with his presence' (11). The author's autobiographical impulse – to define and pay tribute to his father's ethic of renunciation – cannot be adequately represented in the narrative genre within which Gaita has chosen to write. Autobiography, even relational auto/biography, driven as it is by narratological volition and intention – and particularly a masculine version of this enterprise such as the Son's Book of the Father – struggles to create a space for the kind of father Gaita wishes to celebrate. These limitations are exacerbated by the author's 'ethical' mode, his commitment to 'tell it truthfully' (*After Romulus* 91) and a resulting inability (or unwillingness) to expose his father's inner life. This leads to a lack, a slippage between authorial intentions and reader comprehension, demonstrated by Gaita's need to continually correct and redirect his readers' responses to his text. This absence can be identified in the text itself, as this reading seeks to demonstrate.

Romulus, My Father is undoubtedly Australia's most celebrated patriography. Since its release in 1998, the book has been reprinted almost every year (on occasion up to four times), totalling over twenty reprints. It received the Victorian Premier's Nettie Palmer Prize for Non-Fiction in 1998, and has been translated into numerous languages. It has since been added to high school curricula across the country and was cemented in the public consciousness with the release of the Richard Roxburgh–directed film version in 2007.

These markers of the book's popularity do not fully elucidate the regard in which it is held. Helen Garner describes the rarefied position *Romulus, My Father* inhabits in the following way:

> The book changed the quality of the literary air in this country. People often take an unusually emotional tone when they speak about it, as if it had performed the function that Franz Kafka demanded: 'A book must be the axe for the frozen sea within us'. Reading it, with its stiff, passionate dignity and its moral demands, can smash open a reader's own blocked-off sorrows. Out they rush to meet those that the book relates. (17)

The text's dignity and moral demands have produced an unusual level of reader-identification: not only allowing one to mourn one's own loved ones,[3] but even to mourn *with* the author for a father one has never met. Garner, struggling to account for her emotional response to the experience of being taken by Gaita on a tour of the sites or 'personal shrines' (21) of the text, realises that, 'Like many people who have read his memoir *Romulus, My Father*, I felt I knew [Raimond] better than I actually do' (16).

Other key Australian literary commentators have been similarly unreserved. During his speech at the launch of *Romulus, My Father*, Robert Manne stated that, 'even though this story shaped the life of a dear friend and even though it is told with a transparent desire for plain truthfulness to the facts, it had for me the simplicity of myth and the force of tragedy', before concluding that, 'I know of no other book where the love of a father and son has been so beautifully expressed' (11). Manne contrasts Gaita's moral world with the current age, which 'is haunted by the threat of a collapse into meaninglessness', whereas 'within this story everything has weight' (11). Faced with a narrative of tragedy told with such dignity, fellow writers and

---

3 In his review of *Romulus, My Father*, Ross Fitzgerald pays tribute to those whom the text helped him to mourn (11).

critics, whether friends or acquaintances, cannot but respond in hushed tones. This funeral-like respectfulness strikes a chord here, for it is the terrible weight of the text, its control over the discourses of suffering and dignity, which the following discussion seeks to exemplify. As a eulogy from a son to a father, the work has seemingly become a vehicle for Romulus to be collectively mourned and memorialised.

Autobiography as Tragedy

In elegiac auto/biographies, the framework for the author's desires and intentions in the central narrative are often best illuminated by assessing the tributes offered to peripheral figures within the text. Such is the case with Gaita's short aside about his school friend John Dunstan, who helped the author at a time of great need. Gaita records the details of Dunstan's 'short sad life' because 'his generosity deserves more than its mere recording' (130). The telling of this life of hardship takes a mere page, ending thus: 'He came to Melbourne, failed his matriculation, became lost and unstable and, four years later, jumped to his death from the housing commission flats in Carlton' (130). Coming as it does after the suicide of the author's mother, family friend Mitru and the attempted suicide of his father, Gaita's recording of this premature death, incidental in the course of the narrative, seems almost gratuitous. Its inclusion gestures towards the importance Gaita places on 'bearing witness', to tragedy as well as to decency. But how does its telling (rather than mere recording) repay the debt owed by the author for receipt of his schoolmate's generous friendship? This question relates centrally to Gaita's task of memorialising the father.

Gaita has elsewhere described his text as 'a kind of tragic poem, in that extended sense in which the ancient Greeks spoke of poetry' ('From Book' xii). In the book itself, Gaita writes that 'tragedy, with its calm pity for the affliction it depicts, was the genre that first attracted my passionate allegiance' (*Romulus, My Father* 124), and this discursive mode shapes the tone of the narrative. The bleak and austere portrayal of Romulus's early life in 1920s Yugoslavia, where he 'knew only poverty' (2) emphasises not only the father's suffering, but also his willingness to deny himself for others. This discourse is evident in the opening scene, which depicts a 13-year-old boy willing to flee his home to avoid killing his abusive uncle with a pitch fork:

> To ensure that he would not do so he jumped through the window just before his uncle broke down the door, and he fled, to return only for a month five years later. It was the last of many times that his habitually drunken uncle had driven my father to desperate defences. (2–3)

The complexity of filial relationships and violence is foregrounded, the scene prefiguring a later climax where Romulus threatens his son with an axe, but it is the act of self-denial that is highlighted here: Romulus leaves his birthplace out of fear of the (possibly justifiable) evil he might do. As Parker notes, 'His fear is *on behalf of his uncle* [...] The courageous strength being delineated here by Gaita is not physical but moral. It is the strength of self denial for the sake of another, even another who may not seem to have much claim on his compassion' ('Multiculturalism' 46–7, emphasis in the original).

Gaita's text lists a litany of hardship faced by his young father. The promise of an education beyond four years of school is thwarted by 'an inefficient postal service', leaving an image of the boy crying bitterly, 'because his love of learning would never be fulfilled' (3). The tough physical labour of Romulus's blacksmith apprenticeship, where work begins at 1 am and ends at 4 pm, as well as other deprivations such as a lack of food, are recounted by the narrator in spare prose that heightens the sheer cruelty of the father's life. Romulus's relationship with Gaita's mother Christine introduces further prospects for suffering, the tempestuous affair conducted under the very real threat of death due to 'Nazi racial policy' (7). The historical backdrop of 'the violent destruction of the symbols of order and continuity' explain in part what Gaita calls his parents' 'passionately anarchic way of living' (7) and is offered as justification for Romulus's first attempt at suicide when Christine briefly ended the relationship (8). The first signs of Christine's mental illness and parental neglect surface following Raimond's birth, introducing the relational pattern of the text: Romulus comes to assume the role of primary care-giver, fulfilling the traditional duties of both parents.

Like the opening scene of the book, the author's description of his father walking 80 kilometres in search of milk for his young son reads as an almost biblical act of self-sacrifice for the sake of those he loves: 'Exhausted by his efforts to get food for us and because he denied himself so that I would have more, he fainted from hunger on more than one occasion' (9). Brigitta Olubas figures such behaviour as going beyond 'traditional parental self-abnegation' to embody 'parental care', a concept drawn from sociologist Andrew Metcalfe, which refers to the way 'the parent cares for him or herself in his or her care of the child' (7). In this formulation, labelled by Metcalfe as 'middle-age', the subjects of parent and child are thoroughly enmeshed, 'the "I" or "you" invoked [...] is always both parent and child, and is secure or complete in neither position' (Olubas 3). While a condition of much relational auto/biography, this notion seems particularly apt in describing the bond between father and son in Gaita's text, where Raimond seems to have absorbed so much of the father's way of seeing the world, and where the pattern of parental care is at times reversed, so that the child must care for his parent.[4] However, the contrast between these earlier instances of self-denial and those that deal with Romulus's later life are that the former can be portrayed as definitive, heroic acts. Traditional male autobiography, driven by volition and narrated action, is the ideal genre for representing this form of sacrifice.

While passage to Australia for the young family (against Romulus's wishes) may have offered some hope of improvement, Gaita thwarts this expectation with the prophecy his father received from a tarot card reader that 'he was destined for a journey across a large water, that he would lose his wife and suffer greatly' (10). Nor is it long before this prophecy begins to see fulfilment. While Romulus finds further premonitions in the Australian landscape and foliage, which 'seemed symbols of barrenness and deprivation' (14), these cannot 'extinguish his young dreams of a new life' (16). But it is his mother Christine's very public infidelities, particularly one involving her husband's friend Mitru, which cause the greatest challenge to Gaita's depiction of a masculine self-sacrifice. Fabled acts of renunciation compel the biographical narrative forward. But here, when the model of heroism would demand that a man defend his honour, it is Romulus's lack of action that is most stark. He does not act violently towards his wife or the men who cuckold him, but suffers these humiliations in silence. In his forward to Nick Drake's screenplay of *Romulus, My Father*, Gaita heightens the disparity with reference to the deeply proud and patriarchal Yugoslavian culture from which Romulus came: 'My father was born into a culture in which honour was, at least for men, the focal ethical concept. For that reason, few of his compatriots had much sympathy for his attitude towards my mother and Mitru. Some despised it' ('From Book' xvi).

Gaita's ethics of autobiography – to bear witness rather than speculate, to narrate rather than psychoanalyse – contribute to our lack of access to the father's inner life. Due to these restrictions, it becomes difficult for Gaita, recounting very adult events from his childhood, to present a clear perspective of his father's state of mind at this time, though he ventures that, 'My father must have been heartbroken by this unfathomable, troubled, vivacious and unfaithful wife' (19). In part, this deficiency is a product of the author's self-infantilisation: the adult narrator predominantly limits himself to a child's understanding, or to only those insights that may be gleaned from unadorned narration. The same characteristics for which the book is praised – its 'simplicity of myth' (Manne 11), its presentation of 'figures in a timeless tragedy' (Parker, 'Multiculturalism' 49) – also contribute to the lack of interiority in the text, particularly regarding the figure of Romulus.

---

4 See, for example, 83–90, when Christine's mental illness forces Raimond to care for her and for his half-sister Susan. Also 115–40, where during Romulus's period of insanity, Raimond completes his father's furniture deliveries.

Furthermore, Gaita rarely portrays Romulus as self-reflective, making it difficult for the reader to gain any insight into what motivates him. This is compounded by Romulus's other-focussed nature, which cares most often for the feelings and interests of others, including his son. When he does act, it is often difficult for others to conceive of the reasons behind his actions. 'It was bad enough', his father's compatriots thought, 'that a good friend cuckolded him, but it was shameless to compound the dishonour by paying their rent when they were threatened by eviction' ('From Book' xvi). Clearly the author has a distinct purpose in mind here: delineating the unique moral character of a man defined by the ethic of renunciation. Like-minded critics such as Parker and Manne have responded more favourably than Romulus's compatriots, praising the father's moral strength of character as it is portrayed in the book. 'No one could follow the moral narrative of Romulus's life with attention', states Manne, 'and then fail to understand why it is that Rai has given his philosophic life to the elucidation of Socrates' thought – better to suffer evil than to do it' (10).

It is worth noting that the reference points for these various tributes to Romulus (Gaita's, Manne's, Parker's) are all unmistakably male-centric – made by important contemporary male commentators who invoke the names of classic male philosophers – undoubtedly a defining feature of the Son's Book. The author's attribution of the intention behind his father's behaviour is seemingly an interpretation – Romulus never invokes classical philosophy, nor expresses anything resembling the ethic given above. It is this feature – Romulus's ignorance of philosophy yet his natural embodiment of it – which in part leads Parker to make his universalist reading: 'The goods these men [Romulus and Hora] instantiate, and by which Gaita indentifies himself, aren't *particular* goods […] they are rather *universal* […] these are goods that anyone may aspire to' ('Multiculturalism' 46, emphasis in the original). In his reply to Parker (which is longer than the article itself), Gaita resists this interpretation, stating that 'Ancient Greek ethics was not one thing', and outlining the difference between the Aristotelian connection between virtue and appearance and the Socratic ethic 'of foregoing' ('A Reply' 58). Gaita claims that, 'with some confusion and much intensity, my father lived these incommensurable conceptions of the ethical' (57).

Gaita's delineation here is instructive, for as a characteristic of the central figure of auto/biography, the ethic of foregoing, due to it lacking the 'appearance of virtue', has evidently been a difficult concept for many readers to understand or appreciate. Despite Manne's confidence of its self-evident nature, readers have found many traits in Romulus to admire, but self-denial is not one of them. As Gaita explains:

When I reflect on the many comments I receive about the book, I am struck by how often people praise my father's integrity, his courage in the face of much misfortune, his sense of honour and his nobility. These are heroic virtues. When people say that he was a *good* man, they usually explain what they mean by saying that he possessed these virtues to an exemplary degree [...] if these had been his only virtues, important though they are, I don't think I would have written the book. I wrote it to celebrate his goodness as revealed in his attitude to Vacek. But because it so often requires renunciation, goodness of that kind is not a heroic virtue. And though he was far from being a Sensitive New Age Guy, my father's goodness also showed in his compassionate responsiveness to my mother and to Mitru, to their need that was constant and to their desperate relationship for which he pitied them because he knew it would consume them. His compassion went deep. I have known no one who so visibly felt the pain of others. But it cost him. ('From Book' xv–xvi, emphasis in the original)

Gaita's desire to celebrate the traditionally non-heroic virtues – compassion, kindness, self-abnegation – seems to have been the author's auto/biographical impulse, without which the book would likely never have been written. Why have readers failed to fully discern the author's intentions? At the risk of sounding overly deterministic, I believe it is in part a failure of form; the failure of this form of life narrative to intelligibly represent self-denial to a culture that values more active or heroic masculine styles. The limitations of a traditional autobiographical narrative occlude certain forms of masculinity from being represented. This apparent failure on the part of readers to comprehend Gaita's autobiographical impulse demonstrates these limitations, and highlights the risks involved in putting a life on the public record, even if only the risk of being misunderstood or of a life being erroneously valorised by a reading public. Put simply, as I will continue to argue in Chapter Six, some forms of masculinity elude intelligible representation within patriography. Although, as in Gaita's case, an author may seek to rectify such misreadings. The author's willingness to continue defending and re-stating his intentions over ten years after the book was first published demonstrates the ongoing process of negotiation between readers and writers of autobiography.

Gaita's Father Figures: Mitru and Hora

Unlike *Father and Son*, *Romulus, My Father* is not an only-child's cloistered father–son narrative, and it is in the portrayal of Mitru that Romulus's lack of 'heroic' agency becomes most sharply delineated. In a continuation of complicated filial relationships, Romulus is for a time replaced by Mitru as a father to Raimond: 'During this period, I became close to Mitru and very fond of him. He was gentle, quick to laughter, and with a wit that showed the sharpness and delicacy of his intelligence' (26). Yet while a stepfather complicates this Son's Book, Gaita's focus on suffering remains relentlessly concentrated. In the very next sentence he admits, 'I did not then, or ever, know the full degree of his pain. My mother had other lovers and he was tormented by jealousy. Sometimes he fought with them. He came to the bungalow one night, his face bloodied and his jacket torn' (26). While the narrator can only speculate on Romulus's feelings, veiled as they are by self-denial, Mitru displays his emotion through violent action. His presence in the text is incontrovertible, typified by acts both visceral and irreversible, and most frighteningly demonstrated by his method of suicide. While he may be a pathetic figure in Gaita's narrative, as a subject of auto/biography, Mitru is at once present and accessible to the reader.

Importantly, also, Mitru's suffering at Christine's hand is related in part to his care for Raimond: 'Mitru was [...] deeply troubled by the fact that she did not care properly for me, and that her careless spending undermined his capacity to do so' (26). Mirtu's fatherly feelings for Raimond, demonstrated when he does not reprimand the boy after he is arrested on suspicion of stealing, but instead 'spoke sorrowfully of what I might become' (27), gestures toward a potential purpose of Gaita's narrative: the repaying of a debt from son to a father figure. A further implication is that while Mitru feared his 'adopted' son might become a criminal, Gaita acknowledges that this man has indeed played a role in what the author *has* become, and the recognition of this fact in text may go some way to redeeming a short and tragic life.

For we might ask what else is gained by way of legacy in the telling of Mitru's story? Does it benefit the memory of this man to have his suffering described? Apart from Mitru's obvious care of Raimond and his daughter Susan, there is very little in Gaita's recollections of him to admire. His meagre jobs and inability to control Christine's wasteful spending lead to poverty and shame, such as the experience of Romulus paying for Mitru's rent-in-arrears, an event which causes Mitru's 'humiliated acknowledgement' of Romulus's superior strength of character in stating, 'Your father would know what to do' (82). However, perhaps even during the telling of Mitru's story, the author is interested not so much in the legacy of a father figure but of his biological father. Parker sees Gaita's purpose here as having more to do with protecting his father from humiliation than recounting Mitru's humiliation, reading his 'attribution of humiliation to Mitru' as 'at least partly defensive' of his father; 'displacing any implication' that Romulus himself may have been humiliated by this situation (*The Self* 129). What Parker highlights is the way the Son's Book may exhibit a protective function in its desire to memorialise, insulating the father's legacy from potential harm. It suggests some responsibility on Gaita's part for the absence of his father's interiority in the text.

As a model of masculinity, Romulus himself compares Mitru unfavourably with his brother Hora:

> My father was very fond of Mitru because he was so evidently a good man, but he did not respect him as much as he did his brother. Mitru was softer and also weaker. My father never blamed him for the affair with my mother. He blamed her (in the sense that he saw her as the primary cause) and, because he saw it as an expression of her promiscuous nature, he pitied Mitru. (82)

Denying oneself (as Hora and Romulus do) does not necessarily make one 'soft' or 'weak', just as textual presence is not necessarily evidence of 'strength of character'. Mitru is likewise left out of Gaita's most exalted passage of praise for his father and Hora, who functions as another father figure in the text:

> On many occasions in my life I've had the need to say, and thankfully have been able to say: I know what a good workman is; I know what an honest man is; I know what friendship is; I know because I remember these things in the person of my father, in the person of his friend Hora, and in the example of their friendship. (74)

Yet Gaita further heightens Mitru's presence and the consequent absence of the father's voice by quoting at length from the letters Mitru wrote to Romulus as a 'confession' for his part in the affair with Christine, even though these hardly portray Mirtu in a good light (77–8). Gaita claims to provide us this excerpt to 'convey the quality of his sensibility', commenting, 'His confession was odd, if not disingenuous' (81). While this indeed feels accurate, one may question the equity of quoting from this evidentiary source without being able to provide the reader access to the other side of the conversation, for as Gaita states, 'I do not know how my father responded to Mitru's letters' (81). Significantly, there are no written quotations from Romulus anywhere in the text. The author seems to have had some access to his father's correspondences with his one-time fiancée Lydia, and even suggests that Romulus was an expressive and prolific writer (120). In *After Romulus* he again emphasises the quality of his father's 'erotically saturated prose' in love letters to his mother, yet does not quote from them (185).

Quotations from correspondences are common in relational auto/biography and serve as more than mere evidentiary sources. They give textual voice to those who are represented but cannot otherwise speak for themselves. Gosse quotes from his father's letter to him at the conclusion of his narrative, not 'for entertainment' but 'to call out sympathy, and perhaps wonder, at the spectacle of so blind a Roman firmness as my Father's spiritual attitude displayed' (*Father and Son* 168). Authors cannot ultimately control reader-response, and, as discussed earlier, Henry's words contribute to readers trusting the father's authenticity over the son's. But whatever effect it has, its inclusion gives this father a voice in the Son's Book about him. Gaita quotes at length from Mitru's letters 'to convey the quality of his sensibility', yet seems to withhold conveying his father's sensibility through *his* own words.

Alex Segal suggests another reason for the absence of Romulus's written word within the text: Gaita's phonocentrism. Segal reads against Gaita's conception of the importance his father placed on conversation 'opening up the possibilities of authentic human disclosure' (*Romulus, My Father* 173), demonstrating how Romulus was in fact deaf to those aspects of speech that make it unique, such as the tone of voice that might differentiate an expression of intention from a promise. Importantly, this calls into question Gaita's mode of tribute:

> To the extent that the dominant picture the biography creates hinges on transparency of words to self, it hinges on speech […] Yet such transparency – as it unfolds in the biography – turns out to be predicated on what 'speech' excludes: on the aspect of language that breaks with the context of utterance, with tone, and hence with the speaker. It is predicated on a structural non-presence. Although privileging spirit over letter, Gaita's writing […] testifies in spite of itself to the insistence of the letter, an insistence that displaces the repression of writing, displaces phonocentrism. And this displacement undoes the picture of continuity between father and son. For at stake is the crucial way in which the Romulus Gaita described in the biography could not have understood his son's work: neither the philosophy nor the biography written in tribute to him. Hence, in what is perhaps the most radical of the silences that marks the text, the object of the tribute and gratitude, could not have received them. ('Speaking' 18)

In this way, Segal seems to suggest, Gaita is somewhat divided in his intentions, and his portrayal of the father at least partially incoherent. Would Romulus's letters have given us better insight into the ethic of self-denial and avoided the problem of how to represent it through narration? Would his words have established his presence or volition more fully within the text? It is impossible to know.[5] Regardless, the absence of Romulus's voice must be attributed in part

---

5   *After Romulus* includes reproductions of correspondence relevant to *Romulus, My Father*, including between father and son. The following chapter will investigate whether the inclusion of such meta-textual evidence of existence assists Freadman in giving 'presence' to his father.

to the author himself, perhaps an acknowledgement of language's incapacity to represent or 'speak for' the written other of the father. Providing this form of direct quotation from Mitru further sharpens the sense of Romulus's absence in the text.

Hora's story is also defined by suffering. While his early life is not described in any detail, the narrator contends that Hora is haunted by the 'oppressive apparatus' of communism in Romania (15), which caused him to flee his homeland. During Romulus's three-month stay in hospital following his motorbike accident, Hora assumes the dual role of father and mother to Raimond, due to Christine's ongoing neglect: 'He did everything: made my meals, washed my clothes and prepared my school lunches' (44). In fact the bond between Hora and Raimond becomes so close that his father's return causes conflicting feelings: 'When he came home I was happy, but also a little sad. It was the only time I remember when my love for Hora and for my father caused confused emotions in me towards either' (48). As we see here, even a father figure who complements the father may cause feelings of ambivalence. As we will discover in subsequent chapters, this is exacerbated when these men are not necessarily 'on the father's side'.

Gaita also does Hora the honour of detailing his attributes, particularly in an unbroken passage of praise and reminiscence that lasts for some seven pages (67–74). Here again Gaita is explicit about his purposes, invoking notions of debt to describe the relationship:

> I owe to Hora the development of my interest in ideas. Inclinations to delinquency ran strong in me at the time. At a certain point in my teenage years, intellectual interests ran stronger than they did. More than anyone else, I owe that and the course of my life to Hora. (72)

Yet, possibly due to the happier life hinted at late in the text (170), Hora's story does not contain the same weight of bleakness as the other figures of Raimond's childhood. Another reason for this may be the fact that *Romulus, My Father* was not written in the face of Hora's death. As the only person left alive from Raimond's early life at the conclusion of the narrative, perhaps the responsibility Gaita feels to account for this man's suffering and goodness is not as sharply felt. Without the obligation to memorialise, less seems required of these recollections by way of reparation. An essay dedicated to Hora in *After Romulus* supports this assertion, and demonstrates Gaita's ongoing desire to pay tribute to his complex patrimony. Written almost eight years after Hora died, Gaita describes 'A Summer Coloured Humanism' as an 'elegy to him', and states that, 'In *Romulus, My Father* he is often in the shadow of my father, seen as his loyal friend. I wanted to express my love for, and gratitude to, him alone' (*After Romulus* 6–7). As we shall see in subsequent chapters, this mediation between paying tribute to the father or to father figures in patrimonial life narrative is a central tension of such works.

The Son's Elision of the Mother

However, in these narratives of competing (or even complementary) patrimonies, how does one negotiate a space for the maternal, particularly in the case of a 'failed' or negligent mother? While she is rarely the narrative's central focus, the author takes some care in bearing witness to, rather than diagnosing, Christine Gaita's unique experience of suffering, particularly her bouts of severe depression, and her subsequent suicide.[6] The remoteness of the family's life at Frogmore is debilitating for Christine, who 'could not settle in a dilapidated farmhouse in a landscape that highlighted her isolation' (25). Her neglect of her son makes Christine a pariah amongst the local community and it is this heightened sense of loneliness that leads to her first suicide attempt when Raimond is only six years old. 'She made light of her attempted suicide to me, but her vivacity was gone' (32–3), writes Gaita, describing her subsequent behaviour as 'a strange combination of lethargy and restlessness' (33). The descriptions of her sudden disappearances, her neglect of her baby daughter Susan, and her sexualised behaviour in front of her son (87), illustrate how fraught Gaita's recollections of his mother must be.

Following Mitru's suicide, and the loss of her daughters who become wards of the state, Christine admits herself as a day patient at a psychiatric clinic. She visits Raimond at his school in Melbourne unannounced and he is shocked by her appearance (109). She insists on taking her son to lunch, and in an effort to 'reduce the distance between us' she dances to Buddy Holly in the café. The pathos of the scene 'embarrasses and saddens' Raimond to the point of asking his principal to refuse her any further visits (110). As we shall see repeated in *The Land I Came Through Last*, the double disavowal of a child by a parent and a parent by a child leads to a supremely ambivalent representation of that parent in auto/biography.

It is important that following news of his mother's subsequent suicide Gaita describes being overcome by both 'grief and remorse' (111), the latter emotion hinting at another kind of debt owed to the dead. As an adult looking back, therefore, the author seems often at pains to point out the extent of

---

6   In *After Romulus*, Gaita labels his mother's illness as manic depression, and describes her wasteful spending and promiscuity as symptoms of this condition. He resisted giving a name to her illness in the text 'because I wanted to convey, in ways not obscured or softened by theory, the full terribleness, and the full terror of madness while not diminishing the dignity of those who suffer it' (71).

his mother's manic depression and possible schizophrenia (84), admitting that 'My father, Hora and, I think, Mitru, did not appreciate the degree to which my mother's life and behaviour were affected by her psychological illness' (112). According to Gaita, no other explanation can account for his mother's behaviour, deciding finally that 'No failing of character, no vice, explains or even describes her incapacity properly to care for her children' (112).

A key scene of the narrative in which Gaita moves beyond the period covered in the text reveals again the extent to which reparation drives the auto/biography. Gaita admits that due to 'our intense and conflicting emotions concerning my mother' he and Romulus allowed Christine to lie in an unmarked grave for over twenty years (113). Eventually, seemingly prompted by the shame of this fact, they were compelled to belated memorialisation. Short of money to buy a headstone, Gaita and his father build one together. The author poignantly describes their 'remorseful work' while Gaita's 4-year-old daughter plays amongst the graves: 'Working together, our sorrow lightened by the presence of a young girl representing new life and hope we came together as son and husband with the woman whose remains lay beneath us' (113–14). As Olubas finds:

> This passage is marked by a complex and yet utterly prosaic temporality, where family relations are determined by care and labour on behalf of another rather than simply or onerously by chronology. The persistence of loss, the impossibility of closure over the death of a mother, frames an understanding of family relations in terms of generation as a mode of interrelation. (7)

The work also opens up a space for her life story to be told, the act of building this monument allowing Romulus to speak 'compassionately of my mother's troubled life' (114). The repeated references to 'story', 'life' and 'work' in this short scene seem emblematic of Gaita's purpose for writing. While this act, born out of guilt, means that Christine's story no longer includes the awful fact of an unmarked grave, it is Gaita's story that becomes his 'remorseful work', speaking of suffering in the hope that it may, somehow, redeem his mother's tragic life through narrative, even whilst acknowledging 'the impossibility of closure'.

However, Gaita's work of reparation cannot shake the sense that his attempt to render Christine's story in patriography falls somewhat short. Notwithstanding the concessions offered for his mother's failings, the framework Gaita establishes for eulogising the father figures of his childhood, specifically in regard to the notion of character, leave a figure like Christine with very little space to be properly understood. This formulation of character – celebrated in the figure of Romulus and highly respected by 1950s Australian rural society (which has had much impact on Gaita's conception of the world) – regards suspiciously a woman with 'personality' such as Christine (101). The author describes how this framing of character leads many to regard Christine's 'engaging vivacity as a dangerously seductive manifestation of personality in a woman they believed to be entirely lacking in character – a "characterless woman", as Hora put it' (103). But does Gaita's portrayal of his mother allow the reader to come to some other conclusion than the one given above? Does the author's tragic mode of 'calm pity' afford his mother the same compassionate understanding for her failings as that extended to others? Parker believes not, contending that although it is a 'huge challenge' for an author such as Gaita to give a balanced account when 'his perspective of the world has been so formed by his father' ('Multiculturalism' 51), the author 'doesn't himself provide the framework for us to see his mother's destruction in different terms' (52). He adds that 'one feels sure that Emily Brontë, Tolstoy, or Jean Rhys would have known how to come to grips with such a figure' (52). Gaita is partially aware of his narrative's limitations, Parker concedes, and seeks to counter-balance his representation of Christine by reference to the 'serious possibilities in her that might have been realised in a very different sort of setting' (51). Yet these instances of tribute, such as Mikkelson's recollection of Christine as 'very intelligent and a "woman of substance"' (Gaita, *Romulus, My Father* 31), are too infrequent to balance the ledger. In his response to Parker, Gaita rejects these assertions, emphasising the narrative's commitment to 'truthfulness' ('A Reply' 55) and affirming that 'whatever Tolstoy did with "such a character", the result would not be my mother' (65).

The question of Christine's treatment in the text reveals an instructive limitation of this Son's Book of the Father: the very formulation of the text dictates that the mother's story cannot be fully rendered. Joy Hooton has noted this phenomenon in intergenerational auto/biographies written by women: 'it is a curious fact that a daughter's admiration for her father often involves dismissal of a mother' (150). Hooton also finds that in the Australian context, 'Fathers who inhabit the bush are particularly obliterating of mothers' (151); though it would be an oversimplification to ascribe this pattern to Gaita's text. For Gaita these limitations are of several orders: the author's commitment to 'bearing witness' and refusal to psychoanalyse or fictionalise; his internalising of his father's values; his avowed focus on memorialising the father's self-denial. Yet, they are all generic choices the author makes, in order to, as it were, 'best serve' the father. Gaita concedes as much when he states, 'some lives are lived in such a way one would almost certainly distort them if one referred in any detail to that complexity. This is true of my father' ('A Reply' 66). The defining feature of son–father auto/biographies, then, their strength as well as (at least for the mother) their shortcoming, is the framing of the genre to best fit the kind of image of the father the author desires to portray.

While still defending himself against Parker's claim that 'I am unjust to my mother in the book', Gaita has recently come to something of the same conclusion regarding his patrimonial life narrative:

> One way of making the point I am gesturing towards, perhaps, would be to say that, just as my mother was ill at ease in the actual landscape of Central Victoria, so she is ill at ease as a character in a book whose narrative genre is conditioned by that landscape and its natural congruence with categories of character, fate and metaphysics [...] Perhaps that genre is not one in which she can appear fully individuated, fully a presence in the world, a distinctive perspective on it. I do not know whether that is true, but this is clearly true: genre is essential to narrative and it opens and closes the possibilities of characterisation. (*After Romulus* 116–18)

Gaita is surely correct here, and his sense of the way his mother's non-presence haunts the text is decidedly apt. This realisation led him recently to consider writing a Book of the Mother, and as the author asserts in *After Romulus*, the blurry cover image of himself as a young boy in his mother's embrace is a gesture towards matriography. However, like the smudgy ghostliness of his mother's face in the photograph, Christine remains an unknowable presence in his writing. 'An unassuageable Longing' attempts a kind of reparation of his mother's memory, but as Gaita seems to conclude, repeating the parental tribute in auto/biography is in his case impossible, not only because his mother's 'perspective' remains inaccessible (218), but also because the self in relation to the mother is emotionally out of reach of the author, leading to 'a melancholy and longing that have not diminished' (226).

The Absent-Present Father

Gaita's invocation of genre returns us to the figure of the father. Is Romulus, as he is represented in the text, fully individuated, fully a presence in the world? Perhaps the most harrowing portion of the text, and the one that presents the strongest impediment to the representation of Romulus within traditional autobiography, is that which deals with Romulus's decline into insanity. In a sustained passage that continues virtually unbroken for some thirty pages (*Romulus, My Father* 115–45), Gaita offers both account and analysis of his father's mental illness; a treatment not afforded others. When Raimond visits his father in a psychiatric hospital, the author demonstrates the importance of setting and landscape in 'giving colour [...] to my understanding of suffering', describing the hospital as a place that 'represented a foreign world to me, one whose beliefs [...] I instinctively felt to be in conflict with those that had enabled me to understand the events of my childhood' (123). Seeing his father in a place shaped by 'psychiatry's debunking of metaphysics' leaves no room for Raimond to make sense of this scene. Gaita describes the effect of this experience: 'I left the hospital changed. I had absorbed past sorrows against the sure confidence of my father's strength. I knew that, whatever was to come, I could never do so again' (125).

What is the 'father's strength' as it is portrayed in *Romulus, My Father*? The question goes to the heart of how a particular kind of masculinity or 'male' story might be represented and celebrated in patrimonial life narrative. As discussed previously, feminist theory has forced into the open the examination of the male body in literature, yet the father's body continues to present a challenge to a writer-son such as Gaita. Romulus's absence in the text persists despite the author's attempts to emphasise his physicality. The father's physical strength is foregrounded in Gaita's memory of his father's statement (while they rode on his motorbike) that 'there is no sickness worse than mental sickness':

> I remember his words very clearly. I remember the exact point where we were on the road. Most of all, I remember his strong, bare, sun-darkened arms on either side of me as I sat on the petrol tank. For me to have remembered his words and our surroundings so vividly, the authority with which he spoke must have impressed me deeply. The sight of his muscular arms protecting me against their terrible meaning. (140)

As is typical of Gaita's prose, the pathos is underplayed, yet the scene gathers emotional force in its link with Gaita's earlier realisation of the fallibility of his father's strength, following his father's stay in a psychiatric ward. Tellingly, Gaita returns to an aesthetic examination of patrimonial bodies in *After Romulus*, comparing Romulus's and Hora's 'unusually handsome' faces and muscles while shirtless, noting that 'I was pleased that my father had bigger biceps' (14).

Romulus's struggles with delusions and mental illness may also contribute to his textual absence, and raises a potential challenge to Gaita's attribution of self-denial. During Raimond's visit to hospital, an obviously disturbed Romulus claims to be 'not really ill' due to the fact that he 'could speak normally whenever he made the effort'. Gaita concludes, 'he was quite oblivious to the pathos of that claim' (*Romulus, My Father* 125). Likewise, the complex manner in which Romulus deceives himself and others regarding his part in quarrels reveals a peculiar inability to conceive of his self. 'He was not lying', Gaita insists, 'I never knew my father to lie', yet his self-deception is compounded by an inability to understand the notion of self-deception or even recognise its existence. 'When I told him that there were other ways of being untruthful than by lying, that one might be untruthful to oneself', explains the author, 'he clearly had no idea what I was talking about and could find no familiar conceptual path to doing so' (147). As well as being 'a pathetic state of affairs' for 'a man for whom truthfulness mattered so much', this facet of the father goes some way to clarifying his paradoxical absence in a text whose title purports to tell his story. It is not an absence of biographical narrative, but of a subject as relational auto/biography defines it. While the facts of Romulus's life are present, clues to what drives his actions and intentions are not as immediately accessible. We have no real access to Romulus's interior life, perhaps in part because of his own lack of self-knowledge. For Segal, this is linked to Romulus's inability to distinguish meaning from such things as tone-of-voice, his 'emphasis on literal truth seems to entail a lack of emphasis on the kind of truth-to-self that is essential to individuality' ('Speaking' 11).

There also seems an interesting correlation between Romulus's self-denial and his capacity for self-deception. Romulus's inability to conceive of his own propensity for dishonesty to self might cause us to ask whether such a person can practise self-denial in any conscious sense. If one can deceive oneself without acknowledging that such a thing is possible, can an act of conscious or willed self-denial be attributed to that person? In other words, can an absent or unrecognised self properly deny itself for others? Or does the good of self-denial not hinge on questions of interiority or self-knowledge? This line of argument raises the possibility that readers have failed to grasp the qualities Gaita values in his father because Gaita's ascription of these qualities to Romulus is incoherent. I raise this suggestion tentatively for it is a somewhat more radical explanation for the tensions inherent in the text. Segal comes close to asserting a similar argument in discussing Gaita's evocation of the landscape of central Victoria to shape and inform the book's ethic. While Gaita claims, 'Life in Frogmore, in that landscape and under that light, nourished the sense given to me by my father and Hora' of the 'uncompromising authority of morality' (124), it is this very same landscape that Romulus so despised. Gaita's evocation of setting, then, according to Segal, 'gives sensuous embodiment to Romulus Gaita's values – but with reference to a beauty to which he is blind' ('Speaking' 15).

Related to this is how we might understand the reasons for *Raimond*'s actions within the story. When the visibly unwell Romulus visits his son at school, accompanied by the equally unstable-looking Vacek, Raimond denies to a teacher that either man is his father: 'I was later tormented with guilt and shame [...] but I knew not quite for what I was ashamed because I also knew that, terrible though it was, my denial was not prompted by cowardice' (136). Precisely what Gaita means here is somewhat oblique – what sounds like self-justification is in fact another example of the author's desire to distinguish between highly nuanced philosophical concepts. Rather than being ashamed to be associated with his father, which would be a failing of character, Gaita claims to have been conveying the way that 'when people appear bereft of social standing and suffer affliction that obscures all trace of dignity, it is almost impossible to see the good in them' ('A Reply' 60). So ambiguous is Gaita's reasoning within the book, that in the German translation the phrase 'my denial was not prompted by cowardice' was removed, Gaita describing it as 'too compressed' (*After Romulus* 68). Nevertheless, according to Segal, Gaita's failure to impugn his actions here comes at some cost:

> In part the memoir testifies to how its author [...] grew up to be a decent man; yet it does so from a perspective that, at a decisive moment, radically limits the value of decency: Raimond's blindness to the humanity of his afflicted father has nothing to do with a lack of decency. ('Work' 32)

The next scene in which Raimond accompanies Romulus on a trip to Sydney, even though his expressed intention is to murder Lydia's husband, may be read as an attempt to atone for his denial of his father. Somewhat surprisingly, Gaita is not 'morally appalled' by his father's intentions, seeing such an act as justifiable for 'a person passionately in love' (137). Such a justification is not made because the intended agent of such an act is his father: 'I would have refused to condemn anyone in a similar condition to his' (138). Nevertheless, filial duty does play some role, for Gaita states 'The fact that he was my father was the reason I felt obliged to accompany him'. The father's desire to exact revenge on the man who betrayed him abruptly enacts a reversal of his previous lack of agency; his violent intentions, though disturbing, confer something of the visceral presence embodied by Mitru upon him. However, in a typically admirable yet confounding fashion, the father does not follow through with his intentions. When he arrives, Romulus is 'disarmed' by Lydia's husband's 'courtesy' and 'saved' from becoming a murderer by Lydia's beauty (139). Gaita explains, 'There were no shots, not even very angry words' (139). Once again, Romulus's preference to suffer evil rather than do it curtails his presence in the text.

The employment of this Socratic ethic, along with the author's comparison of his father to 'a Biblical prophet, someone whose fierce purity made him transparent to the reality of the values he professed' (174–5), gives some indication of how Gaita intends his memoir to be read. Attributing Plato's ethic from the *Gorgias* to Romulus and describing 'the God he prayed to' as 'the God of Abraham, Isaac, Jacob and Job' (169) places the figure of Romulus within a philosophical and religious tradition of the virtues of affliction. It is as if we are invited through these intertexts to see Romulus's story as another in a long line of grand suffering narratives stretching all the way back to Job. Despite these intertextual cues, Gaita has staunchly resisted Parker's over-evaluation of the book's universalism, rejecting his suggestion that 'it is not the historical people who are under question but the textual people', because the historical subjects 'are beyond all reference' ('A Reply' 53). Encouraged by Gaita's employment of 'the language of religion and metaphysics', Parker believes Romulus should be read as 'a figure in a timeless tragedy', that he deserves to be described and judged by 'an older, more universalistic language that discloses [his] "common humanity"' (49). In his reply, Gaita argues strongly for the specificity of the book's subject matter:

> I take that to mean that in *Romulus, My Father*, the names 'Romulus Gaita' and 'Christine Gaita' do not refer to actual human beings who lived and were called by those names. They refer instead to mere 'characters', whose being and identity [...] exist only in the realm of narrative [...] I am quite sure that the way people have been moved by the story told in *Romulus, My Father* is a function of the fact that they trust that I have tried to tell it truthfully and that it is truthful. ('A Reply' 55)

Gaita's employment of such canonical intertextual reference points – to Greek Tragedy, classical philosophy and Old Testament prophets – seems at odds with his desire for his text to be specifically referential, to be about 'actual human beings who lived and were called by those names'. If Parker is not alone in universalising *Romulus, My Father*, some responsibility for such a misreading must fall to the author himself.

A further ambiguity of the text centres around the normative application of Gaita's intertexts. As the author's references to the Bible and *The Book of Common Prayer* exemplify, Romulus's self-conception was intimately bound up in his religiosity: 'The God he prayed to was the God whom he encountered in the Bible stories of his childhood which came mostly from the Old Testament' (169). Like Smith's mother and her Irish Catholicism, Gaita's immigrant father continues to identify with the Orthodox faith of his cultural heritage, notwithstanding certain ambivalences towards organised religion: 'He thought it absurd that God would listen only to the prayers of those who belonged to particular institutions' (168). Despite this, he begs his son to pray, and is dismayed when he cannot (169). Like Smith, Gaita enacts a more gentle form of rejection of a parent's religion than the one portrayed in *Father and Son*, a feature perhaps common for many second generation migrants to Australia.[7]

---

7   There are in fact some minor resonances between Romulus Gaita and Henry Gosse. Both eschew 'worldly' ideals such as the value of appearances, are suspicious of mainstream religion, have exacting standards and are criticised by their sons for their judgementalism. The 'Puritanism' of the elderly Romulus's house (*Romulus, My Father* 171) accords with the picture given in *Father and Son* of Henry Gosse's sparse dwellings.

Yet the importance of the Bible to Romulus's identity may cause us to question the terms of the author's key tribute to his father. Gaita detaches his father's moral character from any notion of his religiosity, and instead employs the Socratic humanist ethics to which he subscribes. It seems fair to wonder whether Romulus may have preferred an epitaph drawn from Job rather than Plato.[8]

Gaita's final act of bearing witness is to his father's death. The final stages of Romulus's life hint at a resolution of sorts following his marriage to Milka and a period of psychological well-being. Romulus's decline into death is sudden, hastened by the misdiagnosis of his 'dead gut' as the flu: 'They thought it unlikely that he would live for more than twenty-four hours' (202). The time allows for Raimond's daughters and Hora to say fitting goodbyes, though Romulus's comatose state prevents much interaction. Considering such limitations, it is telling that Gaita seems to invest such importance in the recounting of this event. Left alone to wait with his father 'for his death', the author notes the appropriateness of this final communion:

> I reflected that just as I had been alone with him at Frogmore during the time of his terrible affliction, so I was now alone with him in his mortal agony. And, as in my childhood, I spoke to him in German. I told him many times, *'ich liebe dich, mein Vater'*. At first he opened his eyes each time I said it, but after a time he made no response.
>
> My father died just past midnight, as they predicted twenty-four hours before. I kissed him and sat with him for another half-hour before calling the nurses. (205)

As with his eulogy, the task of bearing witness to his father's final breath is seemingly performed because 'there was no one else who could do it'.

Conclusion: A Public Legacy

What, then, is the work of Gaita's text? How is the debt owed to the father repaid by the retelling of his story of suffering? If Romulus seems somewhat absent in his own life story due to his capacity for self-denial, perhaps the work of Gaita's narrative is to reverse this self-denial, to constitute a 'textual' self for Romulus that he refused himself in life. The memoir has indeed done this: *Romulus, My Father*'s cultural *cachet* testifies to autobiography's ability to

---

8 Job 41: 34 encompasses something of the ethic of renunciation embodied by Romulus: '[God] Looks down on all that are haughty; he is king over all that are proud.' John 15:13 expresses Romulus's capacity for self-sacrifice: 'Greater love has no one than this, that he lay down his life for his friends' (*New International Version*).

publically memorialise a father's life. Yet Gaita's handling of his chosen genre – the son–father auto/biography – poses certain problems of representation, specifically regarding the portrayal of a renunciatory ethic. If the text had offered more insight into Romulus's inner life, if Gaita had done more to convey Romulus's interiority, one wonders whether this ethic would have been more visible to readers. But in order to do this, Gaita would arguably have had to have taken more liberties as a memoirist – to speculate, to psychoanalyse, perhaps even to invent – modes that the author explicitly eschews. The necessity for the author to continually reiterate his intentions demonstrates the limitations of his chosen form. Though this is not to argue that the text fails as such. As Segal finds, such tensions 'are central to the fascination of the memoir, with its oscillation between self-realisation and self-effacement' ('Work' 32).

In fact, Gaita may view the failure of readers to grasp his motivation for writing as due to a 'blindspot' in the culture within which the text is read rather than any lack or absence in the book itself. His comments about the work seem to indicate that he is neither surprised nor particularly embarrassed that readers have missed what most concerns him. That readers have been more respondent to Romulus's heroic virtues, such as his resilience and courage than his compassion or renunciation, may, for Gaita, reflect the way we live in a time and place that is blind to the value of these less 'showy' virtues. In this way, then, the text aims to expose a *cultural* absence, and the author's subsequent utterances on his readers' misunderstandings serve to reinforce our blindness. This purpose accords with Aristotle's original intention for epideictic oratory. According to Lawrence Rosenfield, the etymology of the term 'epideictic' 'suggests an exhibiting or making apparent (in the sense of showing or highlighting) what might otherwise remain unnoticed or invisible. Epideictic, therefore, acts to unshroud men's notable deeds in order to let us gaze at the aura glowing from within' (135). In this way, Gaita's eulogy at his father's funeral, then its transmutation into memoir, then his reiteration of his intentions in public debate, are part of one author's ongoing attempt to highlight that which remains invisible.

Interestingly, much of *After Romulus* addresses issues of representation and misreadings not of the memoir but of the film version of *Romulus, My Father*, demonstrating the way the remediation of autobiographical narratives into other media further complicates issues surrounding genre and truth telling. Of particular relevance to Gaita is the fact that critical acclaim for the film has focussed around Eric Bana's 'screen presence' in portraying Romulus, and the fact that his entire life story from the memoir has been compressed into three years in the film ('From Book' 136–9). Critics have praised the actor's 'gravity and emotional resonance' (Rigg), his 'unsuspected range' (Roach) and his 'moving, highly affecting performance' (Mitchell), though Sandra Hall echoes the etymology of 'epideictic' in juxtaposing the image on the book's cover with the actor, finding that Bana

> seems much too wry and sunny to get under the skin of such a man but that's all right. You need a little lightness to lift the sense of quiet desperation running through Gaita's story. Only by dispelling it from time to time can you glimpse the strong vein of hope that's pulsing beneath that dour gaze. (1)

While 'presence' on screen may seem to overcome some of memoir's problems of representation, what Bana's Romulus actually depicts may still elude Gaita's chosen ethical frame. As with readers' responses to the book, reviews of the film seem more likely to praise Romulus's 'courage in the face of adversity' than celebrate his powers of renunciation.

Even if Gaita's attempt to valorise self-denial must in part fail, due to the challenges of portraying it in memoir (or in film), Romulus's prominence in the public consciousness makes the success of this patriography in preserving a legacy irrefutable. During his acceptance speech at the 2007 AFI awards upon winning best actor for his depiction of Romulus, Bana thanked the 'real' Romulus for living a life so worthy of portrayal. As far as a text creating a public legacy goes, such an accolade would be difficult to match. It is interesting, then, that, as is the case in our next Son's Book, the work of constituting a father in text who was 'less than he should have been' in life only begins after he has died.

Chapter Four

'I REALLY WAS THE SON OF SUCH A MAN': REPLACING THE FATHER IN RICHARD FREADMAN'S *SHADOW OF DOUBT: MY FATHER AND MYSELF*

If I didn't have the story appointed for me by my father, did that mean I didn't have a story? Not a Story: I realise now that Dad was calling the shots more than twenty years after his death. Fathers choose our stories for us […] and if we refuse the choice we go without.
—Paul John Eakin, *Living Autobiographically*

My greatest debt is to my father – for what he said, wrote and did while he was alive, and for what he left behind. I dedicate the book to his memory.
—Richard Freadman, *Shadow of Doubt*

The Child is Father of the *Man*;
And I could wish my days to be
Bound each to each by natural piety.
—William Wordsworth, 'My Heart Leaps Up'

Roger Porter's recent *Bureau of Missing Persons: Writing the Secret Lives of Fathers* describes how a number of contemporary autobiographies and memoirs focus on fathers who engaged in lying or fabrication, intentionally concealing their identity from their families by various means. In the sub-genre he terms 'The Child's Book of Parental Deception' (*Bureau* 2), Porter shows how the autobiographical act is not only about unveiling the secrets and lies of the father, but a narrative of the son's or daughter's search, as the author becomes a kind of detective in a crime story: 'Amassing clues, data, and facts, these writers, sleuths of selfhood, gather and sift evidence in the documents, attempting to establish a degree of certitude' about the father's identity and hence, their own (10). This chapter focuses on life writing about the father that shares many of the characteristics of Porter's sub-genre, but does not focus on lying or deception *per se*.[1] Rather, in this instance the author wishes to uncover something at once more benign and more confounding: a father's identity that appears hidden or shadowy as a result of failure and elusiveness; a kind of paternal absent-presence. In Richard Freadman's *Shadow of Doubt: My Father and Myself*, the father is not charged with wilful deception (in fact his capacity to be *wilful* is very much under examination), instead he is described as 'self-thwarting' (81), hiding behind the ethos of decency both for fear of failure and to excuse his failures. As Freadman readily acknowledges in his memoir, there are some particular challenges and ethical quandaries in this brand of auto/biographical search. This chapter seeks to explore these challenges, and to show how Freadman's representation of his father's elusive identity relates directly to his criticism and even to his vocation as a life-writing theorist. Rather than simply uncovering the archival evidence, as Porter's 'sleuths of selfhood' do, Freadman actually commissions and controls much of his evidentiary sources, demonstrating an unusual level of command over the telling of the father's life narrative.

Late in *Shadow of Doubt*, Richard Freadman describes a seminal moment in his adult life when at the age of 26 he wrote a 'watershed letter' in which he instructed his father that his advice concerning important life decisions was no longer welcome. This act formalises an inversion that has patterned his relational auto/biography since its first page, the author stating, 'henceforth, I became the father, he the son' (209). This reversal is central to Freadman's text, and to his construction of his father and himself within it, yet it is done in a book that explicitly desires to honour the father for what he has passed on to his son. The following discussion explores the way Freadman enacts a unique and thorough inversion of the typical intersubjective structure of the father–son relationship as portrayed in the tribute mode of the Son's Book. This inversion is enacted, perhaps reluctantly, as a device for constructing a viable textual identity for the figure of the author's father Paul Freadman. Caught between wanting 'to pay him a tribute that puts his honourable, interesting, sad life on record, but without falsifying that record' (12), and confounded by his father's self-sabotage, the son must foreground the 'self' of his auto/biography in order to construct an identifiable textual presence for the elusive 'other' of his father. Rather than the son's self-portrait emerging from his

---

1 Porter's study includes a chapter called 'The Men Who Were Not There' (99–136), exploring memoirs of elusive fathers where the task of the author is 'describing the indescribable' (99). These memoirs share a number of the key features of *Shadow of Doubt*. Yet Freadman's text cannot be considered a part of Porter's sub-genre, as the father in this case could not be described as 'deliberately unaccountable' (101).

representation of his father, as we saw in *Romulus, My Father*, Freadman in essence 'fathers' his father. Only by asserting the *autos* of the narrative, the self of the author, can the *bios* of the subject come into being. It is this reversal, the son's fathering of his patrimonial legacy, which I argue defines Freadman's achievement in his text.

Empirical Human Beings

Richard Freadman is one of Australia's foremost life-writing scholars. Appointed director of Australia's first Unit for Studies in Biography and Autobiography at La Trobe University in 1996, he is a founding member of the International Auto/Biography Association and author of numerous articles of life-writing criticism. In 2001 he published *Threads of Life*, his first major study of autobiography. Two years later Freadman published *Shadow of Doubt*, a memoir he terms a Son's Book of the Father, in the tradition of Philip Roth's *Patrimony*, J. A. Ackerley's *My Father and Myself*, and the work he deems 'the paradigm case' of this sub-genre (177), Edmund Gosse's *Father and Son*. Like these books, Freadman's text exhibits a definable tension between the desire to honour the father for what he has passed down to the son, and the need to address the father's failings, and even ultimately perhaps, to triumph over him. In other words, as a 'monument' to the father (as Gosse claimed of his work), this mode of Son's Book is marked by an intense ambivalence, leading one to wonder how these fathers might have received such memorialising.

It is worth noting that Freadman is one of a small but significant group of prominent autobiography scholars for whom this friction between theory and practice seems to coalesce around notions of patrimony. Towards the end of his most recent book of criticism *Living Autobiographically* for example, Paul John Eakin suddenly slides into writing auto/biographically about his father. In an extended passage of auto/biography, Eakin outlines the extent to which his father's influence compelled him into life-writing criticism whilst at the same time fuelling his aversion to personal disclosure. In doing so, he succinctly expresses many of the key elements to be explored here, such as the father's indistinctness, the burden of expectation felt by the son (what Eakin calls 'the success plot' (131)), and the insurmountable reality of death:

> For years, ever since I began to identify my professional work as concerned with autobiography, why some people write it and others read it, people would invariably ask me whether I had written autobiography. I would put them off by saying that I was a kind of crypto-autobiographer, someone who wrote his own story indirectly, obliquely, by writing about

other people's lives. But why didn't I write my story? [...] What, then, was holding me back from writing about my father? Well, to begin with, there was the illusion that there was nothing to say because Dad seemed to be an unknown quantity. There was also my uncomfortable feeling of inauthenticity, of lack, which my misgivings about vocation seemed to confirm [...] And deeper still, there was Dad's disquieting death, in 1980. It had not been a good death, and I wanted to put it behind me [...] The blessing and the tremor: so being like Dad was good and also dangerous. (142–3)

Living Autobiographically carries the dedication: 'In memory of my father'. Likewise, in the recent article 'In My Father's Closet', G. Thomas Couser describes discovering a tremendous cache of his father's correspondence after his death, which has led him, after over thirty years of life-writing criticism, to finally turn practitioner. The critic's intention is to 'let the documents tell the story' (892), making these letters the focus of a forthcoming biographical memoir, or what he has coined a patriography. For Couser and Eakin, as for Freadman, the figure of the father seems to have proven auto/biographically inevitable.

An avowed humanist scholar, Richard Freadman has championed and written 'ethically oriented' literary criticism for over twenty years. In 1992's *Re-thinking Theory*, Freadman and co-author Seumas Miller launched a sustained attack against what they termed 'constructivist anti-humanism' which they believed was 'now so pervasive in literary studies' (194):

> We contend that the 'theory' paradigm comprises three constitutive elements [...] One, a repudiation of substantial conceptions of the human subject, be it of authors or of social beings in general; two, a denial of the referential power of language and of literary texts; and three, a repudiation of substantive discourses of value, both moral and aesthetic. (4)

Of particular relevance to the current discussion is Freadman's reassertion of the self: of a subject's capacity to contain, even to control meaning, and of literature's ability, through 'referential' language, to accurately represent that subject. Freadman and Miller propose an approach that 'accords centrality to ethical concerns in literature; it also ascribes to authors, and thus to their texts, the capacity at least partially to transcend ideological conditioning and so to attain access to significant truths about the world, in particular ethical truths' (6). Since the publication of *Re-thinking Theory*, Freadman's academic work has turned increasingly towards autobiography, while preserving his ethico-humanist mode, and significantly, his commitment to the human subject, or in his preferred terminology, the 'self':

> When I speak of the 'self' therefore, I am not speaking of an alleged philosophical construct such as the 'subject'; I am speaking of real, empirical human beings who possess an extraordinary range of attributes (psychological, physiological, cultural), whose lives in cultural situations evince a vast array of forms of participation in and connection with those situations, and whose characteristics admit of various forms of theoretical description. (*Threads* 31)

Such assertions regarding the authority of authors and the authenticity of selves is in evidence in *Shadow of Doubt*, at least in the figure of the son, however as we will discover, this positivism is to the father's distinct disadvantage. A key question Freadman's theory raises for this representation of his father's absence and failure is one of benchmarks: by whose criterion is a self deemed elusive or a life judged to have been unsuccessful? I will analyse the models Freadman uses to assess his father's 'failed life', and explore how his assertion of his own successful life functions as a foil for the father's desire for esteem, whilst simultaneously being offered as alibi and recompense for the father's absence and failure.

Freadman's first (and to date only) foray into autobiographical writing is in many ways a peculiar creation. Described on the book's cover by friend Alan Shapiro as 'memoir at its best', the text is an odd mix of tones and styles, unapologetically blending narrative and reflection (or analysis), where the former is the subordinate feature. As the author alludes to in his text, many of his insights regarding the father–son relationship came about through psychoanalytic therapy he sought as an adult (273).[2] Though it is a work of tribute, Peter Rose describes *Shadow of Doubt* as 'an uncomfortable book to read, even for an outsider' ('Disappointed Man' 46), while Chris Wallace-Crabbe calls it 'tonally or structurally strange, at once moving, zigzag, personal and inescapably melancholy'. Wallace-Crabbe then states bluntly, 'This is a genuinely unusual book, which looks more traditional than it is' ('Wrestling' 4). The narrator adopts a peculiar voice, not only conversational and personal but also measured and academic. Keenly self-conscious of the theoretical discussions surrounding autobiography – its capacity for truthful representation, the ethical constraints entailed in writing about others – Freadman's autobiographical act has a strong sense of being

---

2   Reviewers such as Wallace-Crabbe seem perturbed by the 'Americanisms' in the text, a seeming discomfort with Freadman's embracing of 'therapy culture'.

situated, both in its cultural moment and its literary ancestry. He writes as one aware of others looking over his shoulder: his family, his colleagues, his own critic self. As I will assert, Freadman's commitment to reflection and to ethics both enriches and limits his book: it provides valuable insights to discussions central to this book, yet in some ways it disempowers the text's ability to represent inventively, perhaps even fictively, this shadowy, haunted, self-denying father.

Recording and Recognising the Troubled Inner Life

Shadow of Doubt is an eldest son's tribute to 'a disappointed man' (14), whose early life and academic career promised much, but who, bewilderingly, failed to live up to such promise. In framing his project as 'a quest for an elusive, perhaps illusory "moment"' (96), the author casts himself as a detective, sifting through memories, photographs, letters and interviews for reasons for the father's failure. Crucially, however, as we will discover, much of this archival evidence was actually commissioned by the author himself – or constructed by others at his behest – demonstrating the extent to which this portrait of a father is created and controlled, even 'willed', by his son. What does it mean to discover or even 'recognise' a person in such documents? Elsewhere Freadman has described memoirs such as his as 'recognition quests – journeys towards greater awareness, realization, understanding' ('Recognition' 136). While he elucidates the many 'semantic and experiential registers' of the term 'to recognise', its two key senses in auto/biographical narratives in relation to others are to 'learn well' or 'become thoroughly acquainted with' (136), and to 'see anew' that which is familiar (137).[3] As this discussion seeks to demonstrate, it is arguable whether Freadman achieves either notion of recognition in *Shadow of Doubt* in relation to his father. Nevertheless, in examining and seeking to name the causes of his father's failure and disappointment, Freadman points ultimately to a corrosive pattern of self-doubt, self-thwarting and depression, cloaked in the ethos of decency. The renunciation embodied by the father and memorialised here is of a less heroic order to the Socratic form valorised in

---

3   Freadman's lengthy article is a dense and nuanced philosophical examination of 'recognition' as it pertains to autobiography, and even if I felt able to do so, there is not the space to properly engage with it here. My concern relates primarily to whether any of the many senses of the term recognition as Freadman describes them are possible in a narrative where the author has had such a guiding hand in the creation of his archival evidence. Can an autobiographer see his subject 'anew' in such documents? Do the presuppositions about his subject that underlie his 'commissioning' of some of these sources impede his ability to 'learn well' from them?

the figure of Romulus Gaita. Describing the influence of this 'pervasive family virtue' on his life-writing project, he writes that:

> To grow up in Australia is to know that the notion of decency has played, and continues to play, a key role in the culture. For men of my father's generation particularly, it was immensely powerful in conditioning the way they saw themselves and their place in the world [...] Like many Australians, Paul would often speak of the need to 'do the decent thing', or of someone being 'a decent bloke' (in Australia, at least, decency is a highly gendered term, mostly applied to the civic and interpersonal worlds of men). Paul was later to encounter the ethos of decency in some of its most familiar breeding grounds: Protestant schools and the Boy Scout movement. The ethos consorted well with the laconic egalitarianism of Australian culture: its shyness of the heroic, its distaste for showiness. It came principally from England, where it's long had currency right across the class spectrum. Little wonder that it ran deep in Paul's Anglo-Jewish Australian home. (*Shadow of Doubt* 34)

Freadman finds much here to admire, though he believes the ethos exists (at the time of writing) in Howard's Australia 'in a debased form' (34). Yet it is Paul's particular strain of self-effacing decency that presents such a formidable challenge for life writing that aims to give insights into a subject's inner life: 'One of my reservations about it is, precisely, that it needlessly, and at times harmfully, conflates the notion of decency with the notion of privacy: it seems to suggest that to reveal one's inner self is to do something *in*decent' ('Decent' 133, emphasis in the original). It is one kind of challenge to seek to understand and represent such a father's interiority. It is quite another, according to Freadman, to expose it to the public by publishing a memoir: 'My father was a very private man who would not have wanted his troubled inner life put on public record. But he was also a person who craved *recognition*' (*Shadow of Doubt* 12, emphasis added). While these two competing desires ascribed to the father, for privacy and recognition (here meaning something like public acknowledgement) are fleshed out significantly in the book, the very existence of the published work demonstrates which one the author has chosen to fulfil. Of the many notions of 'recognition' nuanced in Freadman's theory, this final description is perhaps the most incompatible with his memoir in relation to what it achieves for the father.

'Similarity, Influence, Difference'

That this narrative is framed by particular notions of what constitutes a successful male life is established in the book's preface. The author recounts an enduring memory from his childhood, where his father appealed for assurance of his son's admiration:

> One day, when I was 11, my father sat down beside me on a sofa in the formal living room of our house. After some inconsequential chat he looked at me and said: 'You know, I'm quite a successful person.' Then, referring to his best friend Zelman Cowen, he added: 'Quite successful, but not as successful as Zelman. I hope you don't mind'. (11)

'Puzzled and disturbed' by the father's comment, whose 'strong blue eyes were clouded with doubt as, almost imploringly, they sought contact with mine', the son looked away and replied, 'Na; it's okay by me' (12). Freadman describes being deeply affected by his father's doubt and shame: 'I felt a sickly gloom settle in my stomach, seep into my soul [...] How could you feel safe in the world if your father felt like this?' (11). Like Gaita's realisation of the fallibility of his father's strength, the son's great unease is caused here in part by the father's relinquishment of a kind of God-like status – a self-sufficiency, dependability, primacy – as he reveals an inner self in desperate need of reassurance: 'He was forty-seven at the time, and I felt the enormity of his adult need bearing down on me' (11).

Freadman's preface also establishes the central mode of determining a worthy male life in the text: the author will judge the father's life against other proximate male lives, 'to see the patterns of similarity, influence, difference, across the generations' (13). According to Porter, this device is commonly used in memoirs of fathers who were 'deliberately unaccountable', where multigenerational stories are emphasised, 'as if seeing across time might explain what seemed mysterious' (*Bureau* 101). Zelman Cowen continues as an unassailable mirror in the father's estimations of himself; but Freadman introduces other counterpoints as the narrative unfolds. Among them are the author's maternal grandfather Roy and his paternal uncle Ralph, but ultimately the central comparison is that between the father and the son, a reflexive assessment that propels the narrative. As Freadman notes:

> Now 51, a little older than my father was then, but like him an academic, a father and a restlessly ambitious man haunted by a sense of life's insufficiency, I feel moved to write the scene through; to trace it back into family history, and forward into the decades that were to follow. (12)

The history of the intersubjective male relationships of the Freadman family provides ample evidence for the ambivalence the author expresses about his patrimonial inheritance. For reasons that could easily be attributed to the author of *Father and Son*, Freadman's grandfather Henry 'didn't greatly esteem' his own father Jacob because he 'spent too much time with sacred texts, too little on his family's operational and emotional needs' (32–3). Likewise, Paul repeats this pattern into the next generation; his relationship with Henry described as 'problematical' (34), or in the author's mother's words, Paul just 'didn't like his father' (38). Such a pattern greatly disturbs the author: 'not to like your father – that is a momentous thing, unless the father be a monster. There's no suggestion that Henry was anything of the kind. He seems indeed to have been a fundamentally decent man' (38).

Importantly, the author's assessment of his grandfather is not based on personal experience (he died when the author was four), but is largely formed from the competing view offered by Freadman's uncle: 'Ralph talks affectionately of Henry, recalling a genial man' (33), and has 'happier memories' of his childhood (30). Freadman justifies his use of this evidentiary source, or what he calls 'transmission chains', stating, 'There's nothing unusual about this degree of dependence on the stories of others' (45). Ralph is another, though minor, counterpoint to Richard's assessment of his father; his uncle enjoyed a successful career as a lawyer, and 'suspects that Paul was "mildly envious" of his more settled professional life' (47). The author places much stock in Ralph's testimony because 'I know him to be an honourable, unsentimental man with a deep regard for truth-telling' (45). While he admits that 'like all testimonies, Ralph's has its limits' and proceeds carefully to set out the complexity of the relationship between Ralph and Paul (45–8), Freadman's reliance on his uncle's oppositional history highlights a key silence within his text: the lack of his own brother Andrew's perspective. In his acknowledgements he explains that 'Andrew [...] is a private man and it is not for me to presume to tell his story. If at times the book reads as though I am an only child this is misleading' (9). While typically cautious about the ethics of speaking for others, the absence of Freadman's brother within his book is enlarged by the presence of Ralph's counter-story of the author's grandfather: the reader must always wonder how Andrew's conception of their father might similarly differ from the author's own.

As Barbour has noted, a writer-son's judgement of his father's failure is often 'tempered' by exploring the 'causal influences' from the past ('Judging' 79). Freadman assesses Paul's experiences in World War II and his knowledge of the Holocaust as factors that contributed to the course of his life. Paul acted as a flight lieutenant and navigator in bombing raids over New Guinea and lost many colleagues, 'including those he was closest to' (57). Freadman quotes from poetry his father wrote during this time, offering it as evidence of 'a more recessive, more troubled, inwardness' (57), and while his military service is described as 'one of the great imponderables of his life-story' (56), the author concludes that the war left his father with 'profound guilt at having survived when many of his comrades, some of them already family men, had not' and 'susceptible to depression and high anxiety' (58). Added to this was his dawning understanding of the Holocaust:

> Paul once described to me the stunned, horrified, sinking incredulity he felt as he became aware of the enormity of the catastrophe. From that day on, life for Jews – and for many others – was to be lived in shadow, no matter how successful, how happy in other respects those lives might be. (68)

The Holocaust was a kind of family secret in the Freadman household, as it must have been in many homes of the Jewish Diaspora after World War II. Freadman's account of finding Lord Russell's *The Scourge of the Swastika* hidden on top of a cupboard as a 12-year-old is one of the more poignant in his narrative: 'For me, it was an absolutely defining moment. The world had changed' (111).[4] With eyes 'subdued to an anguished kindliness' (109), Paul does an admirable job of explaining to his son the 'sadistic cataclysm' (111) the book had revealed, the author moved to offer one of his many touching yet qualified tributes:

> The genuinely decent person can readily be moved to intercede, to lend comfort or support if someone seems to be in need. My father was decent in just this sense. But alas, among the few people from whom he withheld his solicitude was one who needed it most: himself. (112)

Indeed, while Paul's disappointed life is attributed in part to forces outside of his control, what causes the greatest challenge to the author's attempt to honor his father is the fact that Paul contributed in various ways to his own failure. This is evidenced early in his marriage, when as a bright and ambitious young scholar Paul turned down the offer of a Harkness scholarship to attend Harvard University in order to remain working as a statistician for the Australian Broadcasting Corporation. It is an act that has enduring significance, the author describing it as 'part of a bewildered family mythology of failure and missed opportunity [...] It was clearly a defining moment; a fateful, foolish decision for which he paid dearly' (91). While stories told down the generations usually function to preserve and explain family history, in Paul's case they offer

---

4 The impact of this formative experience is demonstrated by Freadman's latest academic study, *This Crazy Thing a Life: Australian Jewish Autobiography* (2007), which explores in much detail the impact of the Holocaust on Jewish life writers including Lily Brett, Jacob Rosenberg and Arnold Zable.

little insight but act only to confuse the logic of this life narrative. Importantly, Paul's decision is affected by his consideration of others, particularly his ailing mother, his new wife and his unborn child, and so can be construed as an act of self-denial: 'the decent man is not expected to indulge in showy self-assertion. Decency provided the perfect ethos for the under confident man: he could indulge his timidity without losing moral force' (93).

Paul Freadman, then, like Romulus Gaita, though possessing virtues worth celebrating, is a confounding biographical study due to his lack of agency in the text, or more accurately in this case, an agency that works against the self, that undermines the desires of the self that possesses it. 'There is in Paul's later life an undeniable pattern of self-thwarting', writes the author. 'Was he self-destructive?' (81). One is reminded of the early literary notion of self-denial as the self's opposite. In a typically probing passage, Freadman spends an entire chapter assessing the possible causes of Paul's 'fateful, foolish decision' (89–98), including his 'leaky' self-esteem, his timidity masquerading as decency, and his Sartrean 'bad faith' which feared the 'opening up to his "possibilities", deciding in the direction of an open-ended freedom, full-bloodedly pursuing his quest' (92). Astutely, the author notes how important such perplexing patterns have been in his own life: 'It's perhaps not surprising, indeed it is an aspect of Paul's emotional patrimony, that my academic work has often focused on human deliberation and volition' (91).

'An Inalienable Power of the Self'

One can indeed identify a great many of these questions about the father's agency as the driving force behind Freadman's *Threads of Life*. In fact, his study of autobiography and his auto/biography can be read as companion pieces, with the author's theoretical conceptions illuminated, and at times undercut, by his narrative. In *Threads of Life*, Freadman contends that 'the issue of the human will' has been 'central to Western autobiography since its inception', though it has been largely ignored and untheorised within the field of autobiography studies (1). Arguing against modern and postmodern thinkers who believe '"that there is no such thing as the will", there's no such "faculty" in the human person' (7), Freadman analyses a series of predominantly modern autobiographies to demonstrate how the will is conceived of and explored by life writers (even by those who deny its existence), and how the will can be identified as the motivating force behind the construction of a life and a life story, or as the author describes, the 'powers [that] enable the weaver to shape the pattern that is his or her life' (284). While conceding that the will is 'in varying degrees constrained by specific practical, and in particular ideological, contexts' (283), Freadman's study is a thoroughly positivist conception of human agency.[5] He believes, in other words, that the will is real, that it is most free 'when it is instantiated through engagement with rationality' and that it bequeaths to the self ('the weaver') 'certain powers to shape and create' a life (284). In Freadman's estimations, the will is 'an inalienable power of the self' (283).

The term Freadman proposes for the writer who 'achieves a reflective distance from conventional ideological attitudes, and who uses autobiography to explore, critique, and sometimes reformulate cultural understandings of the world', is a 'reflective autobiographer', identifying St Augustine as the reflective autobiographer *par excellence* (283). In *Shadow of Doubt* Freadman aims to be just such an autobiographer, the agent of his narrative who arguably spends more time interpreting and reflecting than he does narrating. The general picture that emerges of the Richard Freadman of his text is of a man possessing a strong and powerful will who (notwithstanding the self-doubt which is part of his patrimonial legacy) controls his destiny (including his ambition to become a life-writing scholar), and who is also firmly in control of his narrative. Yet this is precisely how the son's story diverges from his father's, and how Paul becomes such an elusive biographical study. The question driving the son's search is what became of his father's will? What happened to make him such an ineffectual man?

Freadman's portrayal of his father accords with his exploration of 'weakness of will' in Stephen Spender's autobiographical oeuvre. Freadman argues that Spender's *World Within World* portrays the movement from a decentred self with a 'weak will' to a more concrete self, where the will is exercised 'in a more deliberate, rational and existentially grounded way' (10). This shift can be identified in *Shadow of Doubt* not within the person of the father (whose will becomes weaker and self more decentred as his life progresses) but is enacted from father *to* son, with the author figured as the subject who overcomes the self-doubt and self-thwarting traits inherited from his father to become not only a conventionally successful male but also one who 'doubles the success' by willing his life story onto the page. Paul and Richard, as actors or agents in the memoir, can be placed at either end of Freadman's 'graduated conception of the will'; Paul at the end where the 'will is instantiated through engagement with id, the unconscious, unreflective affect'; Richard

---

5 Though positivist, *Threads of Life* does acknowledge the ineffability of some questions surrounding the will. Of the spiritual dimension of the will, Freadman writes of 'its haunting presence at the heart of our experience in a world we cannot fully fathom; a world from which we want so much, but in which we often find that our efforts are compromised, imperfectly rewarded, or even unavailing' (287). One can easily identify the figure of the father lying behind this statement.

at the other end of the spectrum where the will 'is most "free"' and 'it is instantiated through engagement with rationality' (*Threads* 284). Perhaps this is an oversimplification, for Paul is also shown to be an occasionally rational and reflective man. However, while Richard's battle to liberate his sense of agency from the legacy of his father's impeded will has arguably contributed to his insightful exploration of the many autobiographical manifestations of human agency, it is equally true that Freadman's overarching conception of the will's ultimate freedom (and his demonstration of it through his successful life) becomes a kind of unassailable yardstick with which the son measures his father's life. Is the author too hard on his father? Peter Rose describes *Shadow of Doubt* as 'punitive and harping at times' ('Disappointed Man' 46). To his credit, Freadman admonishes his younger self for behaving arrogantly towards his father (181), yet it is difficult to dispense entirely with the feeling that the motivation ascribed to the teenaged Richard of 'a sense – albeit guilty – of triumph over the Father' (182) does not still drive the current exploration.

Whatever the case, the absence of Paul's will becomes further pronounced the more it is contrasted with the son of this disappointed man. For while Richard shares some of his father's self-doubt which has 'shadowed my own life' (17), the son of this Son's Book is represented as a bright and ambitious young scholar who, unlike his father, seizes his opportunities and becomes both a highly successful academic and, in text, a fully rendered autobiographical self. Tellingly, Richard's professional career flourishes *despite* Paul's attempts to dissuade him from studying overseas; first, when Richard is offered a scholarship to Brandeis University upon completing high school (155), and when he later receives an offer of admission to Hertford College, Oxford (182). In both instances the author speculates as to his father's motives: 'Paul opposed my going to Oxford on financial grounds. Again I wonder what other motivations might have been involved. Envy? A fear of the feelings that might be associated with being overtaken, "shown up" by the son?' (182). These accord with the motives ascribed to Richard's grandfather for thwarting Paul's own educational opportunities (42). Importantly, in rebuffing his father's advice, Richard makes the link with his father's history explicit:

> You knocked back a chance to go to Harvard, and now you want me to knock back a chance to go to Oxford. It's pathological [...] Maybe you can't see that you need to take your chances in life, but to me it's as plain as dog's balls. I'm off. Fuck it! (183)

Despite such bravado, the author demonstrates how his father's self-doubt continued to haunt him during his studies overseas 'and well into my twenties', when, for example, a 'sanctimonious American academic' demeans his thesis topic, causing the 'family anxiety habit' to 'hit with a vengeance' (191–2). Interestingly, the correspondence between father and son during this period reveals an empathetic bond revolving around sharing advice and counsel about how to manage their anxiety and depression. In Paul Auster's *The Invention of Solitude*, according to John Barbour, the father–son bond centres around the shared experience of solitude, eventually redeeming an otherwise broken relationship ('Judging' 78–9). Is this true of Richard and Paul in relation to self-doubt? Reading back on the letters, this 'partners-in-gloom theme' makes Freadman feel uneasy: 'while it reflects a genuine closeness and solicitude between father and son, it bespeaks a relationship that is too much rooted in lugubrious anxiety, too little in confident pleasure and self-esteem' (180–81). However, a 'watershed letter' Richard writes at the age of 26 alters this pattern, when the son requests that his father stop giving him advice about major life decisions. As the author describes, 'The re-defined father–son configuration was such that I was prepared to go on being consulted by my father, and to give what support I could; but it was to be one-way traffic […] henceforth I became the father; he the son' (208–9). As Freadman flags here, this crucial inversion becomes more pronounced in the final years of their relationship, though one can see evidence of it throughout Richard's life story. The author notes for example that, 'well before my teens, I started calling both parents by their first names. Never Mum or Dad' (209).

'The Embodiment of the Successful Career'

One way this inversion is solidified is in the portrayal of Richard's developing relationship with Zelman Cowen, the other fully realised male subject whose achievements draw Paul's lack of agency into sharp relief. A friend from Paul's youth, Cowen went on to study at Oxford University before serving as a dean and vice-chancellor at prominent Australian universities; he became one of Australia's foremost scholars on constitutional law, and was ultimately appointed as governor-general of Australia between 1977 and 1981. It is this final, unassailable achievement that confers a kind of symbolic value to the juxtaposition: 'Zelman wasn't just his best friend; he was the embodiment of the successful career, of the world's good opinion' (230).

Late in the narrative, as Paul lies debilitated and dying, 'Zelman and I sought relief with a walk around the local streets' (223). While the occasion allows the author to explore the extent to which Paul's disappointment may have been worsened by Zelman's success, it also evinces the extent to which Richard and his father have swapped roles. While Zelman and Richard seek each other out for advice over a 'man-to-man' chat, Paul lies as incapacitated as a child. This pattern is repeated when the author compares the way his father did not listen to the counsel of both himself and Zelman, enshrining the inversion of the power relation between father and son (228).

Seeking reasons for the way his father's and Zelman's lives diverged so markedly, Freadman returns to his conception of decency: 'Zelman has a resilient ego; his attraction to decency has, so far as I can see, very little to do with its treacherous allure of self-deception' (227). On the other hand, decency appealed to Paul because of its confluence with low self-esteem:

> For such a man, decency, with its eschew of the big ego, the triumphal Virtues, its ethic of service, self-sacrifice, emotional restraint, can be a real trap. It can be used to rationalise self-denial, self-flagellation, a strange alchemy of suicidal solicitude. It can become the godless religion of the self-thwarting man. (227)

What is at work here is a kind of counter-heroic masculinity: an ethos of renunciation that claims the moral high ground by stating (to the self) something like 'I'm man enough not to have to assert myself'. While in Paul's case, according to his son, such rationalisations are self-deceptive, this does not necessarily render such counter-notions devoid of value. Freadman signals from the outset that, informed both by his subject's life and his own autobiographical intentions, this will be a particular kind of male narrative – one not focussed on 'deeds':

> This is not a book about the Great Man and his deeds [...] It's less about deeds than about how we assess what we do and who we are; about what we value in people, and what we should value in them [...] Memoir, like any form of narrative, depends heavily on deed; but deeds come in many forms, some of them – acts of moral solicitude, for instance – so far removed from the heroic as to be almost undetectable. (16)

Like Gaita, Freadman wishes to bear witness to a virtue that rarely receives recognition, in both life and in narrative. Yet his claim that his patriography is an example of a generic 'shift in focus from towering deeds to intimate texture' (16) feels only half right. Indeed, the text is stretched awkwardly between these poles: while it does involve itself primarily with the intricate minutiae of intersubjective relationships, in order to enunciate the father's failure it continually returns to Eakin's 'success plot'; Zelman's success sub-plot being only the starkest example of such a discourse.[6] The book itself is framed by evidence of the author's deeds: the brief but impressive 'author's bio' offered on the title page (1), the listing of Freadman's academic publications (2). In this way, the narrative is prefaced by the son's ability to triumph where the father failed, before Richard's autobiographical presence is offered as a kind of 'stand in' for Paul's textual absence. Ultimately, Zelman's life is somewhat of a prelude for Freadman's assertion of his own self, for it is the son's life that becomes the fundamental measure of the father's, and against whom the father falls short.

Importantly, Freadman's portrayal of his father's relationship with Zelman's own son Shimon highlights this contrast. Shimon, a Hassidic Jewish Rabbi, describes having been the beneficiary of Paul's 'humility' as a young man (276), and what Richard calls his father's 'disappointing record of worldly achievement', Shimon describes as 'his success' (277). These divergent views perhaps suggest a unique disadvantage the father faces in being esteemed by the son: the propinquity of the relationship denies him the latitude offered to other men of influence upon the son. Freadman's incorporation of Shimon's view of Paul raises another silence in the text: Shimon's tribute to Paul's humility must cause us to wonder about his view of and relationship with his own father Zelman. Would Shimon's Hassidic standpoint have maintained the air of 'objectivity' attributed to it here in relation to *his* father? Such information may have acted as a useful counterbalance to Richard's view of Zelman. Tellingly, Freadman attributes Shimon's turn to Hassidic Judaism in part to Zelman's success at having achieved 'the perfect secular professional life': 'Within the paradigm that his father had embraced, there was nothing left to do' (279), constituting 'a form of permission to switch paradigms' (280). Such statements speak volumes about the symbolic importance Freadman places on his career, the narrative of which is offered as an atonement for the father's lack of 'worldly achievement'.

---

6   Perhaps unsurprisingly, Cowen's memoirs *A Public Life*, published in 2006, exhibits all the hallmarks of the 'great man and his deeds' style of autobiography. The structure and chapter titles display a logical progression from brilliant and ambitious young student to eminent Dean and Professor and ultimately to the post of Governor-General. It is exactly the kind of self-portrait Misch would have deemed a 'representative life'. Cowen's memoirs include a short tribute to his 'enduring friendship' with Paul Freadman and he admits that as a younger man 'I looked up to him with admiration and a little envy' (53). Yet while Cowen describes many of the famous and not-so-famous people he encountered in his life, his focus is not on the 'intimate texture' of life writing, but on the successful life. Cowen admits to being 'grateful for the wise counsel of Richard Freadman, who read an early draft of the text' (ix).

'The Son of a Man Who Could Write This Well'

Another key patrimonial evaluation is enacted between Paul and Richard's maternal grandfather Roy. In fact, the author figures these relationships as 'a pattern of triangulation. Within the triangle each person's relation with one of the others were mediated by his relation with the third' (120). The author recalls Roy with much affection and less ambivalence than in his portrayal of his father. Following the narration of a particularly bruising encounter between father and son, which is read by the author in Freudian terms, Freadman states: 'The emotional temperature of the home being what it was, Roy's presence in the family was a godsend for me. He was accepting kindliness itself' (118). Importantly, the tributes offered to Roy are unqualified. Roy is praised for being 'attuned to need [...] solicitous towards the most humble wish' (119), which mirrors (though without qualification) the tribute to Paul quoted earlier. There are further links to be made between their failings: Roy's timidity causes him to be bullied into selling his business for less than its worth (130), while he is 'so indiscriminately tolerant, that his tolerance seemed to surrender its own virtue' (127). This latter insight is offered by Paul, who is not as forgiving as Richard of his father-in-law's foibles. Seeking to account for the discrepancy in how these men fare in his memorialising, Freadman concedes to the limiting nature of his childhood recollections, and avers ultimately to the positive effect Roy had on him regardless of what may have motivated his solicitousness: 'for me the really important thing has always been those feelings – gentleness and calm – that he radiated to me' (122). Interestingly, this is the same argument Shimon offers regarding Paul's humility: 'seen from his Hassidic standpoint, "the net result was a very good one"' (277).

Surprisingly, a sense of Paul's absence prevails throughout the narrative despite the fact that Freadman gives us direct access to his father's words. Unlike Gaita in his representation of Romulus, whose letters we are not allowed to see, Freadman quotes at length from autobiographical fragments Paul wrote, at first by his own choice, and later, during a period of severe depression, at his son's prompting. While the initial subject of these fragments is Roy, again complicating the biographical dimension of this Son's Book, as Freadman notes, the process becomes an attempt to talk the self back into existence: 'Like so much biographical writing they are also a constituent part of a conversation with self about self. To write about the other is often, however tangentially or unwittingly, to write about the self' (126). But while Roy, as the subject of Paul's relational auto/biographical writings, is largely accessible to the reader despite his own self-deception, a textual presence animated by his 'pithy chuckle' and his conversation that 'bespoke an active and sometimes exotic earlier life' (118), Paul's self-appraisal remains faulty and misleading. 'His self-condemnation is punitive', comments Freadman of Paul's assessment of 'the poverty of my contribution [to Roy's life], of my failure to enter into his inner being', while his relation to self 'is bruisingly judicial: "I pass judgement on myself"' (128).

Despite such criticisms, Freadman's evaluation of his father's capacity to write autobiographically is instructive. His writing has 'deft phrasing and sentence rhythms' where 'the past shimmers in consciousness, beckoningly there yet evanescent' (64), his 'mode of telling combines unflinching honesty, compassion, insight and grace', and the author states that, 'I receive it as a gift. This too is part of his complex patrimony' (126). In his essay, Couser expresses a similar admiration regarding his father's cache of letters (895). Such familial pride demonstrates a desire to honour the parent, yet it also contributes to a sense of the son's superiority, as the 'learned' critic stands in judgement of his father, even if his critique is positive. This patrimonial reversal is most stark when Freadman analyses his father's scholarly writing: 'what a curious feeling to sit in my book-lined study passing judgement on my father's Honours dissertation! [...] He was 31 when he wrote it; I'm reading through the eyes of an older man – a man of 51, and a seasoned academic' (76). To his credit, the author probes his motivations for both praising and criticising his father's dissertation, as well as the efficacy of quoting from it:

> A part of me wants – even needs – to find fault, to feel superior, as if to say, 'You let yourself down by not staying with your academic career. I've gone the whole hog. I've put that to rights. See what I can do with pen in hand. See, I'm the better mind.' And then I feel guilty as hell. Guilty for needing to prevail over a dead and disappointed man; guilty for reporting in print on an essay he didn't intend for publication.
>
> Yet there is some first-rate work in these dusty carbon pages, and another part of me is pleased to find patches that are better than I could write. Pleased for him, but for myself as well – pleased to know that I am the son of a man who could write this well, and to see that the doubt and disappointment that shadowed so much of his life, and darkened my own, was unwarranted. A least in part. And threading its way through all of this is a feeling of something like self-disgust which says: 'Why don't you just lift your focus from your navel. Quit this agon of self-absorption, and be more like Paul and his friends? Get on with the business of living. Stop probing, prying. Respect other people's privacy. Your life has become one long sophomore year.' But it's the way I am. The story demands to be told… (77)

This is a revealingly conflicted passage, oscillating between the desire to celebrate and to triumph over the father; between the need for an expressive and successful father 'who could write this well' and the necessity of telling one's own story; between respecting the father's privacy and obeying the autobiographical impulse to make use of such documentary sources, and ultimately, to publish them. In comparing his generation unfavorably with his father's, Freadman alludes to the *raison d'être* for the rise of the son–father auto/biography, and perhaps life-writing studies generally: while Paul's generation got on with the business of living, Richard's is propelled towards the 'self-absorbed' act of writing and analysing it. Despite considerable probing of the ethics of his act, Freadman concludes ultimately, 'the story demands to be told'.

Freadman extends his intergenerational exploration of patrimony by assessing his own experience of fatherhood, and in so doing gives valuable insights into the uses and potential dangers of the son–father auto/biography. The author examines his relationship with his 6-year-old son, expressing relief that Elliot, 'one of life's great enthusiasts' (168), is a less anxious child than Richard himself was. Their conversations revolve largely around Ellie's interest in 'Poppa Paul', whom he never met. Though the young boy seems equally fascinated by notions of patrimony – what Freadman terms 'his need for a coherent narrative of family' (170) – one wonders if the author is projecting. Nevertheless, Elliot is offered as evidence that the pattern of fraught father–son relationships might well end with Richard and Paul. Equally instructive is Freadman's portrayal of his close bond with his daughter Madeleine. In a chapter called 'Father and Daughter' the author expresses his anxiety that his oldest child might feel alienated by his narrative of patrimony: 'I want Madeleine to know that I didn't write a narrative about the men of the family because they matter more to me than the women' (159). Addressing his daughter directly, Freadman faces the question of why his memoir is not a Son's Book of the Mother: 'Will I write a book about Fleur and me, with long chapters on Ess, your mum, *you*? Nanna Fleur and your mum have made it abundantly clear that they want no such thing. I think that you too would have some doubts' (160, emphasis in the original).[7] Crucially, in a recent discussion with the author on the 'after-life' of his text, Freadman claims that his anxieties have proven unfounded: his daughter, now an adult, maintains that reading *Shadow of Doubt* provided much insight into her herself and her own relationship to her heritage.[8] Perhaps narratives of patrimony may be less exclusive than they seem.

---

7   In his acknowledgements, Freadman utters the phrase 'my greatest debt is to' twice; first inscribing indebtedness to his mother (9), then concluding with the accolade to his father quoted as an epigraph to this chapter (10). Leaving aside the obvious contradiction, perhaps this gesture is the shorthand equivalent of dedicating a Son's Book to both parents.
8   Personal conversation with the author, May 2010.

Representing the Elusive Life

The way Paul's deferential decency impedes the creation of a viable identity, one that can be known or recognised by others, is articulated by Freadman's friend Mark Maimone, who met Paul while accompanying the Freadmans on a holiday to the Lake District in England. *Shadow of Doubt* quotes at length from an account of this experience that Mark writes at the author's request. The fact that the author once again commissions this 'supporting evidence' should cause us to remember how tightly he has controlled the production of his secondary sources. In his recount, Mark quickly picks up on Paul's propensity for self-denial: 'What I found was the attention to others I saw immediately, and found so sympathetic, was usually taken to extremes. He was so anxious and concerned for others, that he ignored his own needs' (194). Likewise he describes expressing interest in Paul's academic work, but Paul was reticent to talk about himself (193). Ultimately, Mark's brief recollections conclude by calling attention to Paul's indecipherableness: 'tensions within the family [may have] blocked my ability to get to know him, but the fact remains that I don't feel I did know him. More remains of our discussions of him than do actual images of our time together' (195–6). Importantly, Richard's portrayal of his father in conversation is more enduring than an actual experience of meeting Paul. While Mark begins his vignette by foregrounding the unreliability of Richard's perspective – 'the very coloured lens of his son'; 'My somewhat ill-informed image was finally confronted with reality' (193) – he ends by reasserting his faith in Richard's version of the father. This suggests that an account of a subject can sometimes overpower an encounter with the subject himself.

And then the war

Paul, c. 1935

It is telling that so much of *Shadow of Doubt* strains towards constituting a viable textual presence for Freadman's father that the author cannot bear witness to in memory. The photographs used to begin each chapter at times enact an incongruity with the writing that follows, the author often referring back to them in order to underscore this paradox (75). These photographs seem so important to Freadman because, as Linda Harverty Rugg remarks, 'photographs as physical evidence re-anchor the subject in the physical world, insist of the verifiable presence of an embodied and solid individual' (2). How much greater the need to re-anchor the subject when he seems precisely the opposite of this: unverifiable, unembodied, opaque. Freadman describes images of a young Paul looking 'happy and confident, his thin black moustache, formal attire, wavy black hair and slender wiry physique redolent of wellbeing' as 'tantalising' (41). Why tantalising? One answer may be because of these photographs' ability to capture the father Richard never knew, the man 'fired by a sense of commitment, yearning, willpower' (17). Another may be because, despite himself, Freadman is all too aware of photography's ability to distort or 'invent' reality quite as much as autobiography. Timothy Dow Adams makes explicit the link between the two, writing that 'sophisticated theorists of photography, imagery and semiotics have repeatedly demonstrated, in a history remarkably similar to that of autobiography, that photography is equally problematic in terms of referentiality' (3). As Roger Porter has noted of the ambiguous photographs included in *The Invention of Solitude*, 'such "evidence" can hinder the autobiographer's task as much as it abets it' (*Bureau* 105). Interestingly, Freadman's use of photographs in his text is almost entirely untheorised, despite his knowledge of autobiography scholarship. Due to his otherwise masterly incorporation of theory in his account, this omission seems telling. Some of the photographs included, such as that used to introduce the chapter 'And then the war' (49), contain 'signs of life' beyond the visual image, such as a tear or a scrawled name visible in the reproduction. These become meta-texts that bear witness to Richard's search and Paul's life in a way that the writing, seemingly, cannot. Having failed to adequately capture his father in words, perhaps Freadman's appeal to the visual image demonstrates his anxiety about language's capacity to represent a denied self. At the very least, like the book in which they are reproduced, these photographs demonstrate and bear the marks of the various uses (and potential misuses) of *aides memoire*.

The written word, however, becomes obligatory when Paul seeks help in finally and irrevocably denying himself life. Late in the narrative, as cancer and Alzheimer's disease claim his physical and mental health, Paul raises the possibility of euthanasia:

> His way of putting it was 'I want out' [...] Before taking it any further I felt we needed Paul to write down what he had said, and somehow to demonstrate that it constituted an ongoing and repeatedly verified wish. And so, propped up in bed, with Fleur holding the pad, he managed painfully to write 'I want out.' He then dozed off. Next day I broached

the issue again, reminding him of what he had said and written. He looked blankly at me. He had no recollection of it. He'd gone beyond the point at which the notion of 'my life' had any stable meaning. (244)

Here Freadman succinctly offers insight into the purpose of his life-writing project. Only the written word can demonstrate the 'ongoing and repeatedly verified', but having experienced the uncertainty of seeing a father 'consumed from within' by 'three colossal forces [...] cancer, Alzheimer's, and self-doubt' (265), the author's own written word becomes a way of attesting to 'his life' with a 'security of meaning' that his father could not express (244).

Tellingly, this pattern of 'speaking for' his father, or of writing his words for him, is established even before Paul's death. When Paul is honored late in life for his contribution to adult education, the author admits to writing his father's acceptance speech 'with – largely for – him' (251). During the ceremony, as his father 'haltingly' follows the script, Richard sits beside him with his own copy, 'ready to assist if need be' (255). The author cannot resist taking credit for the 'simple formality and grace' of the turn of phrase used to pay tribute to Zelman Cowen in the speech (256). This pattern of the author constructing the father's life for him in writing is alluded to throughout the memoir. Even the act of encouraging his father to write autobiographically, only to incorporate and analyse these fragments in his text, speak of an encompassing level of the son's control over the telling of both life stories. In other words, the father–son inversion enacted by Freadman in his text exists at a meta-textual level as well.

Considering the severity of Paul's decline in later years, it is telling that Freadman spends so much of the early part of his narrative dwelling on the period of his father's life where he describes him as 'formidable' and 'flourishing'. Freadman begins his memoir by recounting a defining memory of his father playing a skilful leg glance during a game of park cricket when Freadman was a boy. Importantly, the father directs his shot towards where Richard is fielding: Paul's leg glance is undoubtedly a performance, but it is also a challenge. Forty years on, Freadman speculates on his contradictory feelings at this defining moment:

I'm sure I felt awe at the power and finesse of the shot. Also a kind of admiration that bordered on pride, that my father possessed such prowess. There was the fear of being hit, but also a deeper, more pervasive fear: I'd come face to face with his manly power, the steely strength of those wrists, with skills he learned *before my coming into being*... I felt enervated by what he could do, his strength, his immense reserves of expertise. (24, emphasis added)

It is a rare admission of inferiority: an acknowledgement that this son does indeed come after his father. The author also speculates upon his father's intentions as being a 'demonstration', a way of 'courting my admiration' but also of '*asserting* the power, the primacy, the force of the father' (24, emphasis in the original). According to Freadman, such memories that 'seem unbidden come in response to some current need' (25). In this case the author sees the memory as being 'about retrieving that father who was very good at many things, even masterful, in his prime. The man he was before he became the person he was to become' (25).

It is this same father that Freadman encounters in a dream a few months before beginning his memoir, a younger Paul who 'walked quickly and confidently and seemed to exude assurance' (26). The author's description accords with the photograph used to introduce the chapter (21). Tellingly, the Richard of the dream is 'at once my current adult self, and myself as a child', again an acknowledgement of the originary status of the father. While the author cannot recall what the father actually did in the dream, he recalls feeling relief that his father 'was returned to a kind of flourishing; and the two me's in the dream seemed almost to be comparing notes, checking to see that it could actually be that Paul […] really was okay, that I really was the son of such a man' (26). The author's yearning to retrieve this version of his father, to convince himself and us that he existed, is palpable. But Paul's is perhaps an extreme case of what is true of most lives, and therefore the bind of many auto/biographical narratives: while it is the 'formidable' Paul that Freadman most wishes to represent, it is the image of the diminished father of late life that ultimately endures. Sadly for Paul, life cannot be lived in reverse.

As in Gaita's text, the final act of bearing witness is to the father's death; or in Freadman's case, to the gradual extinguishment of the 'signs of life'. Paul's 'terminal event' (262) is slow, drawn out and unflinchingly recounted, the author describing it as 'one huge task left to perform. It was astonishing how many systems had to be shut down before he could rest' (263). As with much of his melancholy account, Freadman resists attributing consolatory resolution to his scene, demonstrating once again how the desire to 'tell it truthfully' is not always an aide to memorialisation:

> I sat and watched, thinking back through the many Pauls I had known, trying to reconcile them with the figure that lay dying inches away; trying to get to grips with the stupefying fact that it had come down to *this*. My God! Why do we pour all of this energy, passion, good faith into our few fleeting decades when this is where we are headed? I wanted to make some sort of sense of it, but there was simply none to be made. (262–3)

Conclusion: An Inside Job

The desire to 'retrieve' and 'return', to reconstitute a subject diminished by self-denial, self-thwarting and self-doubt is central to Freadman's purpose in writing *Shadow of Doubt*. But central also is the question of which of his father's selves is ultimately retrieved, and whether any of these selves would have wanted his life story published. Would a self-doubting and private man such as Paul Freadman ever desire to have his disappointed life committed to print? Despite these concerns pervading the memoir, embedded within the numerous instances of ethical reflection, it is telling that the author felt compelled to repeat this mediative act in his essay 'Decent and Indecent: Writing my Father's Life'. Originally conceived as a postscript during the writing of his memoir, because 'I'd been so disturbed by what I was doing that [...] I suspended work on the narrative and wrote the coda on ethics in an attempt to decide whether the project was morally acceptable' (121–2), the essay was omitted and later published in Eakin's *The Ethics of Life Writing*. A curious document in many respects – typically philosophical and probing, it also integrates a much greater imaginative dimension than the author allowed himself in memoir – the essay reads as an attempted justification for the decision to publish *Shadow of Doubt*. It is worth remarking that along with Freadman's dream, the 'imagined' Paul of this essay (whose conversation with Richard is lively and humorous) is altogether more vivid and 'present' than the elusive father of Freadman's memories and archival evidence. What this indicates is that a stringently ethical approach to 'factual' life writing, to which both Freadman and Gaita subscribe, comes with in-built limitations as well as textual veracity. One wonders whether the more inventive mode of this essay is better suited to reviving the self-denying father. Certainly the inclusion of Freadman's essay as a coda to his memoir would have counter-balanced the prominence of the later, highly anxious and self-doubting Paul.

Following an analysis of his autobiographical act using Annette Baier's conceptions of 'Trust' and 'Antitrust' to ascertain whether he has been loyal to 'the profound relationship of trust between my father and myself' (132), the author resurrects his father for a day at the cricket in order 'to model a situation that might assist with my ethical dilemma: should I or should I not publish this manuscript?' (134). It is a compelling device, and demonstrates both the desire for and the impossibility of deciding the ethics of this kind of life writing from seeking permission from the dead. However, Freadman's invention of his father's speech, as the author of both sides of this conversation, seems at the very least disconcertingly ventriloquistic, and must stand as the most extreme example of his control over his father's story.

In the essay, Freadman is inconsistent regarding when it first occurred to him to write *Shadow of Doubt*. In arguing that his father 'had some slight reason to think that I might write about him one day' he alludes to the project having gestated for almost thirty years: 'in 1976 I asked him to keep my letters so that I could refer to them in sorting out my relationship to my past […] He knew enough about autobiography to know that parents generally figure prominently therein' (127). Freadman, therefore, is perhaps on firmer ethical ground than Gaita regarding whether his father would have understood the implications of being the subject of memoir, or indeed whether he would have recognised the terms of his son's 'impure tribute' (141). Yet at the beginning of his essay Freadman claims 'After my father died in 1993, it occurred to me that I might write something about his life' (121). Perhaps such ambiguity is not unusual, yet in Freadman's case it goes to the question of authorial influence regarding his evidentiary sources, such as his motives for encouraging his father to write autobiographically.

Though this fictional Paul is convinced of the purity of his son's motives and agrees to read the manuscript of *Shadow of Doubt*, Freadman wisely draws his 'fictive modelling' exercise to a close without explicitly granting himself his father's permission ('Decent' 142). While his final choice to publish his memoir hinges on his decision that his father would have trusted 'my trustworthiness' (132), even this cannot ultimately allay the author's fears as he concludes his essay: 'I hope I haven't subjected a profoundly decent man to unreasonable narrative indecency. I hope I have done the right thing in publishing this auto/biography. I *think* I probably have' (145, emphasis in the original). For an autobiographer who reflects on the ethics of his act more than most, Freadman's final word (to date) on the ethical status of his project sounds a thoroughly hesitant note.

However, perhaps this very mode of ethical probing is the greatest contribution a life-writing critic turned practitioner such as Freadman can make. In constructing a memoir like *Shadow of Doubt*, the very self-writing process becomes both a working through and an acting out of the author's criticism. Does this mean we should hold life-writing scholars to a higher standard, whether ethical or aesthetic, or critique their autobiographies more rigorously in light of their critique of others' life narratives? Whilst some tallying of their practice against their criticism is inevitable, perhaps the autobiographical contract is no more or less binding for the signatory who works in the industry. Equally however, Freadman's role in the production of his documentary sources may cause us to wonder whether *too much* inside knowledge of how autobiography works (and the kinds of evidence required for a 'credible' account) can impede its writing in practice. While there is no such thing as 'letting the past tell its own story', and while every relational autobiographer in one sense 'creates' the story of the other, in this case the author was often responsible for the creation of the documents on which the story is based. And when this story sets out to uncover reasons for the father's absence and failure, it seems appropriate to ask whether the measure for such assessments may be too stringent. For the elusive father who led a disappointed life, perhaps such a tightly controlled attempt to recognise and even resurrect him in text by a more conventionally successful son can only serve to further obliterate him.

Part III
PERFORMING MASCULINITY

Chapter Five

A SPEAKING SUBJECT/A WATCHING OBJECT: ADDRESSING THE FATHER IN PETER ROSE'S *ROSE BOYS*

> To really develop the traditional masculine role, the young boy needs to be able to try out different behaviors and feelings, practice and display them, and have an audience – especially a male audience – that mirrors back how wonderful and masculine he is.
>
> —Warren Steinberg, *Masculinity: Identity, Conflict and Transformation*

> ADRIAN. Why do you wanna fight?
> ROCKY. Because I can't sing or dance.
>
> —Sylvester Stallone, *Rocky*

> Yet why not say what happened? […]
> We are poor passing facts,
> warned by that to give
> each figure in the photograph
> his living name.
>
> —Robert Lowell, 'Epilogue'

Rose Boys originated from the eulogy the author gave at the funeral of the central subject of his memoir. Robert Rose's death and funeral conclude this work of tribute by the subject's brother, an inevitable climax to a family narrative of suffering and life curtailed. In describing the service, the author summarises his eulogy, eloquently stating the autobiographical impulse and purpose of *Rose Boys*:

> I was determined to express my revulsion at the suffering inflicted on Robert. I described it as grotesquely cruel, like a stupid, vicious swipe from the gods. I wanted the high ceilings and elongated crosses to resound with some kind of refusal, however feeble. I spoke about Robert's sporting career. Many in the church, I knew, were unfamiliar with his record. I drew on crucial incidents and images, some of which will be familiar to readers

of this book [...] Then I turned to my consolations: Robert's closeness to
Salli and my parents and his genius for friendship. (*Rose Boys* 283)

Three distinct purposes are identifiable, each an insight into the demands
placed on this form of text as it functions in the public realm. The first is
the desire to bear witness to suffering in a way that sufficiently decries such
experience as abnormal, unjust, or inhumane: Rose's desire for the church to
'resound with some kind of refusal'. The second purpose, the central focus
of more traditional sport's biographies, may seem mundane in comparison –
'I spoke about Robert's sporting career' – yet it is crucial in establishing the
narrative of the life curtailed. Much is expressed by Rose's insistence that
'Many in the church, I knew, were unfamiliar with his record'. Finally there
is the notion of tribute, what Rose calls 'my consolations', the documentation
and celebration of the subject's impact on his world that goes beyond sporting
success to memorialise a kind of ethical or moral 'life well lived'. It is these
three features of Robert's life, what the author calls 'the message of Robert
Rose' (26), that form the basis for the tribute offered, but it is in the interaction
of these features, the way they affect and rely upon each other, which makes
Rose's work such a singular achievement.

Yet there is a fourth 'unspoken' but central task and interaction inherent
in Rose's eulogy: the exchange between a speaking and performing son and a
listening and observing father. For amongst the congregation Peter addressed at
his brother's funeral was his renowned father Bob Rose. In fact, there is evidence
that Peter performs this eulogy *for* his father: both in the sense of giving the
eulogy instead of Bob, and in it being addressed primarily to, or guided by
the wishes of, the father. This chapter aims first to engage with the question
of how autobiography functions as eulogy, fulfilling the three purposes alluded
to by Rose in the above quotation. My second aim is to investigate the notion
of the text being both addressed to the father, and a performance for him,
demonstrating that despite its focus on the fraternal relationship, *Rose Boys* is in
fact a unique example of the Son's Book of the Father. For in this book there
are two sons who speak to and about the father. Therefore, this discussion will
finally turn to the question of who is actually speaking in *Rose Boys*, and whether
autobiography as eulogy can be read as the act of speaking *for* another.

The Brothers' Book of the Father

Timothy Dow Adams counsels against a straightforward interpretation of the
photographs used in autobiography, warning that all of the slippages between
representation and reality that we apply so readily to life writing apply also
to the visual image: 'interrelations between photography and autobiography

demonstrate the inherent tendency in both to conceal as much as they reveal, through their built-in ambiguity, their natural relation to the worlds they depict, which always seems more direct than it really is' (xxi). Such caution is perhaps all the more pertinent when dealing with what might be termed the 'iconic' image in autobiography: the photograph that uncannily embodies the text itself, as if summoned by the author by an act of will. The luminous frontispiece of the first edition of *Father and Son* (which is now the cover of many recent editions) – showing Henry Gosse gazing into the middle distance, his arm around the author-as-a-boy, who stands dutifully beside him, following his father's gaze beyond the book (perhaps the Bible) spread before them – is one such photograph. Describing the unusual power of such a confluence of photography and autobiography as 'an intellectual diptych', Peter Steele writes that,

> Whether one thinks of the photograph as accompanying the text of *Father and Son*, or that text as accompanying the photograph, the upshot is an inducement to reflection in the reader as he considers how far the book comes to meet him, or retires from him. (27)

Despite our knowledge of photography's and autobiography's capacity for misrepresentation, sometimes an image in text is just too evocative to resist.

The photograph that introduces the first chapter of *Rose Boys* is just such an image. The man in the centre of the frame is the author's father, one of the 'legends' of Australian Rules Football who, along with four of his brothers, played for the famous Collingwood Football Club in the 1940s and 50s. The 2-year-old boy who is so expertly kicking a football is not the author, whose lack of sporting prowess is detailed in the memoir, but his older brother Robert. This young boy, 'wonderfully blonde' as the author describes him (19), will go on to be a prodigious sportsman himself, playing under his father at Collingwood, but excelling also at cricket. Robert was seemingly on the cusp of selection to play cricket for Australia when, on Valentine's Day 1974, his career was cut short by a car accident that left him a quadriplegic.

As this tragic accident is the central event of Rose's memoir, the opening image becomes charged with loss, suggestive of a great many of the book's key tropes, such as the tribute to the life curtailed. Referring to Robert Lowell's instruction 'to give each figure his living name', Rose has elsewhere stated, 'I too was trying to give each figure in the photograph his or her "living name". This act of remembrance and evocation proved to be the first of my consolations in writing *Rose Boys*' ('Consolations' 30).

The image also neatly (perhaps Dow Adams would say too neatly) portrays what I believe is the fundamental autobiographical exchange of *Rose Boys*, as well as a number of other recent Australian life-writing texts by and about brothers: the exchange between a watching father and a performing son. The genre to which I refer is undoubtedly a patriography, though may be deemed as a subcategory within this grouping: perhaps a Brothers' Book of the Father. Internationally, I would point to Mikal Gilmore's *Shot in the Heart* as another example of a Brothers' Book. Two further Australian examples of this type, to which I will make brief reference, are the Wherrett brothers' *Desirelines*, and the Dack brothers' *Sunshine and Shadow*.[1] At first glance, it might seem more accurate to describe such memoirs as Books *of* the Brother rather than the father, taking as they do the fraternal rather than paternal as their central relational frame. But as Leigh Gilmore states of *Shot in the Heart*, 'there are many ways to tell the story of the father, including telling the story of the brother' (75). Redman erroneously excludes *Rose Boys* from his brief study of son–father auto/biographies on the grounds that the father is not sufficiently central to the text to warrant examination (135). The photograph on the book's cover, depicting a strong and smiling father (once again) crouching above his two young sons, clearly heralds this as a memoir of patrimony in the tradition of Philip Roth's renowned auto/biography. Further, I will argue that *Rose Boys* must be considered a part of this sub-genre because the father is the implied addressee of the text and the act of writing is itself a performance for him.

In describing *Rose Boys*' iconic image some pages after it appears, the author makes explicit the importance of its performative aspect, and of the paternal gaze:

> Dad, very attentive, props on his haunches as the little boy kicks the football. It flies off to the right, catching the sun, perfectly focussed. The expression on Robert's face is remarkable for its portent of what

---

[1] A key difference is that, unlike *Rose Boys*, these texts are explicitly collaborative, the narration shared by both brothers. Yet as I will argue here, Rose frames both himself and Robert as the speaking subjects of the text.

he would become. He grimaces, so great is his intensity. His kicking technique is flawless. [...] Young Robert is kicking for his father, and he knows how to do it. (19)

It is worth remembering that newspaper photographers took many of the images in *Rose Boys* for the purposes of reporting on the sporting careers of Bob and Robert Rose, so they are framed in very deliberate ways. This is a narrative of relationships that take place in the public sphere, and are enacted very much under a public gaze. Therefore, the primary subject of this photograph is Bob Rose, whose act of crouching to watch his son kick is in fact a performance for the camera. Yet as Peter's description evinces, the son's act is also doubtless a performance, though not for the camera – 'young Robert is kicking *for* his father' (emphasis added). What kind of a performance is it? I would like to suggest that this kick and numerous other acts portrayed in *Rose Boys* can be read as performances of sonship: of the son courting the father's admiration and pride, and in doing so demonstrating that he is, like Freadman, 'the son of such a man'. Here I draw on Jungian psychoanalytic theory, primarily the work of Warren Steinberg, who has written widely on the place of the father in a son's development of masculinity. Of most relevance is Steinberg's conception of developmental identification, which he describes as 'the normal process by which the son looks to the father for the provision of a model on which to pattern himself [...] The son wants to be a man, and he wants to be a man just like his father' (69). The aim of this reading is not to test or validate this conception, nor to confirm whether it is 'the normal process', but to investigate the extent to which such an idea is enacted textually in memoir.

This discussion posits the central auto/biographical exchange in *Rose Boys* as an exchange between a speaking and performing subject (in the sons Robert and Peter) and a watching object and addressee (in the father Bob Rose). How is the paternal gaze conceived of and represented in this form of memoir? Can this work be read as a 'performance' for the father? How is the performance of sonship framed and represented? And how is Peter Rose's autobiographical act both a 'speaking for himself' and an attempt to speak *for* his brother. Can a life writer speak for another who has died, or will another to speak through his work? And what are the ethical implications of this attempt?

Before I continue, it is important to contextualise my own 'watching object'. This chapter has been adapted from a conference paper I gave in September 2009 at the Story of the Story: Ethics, Therapy and Life Writing Conference at Flinders University. Amongst the audience that day was the author. Immediately following my paper, I interviewed Rose about his memoir and his practice of life writing more generally. Therefore, this analysis is offered as a kind of dialogue between author and critic. Aspects of my argument have been revised based on my conversation with the author, while the following discussion also incorporates and critiques comments made in interview. Though it is worth keeping in mind that author interviews are a very different kind of autobiographical text, where revelations must be viewed through a vastly more sceptical or at least cautious lens, they are in my opinion a useful and valid way of interrogating an autobiography against its author's stated intentions. However, perhaps more than other chapters in this present study, readers should be alert to the critical frame of this analysis.

The 'Father–Son Rule'

Of the contemporary works discussed in this book, *Rose Boys* is the only one that deals with what may be termed 'public lives'. As publicly recognised achievement impinges heavily on the narrative, it is worth briefly outlining this biographical and cultural milieu. Just as Gosse's father was an eminent Victorian scientist who was already the subject of biography before the publication of *Father and Son*, Rose's father (and to a lesser extent his brother) was a well-known sporting figure in Australia well before his son represented him in *Rose Boys*. In fact, it would not be unfair to observe that in this case the father's fame greatly exceeds that of his writer-son. Considered by many to be the greatest to have ever played for Collingwood, 'the most famous sporting club in Australia' (Freadman, 'Recognition' 133), Bob Rose then coached his beloved team (which for a period included his son Robert) to a number of grand finals throughout the 1960s, 70s and 80s. He was inducted into the Australian Football Hall of Fame in 1996 and the annual AFL Players' Association Award for Most Courageous Player is named in his honour.

Footballing dynasties are a peculiar feature of professional 'Aussie Rules', and in the context of my focus on father–son relationships in Australia, highlight pertinent questions about how patrimonial inheritance functions, including how a son's conception of self and masculinity is formed in relation to his father. So important is the symbolic value of such dynasties that in the 1950s the Victorian Football League formulated the 'father–son rule', which allows clubs to draft the son of a famous former player in order to preserve the legacy of the family name under the one 'jersey'. In essence, the father–son rule enshrines in the code's regulations the importance of a son 'following in his father's footsteps'.[2] The father–son rule has been utilised at least

---

[2] The rule was instigated by the Melbourne Football Club to draft Ron Barassi, whose father Barassi Senior had recently been killed in World War II. One may read Barassi's stellar career (one of the most celebrated in AFL history) as a son's desire to 'make good' on his father's curtailed life. Barassi's autobiography certainly frames his achievement in this way. See *Barassi: The Life Behind the Legend* East Roseville: Simon & Schuster, 1995.

twenty-five times since 1989, perhaps most notably in recent times by Geelong to draft Gary Ablett's two sons, Gary Junior and Nathan, to the club. It is into this contextual frame that Peter Rose's 'essay in fraternal juxtaposition' is written, and underscores the expectation placed on both sons by what the author refers to as 'the birthright' of being 'a son of Victoria Park' (218).

Although he admits to writing fiction as a teenager (tellingly, his first piece of writing was 'a woeful story called "Father to Son"' (42–3)), Peter Rose became a published author relatively late in life, following a successful stint as the Australasian editor of Oxford University Press. He published his first poem at the age of 30, with his debut collection of poetry *The House of Vitriol* appearing five years later in 1990. He has since published four further collections of poetry and two novels. While best known as a poet and as editor of the *Australian Book Review* (since 2001), it is arguably his memoir that introduced Rose to a wider audience. Reprinted over ten times since its publication in 2001, *Rose Boys* has sold in excess of twenty thousand copies. Widely reviewed upon its release in both sporting and literary publications, the text received unstinting praise. Sports writer and former footballer Brent Crosswell described *Rose Boys* as 'a book of immense emotional force that is a eulogy to his brother, a tribute to his parents and a powerful demonstration of the redemptive quality of suffering' (131). Freadman described it as 'life writing of a very high order [...] that combines biography, autobiography, pathography, eulogy, ethical reflection, and an inquiry into Australian myths, ideologies, styles of masculinity, and cultural locales' ('Incongruous' 23–4). It was joint winner of the National Biography Award 2003, and was short-listed for the NSW Premier's Literary Awards and the Douglas Stewart Prize for Non-Fiction, both in 2002.

The Auto/Biographical Exchange

The author establishes the auto/biographical exchange between a speaking subject and a watching object in the opening passage of *Rose Boys*, a prose description of a dream that, through the course of the narrative, transmutes into the poem 'I Recognise My Brother in a Dream' (275). In the dream, Peter is back in his hometown of Wangaratta, where there is a fire at the local library. He stands at street level and watches the fire engulf the building, before becoming aware of three boys watching on from a block of flats down the street:

> I move towards them, studying my excited trio, not the blaze. The boy in the middle is jeering at something in the distance. He is slender and

vivid and blond as an angel [...] I almost recognise this boy, but he is younger than me, which feels wrong. He is clearly the oracle because of his uncanny vision. Creeping to the foot of the flats, I listen to his sunny description of the pandemonium in the library [...] And then, looking over the window ledge, he takes pity on me and addresses me directly. (xiv)

Here the watching object is Peter, who studies the three boys, and almost recognises his brother. The speaking subject is of course Robert, the oracle who narrates what he sees to whoever will listen. Peter the watcher is also obviously listening, but it is his observation of the young boy's performance that seemingly causes his brother to turn and 'address' Peter directly. Importantly, the author does not disclose the contents of this speech, but as this is the last line of what is a kind of preface to the book, we are invited to read the narrative that follows as a kind of transposing of this address, a ventriloquising of 'the message of Robert Rose'.

Of much relevance here is the fact that *Rose Boys* was written following Robert's death some twenty-five years after he became a quadriplegic. As noted, this incident was the trigger for Peter Rose's auto/biographical impulse, the text originating from the address he gave at Robert's funeral. But what exactly is involved in describing autobiography as eulogy? First, it differentiates it from a comparison to elegy or obituary, in that the term eulogy preserves a sense of the text being an act of speaking. As Derrida discovered when faced with the death of and mourning for Emmanuel Levinas, this kind of writing becomes an attempt 'to speak *for* the other whom one loves and admires, before speaking *of* him' (*Adieu* 2, emphasis in the original). Tracing Derrida's funeral orations back to Aristotle's formulation of presence in epideidic rhetoric, Brooke Rollins claims it as the rhetorical form 'most closely linked to the occasion it was delivered' (6). Like Derrida's *Adieu to Emmanuel Levinas*, *Rose Boys* is undoubtedly a work of tribute, but this notion of speaking *for* has other implications. Can an auto/biographer speak *for* another who has died? Can he be an interlocutor through whom the dead speaks?

Secondly, Rose's text is eulogy in the way that it explicitly aims to be both a work of consolation and restitution, engaging in a direct way with the world outside the text. *Rose Boys* heralds itself as a work of tribute to lives curtailed with the dedication: 'For Robert Rose 1952–1999 and Brian Martin 1945–2000.' The latter is an ex-jockey who, like Robert, became a quadriplegic following an accident and was later befriended by the Rose family. Though Martin barely features in the narrative, this dedication to him highlights the author's determination that his text be a work of restitution for those fellow victims of paralysis who have suffered and died along with his brother.³ In telling a narrative of quadriplegia, Rose focuses attention on the indignities of such an experience, and on society's neglect. Describing an under-resourced hospital ward late in the text, Rose states: 'This, you couldn't help thinking, was what society thought of its most powerless members. This was how canny governments treated the unlucky ones' (245). By informing readers of The Robert Rose Foundation, 'a new charity intended to help people with spinal cord injuries to lead more fulfilling and independent lives' (xi), Rose makes his text a work of restitution in a very practical sense, demonstrating, as McCooey describes, 'how autobiography can directly intervene in the public sphere' ('Going Public' 29).

Masculinity and Public Gazing

Before returning to the difficult question of who is 'speaking' in Rose's narrative, we must explore further the representation of the primary watching object of the text: the figure of Bob Rose. Peter discovers the iconic image of his father watching his brother kick a football in one of the Rose family scrapbooks, which the author details at length in his book. 'Curious documents: these bibles of scrap, collages of self-delight', Peter states, 'I have never kept one myself. That would be a thin volume anyway' (3). A great many elisions and tensions underlie Rose's description of what he calls his brother and father's 'voluminous' scrapbooks. As Peter himself observes, he and his brother were vastly different. Robert is described by many as 'a golden youth', the same term applied to their father half a century before. In another image from the book, father and sons perform for the cameras when Bob Rose is first appointed to coach Collingwood, or Bob and Robert expertly perform, while Peter watches on (29). As the author describes, 'They lope along, effortlessly bouncing footballs. I must have lost mine. I grin at them determinedly' (40). As a teenager, Robert is at home in the hedonistic, heterosexual 'world of men' into which he is born, a brilliant sportsman who before his accident embodies, as Christine Nicholls observes, 'an idealised conceptualisation of the "true type"', his 'corporal style is that

---

3   As with Gaita's brief eulogy to his friend John Dunstan, Rose's tributes-in-miniature are an apt summation of his mode of memorialisation. In briefly recounting Martin's story of quadriplegia, the author records the passing of an unnamed friend of Brian's and Robert's who was run over by a train when his wheelchair became stuck at a level crossing. Following Brian's account of the incident, Rose writes: 'We both sat there blinking at the cruelty of it all. There was nothing to say' (233). Despite this assertion, the author demonstrates by writing that in fact there *is* much to say, his text becoming a refusal to stay silent, even when those he writes about are reticent to speak of themselves.

of hegemonic Australian masculinity' (165). Or as the author describes him, 'my eternal adversary, so recklessly impatient to realise his manhood' (119–20). Peter, on the other hand, is an intellectual, solitary, homosexual young man who is at times painfully self-critical. As a teenager Rose prefers sitting in the stands with the footballer's wives than in the dressing sheds with the men. In this way, one might surmise, Steinberg's developmental identification with the father does not apply in Peter's case, who has instead remained attached to the mother. In interview the author appears to confirm this assessment:

> I had grown up around hundreds of men who seemed overly needful of public attention or adulation. I thought it was frankly ridiculous that so much attention was directed at them for kicking a football. As a boy I preferred a more purist kind of silence and reticence, which was my mother's position. (In Mansfield, 'Cathartic' 31)

Evidence of a preference for the mother's position can be found in the text itself. During his exploration of the family sporting archives, Rose pauses to describe his mother's scrapbook, 'the one I treasure most' (12). It details her promising early career as a singer on stage and radio in Melbourne. Two key contributors to this succinct tribute-in-miniature are the mother's reticence to speak about herself, and the fact that her story is also one of a life curtailed. Rose describes how she ended her career when she got married on the advice of a family member: 'For myself, revering music as I do, it seems like a bad joke, the sort of fatuous advice that subverts a life' (15). Though he calls himself 'a son of her sacrifice', one feels that the author slates more blame towards the males of the family who gained such attention 'for kicking a football'.

Fellow poet John Kinsella appears to share Rose's disdain for the regard in which AFL players are held, describing the sport as 'just a bunch of blokes […] kicking the inflated skin of a dead cow, or cows, around a field' (24). In his astonishingly acerbic essay 'Why I Didn't Play Australian Rules Football', Kinsella denounces the code's influence on Australian culture, including the myth of egalitarianism it fosters, its closet racism and sexism, its propagation of 'blind nationalism' and its sanctioning of violence: 'There's not a lot I need to say about "Aussie Rules" being a bloodsport' (21). Interestingly, Kinsella explicitly links his animosity to his relationship with his father and grandfather, and notions of masculinity: 'My father's struggle with his aggressive and semi-meditative side (read: sarcastic, laconic, Australian) found focus in football' (22). The author describes how, after being injured 'on the verge of selection to the big time', his father invested his sporting hopes in his son until Kinsella too was injured while playing AFL: 'now that I was out of contention as a footballer (on any level), it was quickly asserted that my sissyness and pooferism were confirmed. A life of beatings and victimisation followed' (23). Though this revelation provides ample evidence for the author's attitude to the sport, his continued attack on the influence of AFL generally leads him to adopt a vindicatory tone at the conclusion of his essay. Searching for a further rationalisation for his antipathy, Kinsella introduces a fraternal component to his relationship with 'Aussie Rules':

> It's a cruel sport, as most are. So where do I fit in this? Well, my father had another son by his second marriage. This son was more than a promising footballer. On the surface, he seemed to love it, though such tales were always mediated by a desire to prove manliness to my very large father. I suspect there's more to it than that […] On the verge of joining the Colts, one step before my father's achievement, he was badly injured. He lost all – the adulation of girls and women, the approval and admiration of the blokes […] Or maybe he escaped in the nick of time. (24)

In *Rose Boys*, however, the author's relation to his father's and brother's world is far more ambivalent than Kinsella's, or indeed than Rose's own disparagement of the attention his male relatives received for 'kicking a football' would suggest. The author often speaks admiringly, if somewhat equivocally, of the male world of the Collingwood Social Club, described by Freadman as 'a kind of shrine' to 'hegemonic Australian masculinity' ('Recognition' 152). Observing a group of drinkers at his father's seventieth birthday party, Rose writes:

> I watched these jovial survivors – some my age, others quite old. I was struck, as always, by their invincible camaraderie. […] How sane they were, how affable […] I did so without envy, for I have never aspired to this fraternity, but when I pondered my own world – solitary, bookish, egoistic, self-reliant – it seemed impoverished by comparison. Although there was something profoundly innocent, even boyish, about these men as they poured late beers and slapped each other on the back, I felt sure they knew something about kinship and contentment that the poets didn't. (235)

The self-conscious outsider manages an almost anthropological tone here, at the same time chalking one up for the footballers over the poets. In his poem 'Operamanes', which was written before *Rose Boys* and is tellingly addressed to his father, Rose covers similar territory, this time gently parodying the lively discussion of sporting glories he overhears in a pub:

> Another year, serving behind the bar
> at the Collingwood Social Club

> I listened to a core of die-hards
> extolling your prodigious torpedo punt
> in the 1953 Grand Final
> the rare projectile artistry of it. […]
> Marvelling at my half-time rhapsodists
> I mistook them for a coloratura's claqueurs. (*Vitriol* 17)

The poem highlights the 'mixed-blessing' of being son to such a famous father – Rose's tone is itself admiring, though also ironic – a defence perhaps against the experience of being identified with and compared to the 'great Bob Rose'.

Late in his memoir, when Peter's own professional career as a poet and an editor begins to flourish, he must face again the contrast between himself and the other men in his family, when upon meeting influential professors, he is continually asked: 'Are you really Bobby Rose's son?' 'I sensed a kind of incredulity behind their questions', the author explains. 'Could this lean homosexual bookman really be a bona fide son of Victoria Park?' (218).

The ironic tone the author conjures with such ease regarding his later life is tellingly absent in the diaries of his teenage years. Rereading these documents, the author is 'struck by my agitation, my self-loathing, my sense of futility', by 'a profound sense of abnormality or unsuitability' (70). At this age the contrast between himself and his brother (and between himself and his father), is evidently more keenly felt, perhaps most obviously Peter's lack of prowess on the sporting field. Though eager to point out that his father was 'highly civilised, and this was never an issue' (63), the adult narrator undercuts this assertion, confirming the importance of the father's 'attentive' gaze on his own sporting performance in the family archive. Sources of this kind can also bear other evidences, such as a father's love, embedded in the paper. Upon discovering a newspaper clipping in one scrapbook that refers to him as 'a budding champ', the author cannot help but draw our attention to evidence of the father's lingering pride. 'My first clipping', the author exclaims, 'Dad's thumbprint on this piece of journalistic whimsy is as palpable as the musty aroma rising from Robert's scrapbook' (22). Elsewhere Rose is keen to highlight the fallibility of his textual sources, 'the omissions as well as the feats and statistics' (18). However, as with the tear in the photograph of the father in *Shadow of Doubt*, here it is the physicality of such evidentiary sources – the manner in which they become vessels for one's emotions and understanding of others – which is of value; not for the information they contain (or omit), but for their confirmation of the father's attention, of inter-connectedness, as Rose states elsewhere, of 'loving and being loved' (213).

This paternal gaze exists right the way through *Rose Boys*. In a great many of the author's memories of his father, he is portrayed in the act of watching or looking on while his sons perform. Unsurprisingly, the majority of these occurrences are as a spectator of the football-and-cricketing prodigy Robert, yet prior to the author abandoning sport completely in his later teenage years, he describes his father's dependable presence at his D-grade school sporting fixtures: 'To encourage me, but also because he was genuinely interested, Dad always followed my sporting career, such as it was' (67). A particularly striking example is of Peter's father watching him play AFL early on a Saturday morning from 'the boundary of the oval known as Siberia [...] The vice-principal [...] asked dad what on earth he was doing there at eight-thirty in the morning. Dad was coaching Collingwood in the final that afternoon' (68). The vice-principal's incredulity works in two ways: first by establishing a communally held value for professional or 'elite' sport above other forms of achievement, to which Bob Rose is a kind of emblem, and simultaneously placing the father beyond such petty comparisons; a father willing to go to great lengths to watch and support his (at this stage) less successful son.

The importance of the father's gaze on a son's sporting performance is confirmed in two other Australian brothers' stories, though in these cases by its absence. Though the father of Richard and Peter Wherrett's *Desirelines* is a violent alcoholic whose influence on his family is unremittingly destructive, both brothers note with disappointment his nonattendance at their high school rugby matches. As Peter Wherrett explains: 'my father never came to watch either Richard or me play anything. He himself had been such a fine athlete, yet he had no interest in either of us boys following suit. In my memory he never even discussed a game with me' (86). A key moment in *Desirelines* comes when younger brother Richard sets a new school record for the 220-yard sprint, reclaiming his father's record that had only recently been broken. When older brother Peter runs to tell his father, who has missed the race, that 'the Wherrett name' was 'back in the record books' (87), the father's response is notable for its deficiency: 'He said something like, "That's good" and thereafter dismissed me with an apparent lack of interest' (88).

James and Stephen Dack's *Sunshine and Shadow*, another collaborative autobiography written by two brothers, confirms the desire for the paternal gaze of an absent father, even when this father is repeatedly abusive. Interestingly, both *Desirelines* and *Sunshine and Shadow* narrate how, in their teens, both older brothers are forced into violent confrontation with their abusive fathers, recalling Merv Lilley's descriptions of the epic stoushes between his father and older brother. Steinberg describes this phenomenon as 'defensive identification', which 'is not based on love and affection, but is synonymous with identification with the aggressor. It is a way of reducing anxiety by becoming like the person one is afraid of' (69). The alcoholic and abusive father of *Sunshine and Shadow* looms large in the narrative, despite effectively abandoning the family when James was just ten and Stephen five. As Stephen explains: 'I [...] missed a man who I could show off to and impress with my sporting talent, which I exhibited almost from the time I could run. For better or worse he was my dad and I craved his approval' (67). Both narrators record the disillusionment they experience when their father, on separate occasions, fails to deliver on a promise to watch them play football. James recalls waiting on a street corner for his father for six hours, stating that, 'I had long before stopped believing anything my father said, but his no show that day broke my heart' (12). In a scene reminiscent of Smith's childhood memory of his father's sudden brief reappearance in his life, Stephen records his father's unexpected arrival at his football game after a prolonged absence:

> I ran proudly onto the field, determined to play the game of my life for my father. I assumed he'd watch the game then we'd go home together. I played my heart out and scored a try and I looked across to see if he's seen my mighty run to the line. He was gone [...] He made me feel like I was nothing. (39)

In the sporting arena, the father's gaze, or its absence, is evidently keenly felt.

In *Rose Boys*, Peter's memories of being watched by his father are not universally positive. One such instance is Bob's attempt to socialise his errant, awkward teenage son by sending him to a youth club: 'I remember my father's frustration and helplessness – did he stay one night to observe? – as he watched me avoiding the others in my nervousness and shyness' (71). Importantly perhaps, these experiences inevitably reduced Peter to a state of silence, 'incapable of conversation, or touch, or fluency, or dexterity, or speech'. Here, rather than running counter to social convention, the father is the socialising force, an adept media-savvy public figure watching on as his son falls well short of the mark: 'I remember his hopeless and unavailing pep talks, of a kind with which he was doubtless in the habit of inspiring gauche, recalcitrant football recruits' (71). Considering the poignancy of this recollection, it is difficult not to read Rose's subsequent mastery of public speaking and performance, which he describes in interview as 'something I could do now' (in Mansfield, 'Cathartic' 31) as a restitution for his earlier failings.

Peter is not the first to have noted his awareness of the paternal gaze. His older brother Robert acknowledges its centrality in an interview for a local newspaper (following the announcement of Bob Rose as Australian Father of the Year in 1995) for what the author describes somewhat dismissively as 'one of those father–son articles. By now most of the sentiments were as familiar as 'Good Old Collingwood Forever' (225). But what elevates the piece beyond sentimental cliché is Robert's description of the importance of observation between father and son: 'Those days were terrific, being with each other. It was like later on when I kicked on to Shield cricket. I'd always look around at the crowd to see him, and sure enough, he'd be there' (225). Even after Robert's accident, this watching between father and son continued as a mutually sustaining relationality, this time with the father in the role of observant carer. 'I try not to ask too much of Bob', Robert states in interview. 'I try to wait until he gets off his stool or takes a break from gardening or something before I ask for a drink or a cigarette. I watch and wait. And I know he's watching too' (225).

This newspaper article can be read as one of a number of instances of Bob and Robert publically 'performing' the father–son relationship. Just as the photographs of Bob and Robert kicking or bouncing footballs are examples of them 'performing for the cameras', Peter describes how the familiar sight of Bob pushing his son's wheelchair through the crowd at Collingwood fixtures became for many an emblem of the devoted father–son bond. In a letter written to the author, former Victorian Premier Jeff Kennett describes the impact of this scene:

> It was during the countless times I saw your Father behind Robert's wheelchair, ensuring that Robert could see or attend a particular function, that I observed a special relationship, a singular calm, a great dignity. There was never any fanfare…just a Father in love with his son, and that love reciprocated. There was an aura around them, and Robert's condition, and the wheelchair, seemed to be incidental… They set a high standard, a great example for others. I regret Robert's passing, but he and your Father left me with a picture I will never forget. (271)

Despite the lack of fanfare and Robert's incapacitation, Nicholls rightly reads this scene not only as a performance, but also in sporting terms: 'It is as if the two men are "performing" their masculinity as a team, virtually two sides of the one coin, with the father "doing" the physical side whilst the son "does" the courage' (170).

But what of Peter? Does the father continue to 'watch' his youngest son perform once he has abandoned sport and his life has taken a very different path? Can the father's bond with Peter be similarly described as a mutually sustaining relationality, or even as a performance? In interview, the author describes the experience of appearing alongside his father at a writer's festival after the release of *Rose Boys*, though he notes ruefully, 'more people wanted dad to sign my book rather than me' (in Mansfield, 'Cathartic' 31). According to Redman, a key motif of many patrimonial life narratives is the 'dark brother' motif, where 'the author feels he was not the father's preferred son. That status belonged to a now bequeathed sibling, for whom the surviving son becomes an inadequate substitute' (133). Redman points to J. R. Ackerley's sense in *My Father and Myself* of being 'the wrong son' as one example of the 'dark brother motif'. Could *Rose Boys* be read as another? Does Rose's essay in fraternal juxtaposition, informed as it is by the paternal gaze, cast the author as 'the wrong son'? The thought had evidently occurred to Bob Rose himself. During a frank conversation between Bob and Peter following Robert's accident, the author writes:

> Dad became upset. He said I believed he cared more for Robert than he did for me. He had said this once before. I had denied it then, as I did now. Although I knew that Dad and Robert had much more in common than we did, and though I had long thought of myself as a redundant and confusing son, I never felt that Dad favoured Robert. Nor was I conscious of harbouring resentment [...] Had he preferred Robert, I wouldn't have been particularly affronted. But it wasn't Dad's form. I often thought of him as the fairest man I knew. He loved both his sons.
>
> I placated Dad as best I could. (121–2)

One can easily imagine how a male like Peter may have felt superfluous within a famous sporting family such as the Roses, but as readers we must in the end take Rose at his word and conclude that the dark brother motif does not apply in this case, despite the father's fears to the contrary. A good deal of the credit for this must fall to Bob Rose himself who, based on his depiction in *Rose Boys*, was extraordinarily gentle, open-minded and insightful for a man of his generation and cultural background. Rose's choice of words in describing himself as a 'redundant' son is interesting, implying as it does an achievement-based assessment of worth. It may prompt us to wonder to what extent the author's success in the poetry and publishing worlds has been driven by his patrimonial heritage and whether it is viewed by the author or others in sporting terms. Nicholls claims that the author 'is not so different from other men in his family: he too has a strongly competitive streak manifesting itself initially in combative, physical contests with his older brother, and in less obvious ways as he grows up. In certain important respects Peter is also the beneficiary of the family's high public profile, regardless of whether his own sporting ability matches that of other family members' (163). In interview, the author seems to concur, describing his realisation of the patrimony he shares with his brother following his father's death:

> In many ways we were tremendously competitive, both of us. I didn't appreciate that until much later, because I chose other pursuits. Poetry and literature seem so pure, so Romantic. But thinking about it later, I realised that I was every bit as driven as Robert was. You couldn't be around all that energy and drive and not absorb some of it. Sometimes you don't begin to understand your emotional and genetic inheritance until the people aren't there. (In Mansfield, 'Cathartic' 32)

As with much of my interview with him, there is a certain indeterminability here regarding to whom Rose is referring. The quotation begins with a comparison between his brother and himself, yet is a response to a question about his father. Therefore, by the end of this quotation, the 'energy and drive' Rose refers to having grown up around could be both his father's and brother's, and his final reference to a genetic inheritance ultimately shifts the reference point to the father. Such is the enmeshed nature of the Rose boys.

There is indeed evidence that the paternal gaze continues to sustain Peter in later life. Late in the text, for example, Bob watches his younger son 'perform' at the launch of his first book of poetry, though as the author pointedly notes: 'The fact that Dad chose to leave midway through a final in which Collingwood were playing in order to attend the launch proved much more newsworthy than the book's release' (220). Again Bob's actions demonstrate an ascription of value that is in stark contrast to the broader 'football-mad' culture within which he existed, highlighting the uniqueness of this father. Yet can Peter's poetry reading be construed as a performance of masculinity, or even of sonship? Can his memoir? Is there a place within the Australian conception of idealised masculinity for the heroic writer? According to John Hughes, the son–father auto/biographer to whom we will turn in the following chapter, the answer is a definitive no: 'being a writer is about as low a form of masculine achievement as I can imagine in Australia' (in Mansfield, 'Beating' 100). Rose seems not to share Hughes's pessimism in this regard; though growing up around men 'overly needful of public attention' has given him some pause, as he expresses in interview:

> *Rose Boys* changed many things for me. Suddenly there was a certain public interest in my work. I became more aware of the potential to entertain or to stir people. [...] After a while I became quite wary. People's interest was genuine and rewarding, but I tried to keep it in proportion. [...] the public side of it began to feel *actorly*. It was something I could do now, but

I was a little suspicious of it. (In Mansfield, 'Cathartic' 30–31, emphasis speaker's own)

Who is Speaking?

For both brothers in *Rose Boys*, the watching object of the father informs their performance. This is why I conceive of the book as a Son's Book *for* the Father, written about the brother but under the gaze of the father – as Rose makes clear in alluding to the father's expectations of the book while it was being written: 'Am I perpetuating my brother's memory, which is what our father believes and perhaps why he is so enthusiastic about the book?' (149) But whose Son's Book is *Rose Boys*? In an obvious sense, the subject of the work is Robert, the other of this 'essay in fraternal juxtaposition', as the author calls it, and the speaker is Peter. Yet within the work itself the author attempts to frame his brother Robert as the speaking subject of the text. In his dream, the boy Peter recognises as his brother 'turns and addresses me directly'. Pages later, as the author begins to construct an auto/biographical treatise for his work, he asks:

> What exactly is the message of Robert Rose? One year after his death, twenty-six years after just another of our crashes, knowing the effect it had on his family and friends and thousands of others who hardly knew him, I want to go back there and *reanimate* him, despite those callipers and sandbags […] I want to examine his achievements, what he symbolised, what he gave and withheld, what he divulged and what he never said, as a son, as a brother, as a husband, as a mate, as a tragic victim of that second or two in time. […] It is time to listen to my brother whose message, laconic but self-evident in later life, I somehow never fully heeded. If I am to overcome these eternities of maladjustment, as a friend put it when Robert died, I must try. Brothers so close yet so incongruous meet improbably in this shifting text.
>
> Again I turn to the handsome lad, the vaunted youth, the rage recruit, and *will him to speak to me*. (26–7, emphasis mine)

The term 'reanimate' is an evocative and fitting one, for it captures the intense struggle of auto/biography for a writer such as Rose. Unlike the photographs that begin each chapter, the author desires moving images and speaking subjects. Though two brothers meet 'in this shifting text', the message of the book is, according to the author, Robert's message, one he hopes to decipher by 'willing him to speak'. The question underlying this attempt is: what constitutes a speech act in autobiography?

This notion of willing the dead to speak recalls Paul de Man's famous condemnation of autobiography as prosopopoeia, 'the fiction of an apostrophe to an absent, deceased, or voiceless entity, which posits the possibility of the latter's reply and confers upon it the power of speech' (75–6). Rose's address to his absent brother, the calling back from the dead the voice of the addressee, has this specific aim – to make the other speak. Seemingly, Rose does not share de Man's pessimism about autobiography, yet he does struggle with the ethics of his act, particularly with the question of whether the laconic subject can be made to speak, or would want to be spoken *for* in autobiography. How would Robert have felt about being textually reanimated, bedsores and all? A major feature of pathography (or life writing about illness) is the desire to retrieve past lives and bodies lost due to sickness and tragedy, to revive them in the face of death (Couser, *Vulnerable Subjects* 198). Such an act is not without its ethical dilemmas, but when it takes the form of pathobiography, the act is complicated further. It is important to note that Robert cannot be figured as a 'vulnerable subject' of Couser's estimations (x), nor as one of Lejeune's 'those who do not write' (185). Working briefly as a sports journalist after his accident, Robert demonstrates that he was in no way averse to life writing in the public domain, and *Rose Boys* contains some of Robert's own autobiographical reflections written for this purpose (138–40), including work that could be described as autopathography. However, one may still wonder how welcoming Robert may have been of Peter's far more intimate portrait of his disability.

Peter admits feeling uncomfortable upon being told by a family friend that Robert was 'distressed' by the poem 'I Recognise My Brother in a Dream', and that he 'didn't understand it' (150). Further, as the following observation by Freadman implies, the author's desire to 'will' his brother 'to speak' perhaps runs contrary to the verbal reticence Robert embodied in life:

> Peter is in no doubt that Robert's life has a 'message' but the message is somehow 'laconic' (27), wary of speech. It is Peter who feels moved to write, to 'examine' that life more deeply [...] If the transferred pain that comes with re-seeing, re-cognising Robert 'forces upon' Peter the impulse to speak, the writing also springs from a kind of decision: a decision not to consign Robert's life to the domain of the 'laconic but self-evident' (27), but rather to 'reanimate' it, to write it with a depth of *understanding*, a kind of *recognition*, that eludes the laconic gaze. ('Recognition' 156, emphasis in the original)

This depth of understanding, this literary reanimation is one the author evidently recognises and values, but would Robert recognise himself in it? The question again recalls Segal's criticism of *Romulus, My Father* giving 'sensuous embodiment the father's values – but with reference to a beauty to which he is blind' ('Speaking' 15). In attempting to communicate his brother's 'laconic' message, Rose writes his way into an ethical debate about competing *styles* of address in Australian life writing, particularly tributes written by men to other men. As Tridgell observes, this disjunction is most obviously expressed in approaches to communication: 'What happens when a highly articulate autobiographer attempts to represent the communicative style of a subject who does not share or value the autobiographer's discursive style?' (285). It is a central conflict in auto/biographies of this nature, a complex struggle between the rights of the writing self and the written other, between the desires of the literary and the laconic, the erudite and the non-intellectual.

In *Rose Boys* one's voice and discursive approach are heavily gendered things, denoting acceptable modes of masculinity. In a revealing quotation from Peter's diary, the author demonstrates the pressure he felt to conform to a manlier mode of speech:

I realise my voice is too high and suspicious, hence I intend to:

1. go deeper.
2. enunciate less clearly.
3. speak less.
4. speak softer. (70)

These notions of discursive style are relevant to the manner in which Peter chooses to enunciate Robert's message, which is described as 'laconic', wary of speech, yet who is brought to life by his far more erudite brother. In an outworking of the author's adopted mode of fraternal juxtaposition, there are many instances in the book where Peter attempts to preserve and respect Robert's mode of address, whilst at the same time contrasting it with his own. When Peter and his mother first enter the hospital room on the night of Robert's accident, the author poignantly records his brother's understatement – 'I'm in trouble' – at the same time placing it alongside observational prose that is rich in detail: 'Robert was lying on his back, looking rather beautiful. His head was shaved. They had already drilled holes in his skull and inserted callipers attached to eighty-pound weights. Robert's head was pulled back, immovable' (55–6). Likewise, the 'death-haunted poet', as the author describes himself (in Mansfield, 'Cathartic' 27), allows the following simple exchange at Robert's fortieth birthday party to stand for his brother's ruminations on death: 'Later I asked Robert if he was looking forward to another forty years. "No way," he laughed. Twenty? "Maybe ten"' (222).

However, it is worth noting that, despite his care, the author never fully resolves the questions he poses, remaining keenly aware of the ethical implications of 'reanimating' his verbally reticent, quadriplegic brother. In another searching self-assessment of his auto/biographical act the author resolves that:

> I have no intention of writing a second book about Robert. I'm not even sure I should be writing the first. What would Robert have made of my essay in fraternal juxtaposition? Would he have liked my tentative portrait? Would he have approved? Would he have tried to stop me? [...] And what is *my* true motive (if I can be said to have formulated one)? Am I perpetuating my brother's memory, which is what our father believes and perhaps why he is so enthusiastic about the book? [...] Am I trying to reveal the essential Robert, the latent messenger in the *Herald* editorial? Or am I trying to impose a version of him on the public, unconsciously distorting what really happened? Do I still need to recognise my brother, as in the dream? Do I crave his recognition? Is it atonement for things left unsaid and undone? (149–50, emphasis in the original)

Few, if any, of these questions are resolved unequivocally, though in memoirs of this nature such 'self-probing' often appears to serve the purpose of absolving the author of the ethical dilemmas posed – the publication of the memoir possibly demonstrating the author's ultimate resolution of stated quandaries. We may wonder whether simply asking the questions is sufficient. Freadman helpfully answers Rose's two final queries for him, sounding a triumphal note for relational auto/biography's ability to intervene in positive ways for lives and selves beyond the textual:

> The answer to both questions would seem to be 'yes'. Needing as in the dream presumably refers to the sense that one has not quite arrived at recognition, or that 'real' recognition (whatever that might mean) continues to elude the speaker. Writing the poem helps to satisfy that need: the poem re-casts the first contemptuous dream-figure [...] with a more responsible, solicitous brother-as-guide who, unlike the one in the dream, assumes responsibility for narrating the inferno that threatens Peter's erudite world. Writing the narrative further helps to meet that need; the writing is also a way of 'willing' Robert 'to speak,' of restoring him to something of his position as interlocutor in an I/Thou dyad. The writing that restores this sublime reciprocity re-confers life on Robert, and enables Peter to draw again on his brother's extraordinary solicitude, his salving power of recognition. ('Recognition' 158)

Freadman focuses the discussion away from Rose's ethical considerations and towards the question of what autobiography can actually *do* – for relationships and for one's memories of these relationships. Can life writing actually change the world outside the text? Can it bestow on the writer another's 'salving power of recognition'? Can it atone? In interview, Rose remains somewhat ambivalent about such questions. In response to my question, 'Can writing of the past atone for the past?', the author states:

> Well, it simply can't. I'm well aware that *Rose Boys* perpetuates Robert's memory in ways that have been of some comfort to people who loved him, and has advanced the charity named after him. Robert's life, his long struggle, are appreciated now. He is preserved in a book, so to speak, something that I, as a writer who is necessarily interested in posterity, but also as someone who has always been *infatuated* with books, must admire and perhaps, at some level, almost envy. But 'atonement'?… People often ask me, 'Was it cathartic? Do you feel better now?' The reality is that the man died in his forties after twenty-five years of suffering. Imagine waking to that reality every morning. Nothing atones for that. There were certainly things I should have said to Robert, done for him. Writing a book about a person doesn't compensate for that. (In Mansfield, 'Cathartic' 243, emphasis in the original)

The author holds his book's achievements and what it can never achieve, as well as who benefits from its achievement, in uneasy tension. The way he slips between speaking for himself and his brother underscores how difficult it is to determine who is actually speaking in *Rose Boys*, or who is speaking at any given time. Freadman's claim that the text restores Robert to his position 'as interlocutor in an I/Thou dyad' casts the text as a kind of dialogue between self and other, between Robert and Peter. Ten years after Robert's death and eight years after the book's publication, the speaking subjects of the text remain thoroughly enmeshed.

Conclusion: Speaking for Oneself

It is clear that whoever is actually speaking in *Rose Boys*, the watching figure of the father is its addressee and audience to the sons' performances of sonship. The final photograph in *Rose Boys* confirms this reading, exemplifying the notion of a speaking subject and a watching object as an act of mutually sustaining relationality. Watching the son also nourishes the father, and when he outlives his son, the absence comes at some cost. At Robert's wake, a photographer captured an image of the father seeking out his lost son. As Peter describes, 'dad, unaware of the camera, moves through the nebulous company, glass in hand, slightly quizzical, looking for someone. He had pushed Robert around that room a thousand times' (287).

The final speech act of the text is the address Peter gave at Robert's funeral. As a publicly enacted and observed event, Peter's eulogy is also a performance, for as Nicole Loraux writes, 'But what is speechmaking if not an act?' (16). The portion quoted towards the end of *Rose Boys* is another apt summation of Rose's auto/biographical impulse. Far from speaking little or softly as he once intended to do, Peter desires that the 'high ceilings and elongated crosses' of the church 'resound with some kind of refusal, however feeble'. This speech act is one Peter desired to make the moment he first heard of his brother's accident (50), one delivered under the watchful eye of the father, who is also, along with Peter's mother, honoured for their unique bond with Robert, what Peter calls 'a tacit and everlasting pact' (284). In fact, as Rose indicates in interview, he assumed the task of eulogising his brother as a proxy for his father: 'My father was exhausted, and I knew that my mother would not want to do something like that. By then I'd managed to overcome my powerful dislike of performance. I knew I could write something for the occasion' (in Mansfield, 'Cathartic' 25). In this way, Peter becomes his father's representative, and his willingness to speak is another performance of sonship: a demonstration to his father of his superior emotional strength.

Yet importantly, here, Peter is not willing his brother to speak, but speaking for himself. Despite his efforts, Rose cannot ultimately will another to speak, but (like Derrida) can attempt to speak *for* and *of* him, for as Rollins writes of Derrida, 'the eulogist must speak as though guided by the deceased's utter inability to listen or respond' (15). In so doing, Rose intends to perpetuate a memory, fulfil a need and communicate a message. Ultimately, this message can only be read as the author's own. *Rose Boys* stands as an important example of autobiography's unique engagement with the world.

Interestingly, for Peter, memoir has not ended this process of mourning through writing. In 'Ladybird', one of a series of poems composed following the recent death of the author's father, Peter continues to dream of, re-animate, compete and dialogue with his brother:

> You were twenty-two when it happened;
> forty-seven at your death, younger than I am.
> Why is it that only now do I feel
> the full burden of its grotesquerie
> the callous moral heft of it [...]? (*Rattus* 7)

A second poem, 'Facing North' addresses the father directly ('Facing North' 13). In another poem, 'Learning to Surf', which carries the dedication 'for my dying father', the son continues to perform under a paternal gaze:

> Now I surprise myself –
> discover the vessel beneath my feet.
> It's been there all along, unknown to me.
> Even as I flounder it hangs there,
> the beach of comfort poorly focused,
> mere memory. So I traffic
> in those consolidating waves.
> Surf picks me up and cushions me –
> shaky equilibrium. Through the surge
> I waver like a victor on a podium,
> marvelling at my effrontery,
> knowing it leads to a foamy grave,
> mandatory and imminent and grand. ('Learning' 71)

In the film *Rocky*, a laconic, almost inarticulate young man who has gone on to become perhaps the ultimate image of hegemonic masculinity is asked by his muse Adrian, 'Why do you wanna fight?' Rocky's answer is brief and to the point: 'Because I can't sing or dance'. The question underlying this discussion, and perhaps a great many son–father auto/biographies, could be this: why do you wanna write?

Rose's response might perhaps be a variation of Rocky's: 'Because I can't kick a football.' I have been attempting to read the autobiographical act in sporting terms, as a performance of sonship, written as it is under the gaze of the father. This is to read Rose's work, written in the face of death and mourning, as an attempt to reanimate and speak for a brother he has lost, and to continue to perform for the father so that he can, in Steinberg's estimations, 'try out different behaviors and feelings, practice and display them, and have an audience – especially a male audience – that mirrors back how wonderful and masculine he is' (74). It is the son's performance of masculinity and patrimony in Australia that we will now investigate further in John Hughes's *The Idea of Home*.

Chapter Six

CHOOSING PATRIMONY: PERFORMING FOR THE FATHER IN JOHN HUGHES'S *THE IDEA OF HOME*

> You will travel far, my little Kal-El, but we will never leave you – even in the face of our deaths. You will make my strength your own. You will see my life through your eyes, as your life will be seen through mine. The son becomes the father. And the father, the son.
>
> —Jor-El, *Superman Returns*

> You see how our roads diverged, my father's and my own. Though I was like him in a way. For what was the road I sought if not a repeat of my father's, but dug out of the depths of another otherness.
>
> —Italo Calvino, *The Road to San Giovanni*

> …he had an inner life that was not declared.
>
> —David Malouf, *12 Edmondstone Street*

In summing up the task of his collection of autobiographical essays *The Idea of Home* John Hughes utters a kind of 'call-to-arms' of relational auto/biography:

> In setting out to write about my grandfather, grandmother, mother and father I discover that I have written about myself. The writing of this book can in no way be considered a fulfillment of their expectations, yet it is my inheritance: an exorcism and a love letter to the dead. (202)

Within the context of Hughes's fragmentary, circular and theory-laden work, this is a surprisingly self-conscious statement of intent, albeit with the caveat of an eleventh-hour discovery of self through the writing process. As one would expect of relational auto/biography, the author's construction of an identity is produced from his conceptualisation of being born out of and produced by the proximate others of his earliest memories; both the sense of being related to them and existing out of relationship with them. Yet the text is not described as the narrative of what the author has inherited, rather it is framed *as* Hughes's inheritance.

However, the way Hughes concludes with a straightforward roll-call of his subjects – grandfather, grandmother, mother and father – belies the complex and ambivalent nature of the author's relationship to his heritage. As noted in the introduction, very few auto/biographers succeed in honouring their parents or forebears equally in their writing, and as my readings to date have shown, few even make the attempt. Hughes's grandmother is recalled fondly but briefly, and although he dedicates one essay to reminiscence of his mother, *The Idea of Home* is a narrative of patrimony in the manner set out in this study. But it is a Son's Book in which the act of *choosing* plays a vital role. The key figure here is not the father, but the maternal grandfather, who is 'the book's centre, and the mark against which as a young man – and even now perhaps – [Hughes] measures himself' (Johnstone 32). This chapter investigates the notion of competing patrimonial heritages, and the way in which, for Hughes, the maternal grandfather offers a more exotic, less guarded and ultimately less problematic masculine model than that offered by the father. To understand this process of choosing patrimony, we must attend in detail to the various performances of masculinity in *The Idea of Home* (the grandfather's, father's and son's), to discover how they are enacted in various ways both *for* the others in this triangulation, and simultaneously to evade being understood *by* them. The discussion concludes by returning to the central question of whether the act of writing is a performance of masculinity for the father.

The Son's Book of Essays

For most authors discussed in this study, the auto/biographical impulse has led to the creation of the best known and in many cases most well received work of their oeuvre. However, the authors themselves would undoubtedly consider autobiography as secondary to the writing from which they draw their identity: Porter as a short-story writer; Smith as art critic; Gaita as moral philosopher; Freadman as literary critic; and Rose and Gray as poets. John Hughes is the exception. Appearing in 2004, *The Idea of Home* was Hughes's first major publication, although the first three of the five essays that make up the book were published previously in the journal *HEAT*. In the ten years prior to this, Hughes had published only three short stories and three poems, all in Australian literary journals.

Occasionally a writer may appear on the scene 'as one fully formed', and such is the case here. As critics noted upon its release, *The Idea of Home* does not feel like a debut work: ambitious and assured, Hughes writes with the distinctive European sensibility of Sebald or Benjamin. Mark Mordue described it as 'a great book, part of a peculiarly modern genre that mixes memoir, essay and poetic style into something fresh, contradicting the academic heritage of detachment, while profoundly deepening the shallow waters of the modern-day confessional' (9).[1] In *Antipodes*, Charles W. Arnade called it 'wonderful literature in exquisite prose' and remarked that, 'I have hardly ever read a book that has so adroitly fused autobiography with literary criticism' (230). *The Idea of Home* went on to win the NSW Premier's Literary Awards' Douglas Stewart Prize for Non-Fiction in 2005 and the National Biography Award in 2006.

As an autobiographical essayist, Hughes writes his way into a tradition that can be traced back to Montaigne, but within the sub-genre of son–father auto/biographies *The Idea of Home* has some fascinating precursors of its own, most notably Italo Calvino's *The Road to San Giovanni*. Considering Hughes's familiarity with Calvino and his framing of his writing within a European literary tradition, the following reading draws some comparisons between Hughes's and Calvino's representations of the father, specifically regarding Calvino's description of his auto/biography as 'these pages echoing with my father's noisy and distant presence' (15). The discussion is further enriched by investigating resonances with David Malouf's *12 Edmondstone Street*, a celebrated Australian example of the autobiographical essay form, specifically 'The Kyogle Line', Malouf's essay on his father. In order to continue testing my authors' autobiographical acts against their stated intentions, I also draw from the interview I conducted with Hughes in 2009.

Even for the autobiographical essay form, Hughes's text is peculiarly structured. The five essays that make up *The Idea of Home* read like a series of meditations about the same handful of topics over a period of years. Images, places, ideas and people crop up time and again; statements and stories are repeated in a way that gives the work a peculiar circularity. As the author states early in his text, 'I remember bits, fragments, slivers' (6). Crucially, this structure frees Hughes's representations from the demands of narrative, which we discovered in Chapter Three, are often antithetical to the purpose of portraying self-effacing masculine figures. Though far from chronological, the

---

[1] Mordue admits to having known Hughes as a precocious undergraduate at Newcastle University. His review is a revealing appendage to Hughes's self-representation. Mordue describes Hughes as 'the young genius about town' and as 'a young, slightly bitter tongued idealist' (9).

book details the author's upbringing in Cessnock, his education at Newcastle and Cambridge universities, and his subsequent return to Australia following his abandonment of both his academic studies and his search for origins. The first three essays explore his relationship with his grandfather, mother and father respectively, while the final two essays focus more explicitly on the author himself. However, the work oddly coheres around the author's grandfather, who is the driving force behind this idiosyncratic exploration of his heritage.

'Watching Me as I Write'

In 'Country Towns', Hughes's essay on his father, he describes his reticent subject's talent on the football field – a performance not personally witnessed as his 'playing days' predated the author's birth:

> My father will not speak of his prowess in this area, but his friends are strangely lyrical whenever they talk about Cessnock Sportsground and his speed over ten yards, stepping off the sideline on the wing […] dark-haired, wiry, aggressive, like a greyhound himself, and before he broke his legs, brilliant. (86)

Situated within an explicitly Australian context, this display gains the force of an emblem: 'The importance of football to country towns […] should not be underestimated. There is no greater source of identity or self-esteem, no surer guarantee of immortality' (86). Cessnock is a small mining town in the New South Wales Hunter Valley, and the father's reputation within this town has been established through his footballing exploits – the author stating that, 'This is the man my mother would have seen' (86). Yet the author diffuses the reader's assumptions of where this narrative of paternal expectation might be heading, stating some pages later:

> Cessnock was a rugby league town and my brother and I, like most of our friends, wanted to play league. My father, although he'd played himself and was known for it (or rather, because he'd played the game and had the injuries to prove it) […] refused to let us play. He bought us a soccer ball instead. (94–5)

As an important site for the performance of masculinity in Australian auto/biographical writing the sporting arena is highly *codified*: different sports and particularly codes of football are assigned differing degrees of masculinity. This protective father favours the relative safety of soccer over the rugby league he played in his youth, yet the assumption underpinning this comparison is that it is also less masculine. This assumption accords with Gray's experience of growing up in country New South Wales and enduring his father's derision when, as a young boy, he chose to play soccer instead of the more 'manly' rugby (*The Land* 134).

Yet this comparison is of secondary importance to the one Hughes makes between football and autobiography. In a stunning textual manoeuvre, Hughes shifts the site of performed masculinity to the act of writing. Following his description of his father's prowess on the football field, the author writes:

> My uncle told me that their father would stand behind the goalposts and watch silently, amidst the crowd, as my father played. I imagine, sometimes, my father doing the same and watching me as I write. Proving myself, I suppose. (86–7)

The casualness of the comparison belies the pathos expressed here. It is a notion which places a great deal of expectation on the writing process and what it might achieve for the relationship between father and son, particularly for a male writer in Australia. It also raises a number of questions about how masculinity is performed in patrimonial life narratives. What are the key sites for performing masculinity in this sub-genre? How is the paternal gaze conceived of and represented in *The Idea of Home*? How do these displays of masculinity contextualise Hughes both within and outside of an Australian cultural or literary frame? How does the autobiographical act fare as a site for performing masculinity? Is there a place within the Australian conception of idealised masculinity for the heroic writer?

'Performing' Masculinity

R. W. Connell has written widely on what he refers to as hegemonic masculinity which 'embodie(s) the currently most honored way of being a man' and 'require(s) all other men to position themselves in relation to it' ('Hegemonic Masculinity' 832). Connell figures this embodiment or performance as occurring most obviously at socially sanctioned events such as a football game, which 'are not just consequences of our ideas about gender difference. They also help to create and disseminate gender difference, by *displays* of exemplary masculinities and femininities' (*Gender* 4, emphasis mine).[2] In Hughes's case, this notion of

---

2 The specific circumstance that Connell addresses is the American Superbowl, but rugby league is arguably the Australian equivalent, at least for the eastern states. West of what is termed the 'Barassi line' the dominant football code (and site for the demonstration of exemplary masculinities) is of course AFL.

masculinity as a form of display is instructive: though he is fascinated by language, Hughes often focuses on the untranslatability of meaning between languages and so emphasises how meaning is acted out bodily, through gesture. At the same time, a great many of the masculine performances Hughes details are what I refer to as speech acts, where, as Judith Butler describes, 'the pronouncement is the act of speech at the same time as it is the speaking of an act' (198).[3]

Of course a crucial question is who these performances of gender are being enacted for. As Michael S. Kimmel notes, 'We [men] are under constant careful scrutiny from other men. Men watch us, rank us, grant us acceptance into the realm of manhood. Manhood is demonstrated for other men's approval. It is other men who evaluate the performance' (128). The primary evaluator in question for our current discussion is the writer-son, who observes and represents the father's performance in auto/biography, and who must choose to adopt this example or reject it in favour of another kind of performance. But whatever the outcome, it is striking how consistently the writers discussed in this book describe the scenes of fathers and sons in their auto/biographies as *enacted* or *performed* events.

It is instructive to recall Hal Porter's description of his father as 'an inhuman actor', one who evinces a 'hearty participation in the rites of public living – he is, for example, a Mason; he plays golf; he plays cricket; he plays masculinity and respectability and being a good husband, a good father and a nice man' (*The Watcher* 92). Though Hughes's depiction of a father's reputation within a country town was written 40 years later, much of the above quotation still rings true, though without the pejorative edge given it by Porter. Hughes's father fares significantly better than Porter's in auto/biography, though it is difficult to imagine how one could fare worse. This more positive assessment may be due partly to the fact that Hughes posits a more complex paternal legacy than the one described in *The Watcher*. Hughes's maternal grandfather John-Paul is a man with a shadowy past who looms large in the author's life, both for his link to an Eastern European lineage and the sense of foreignness Hughes desires, and for a masculine heritage which is somehow less fraught than that offered

---

3   Since J. L. Austin's (1962) and then John Searle's (1969) designations of speech act theory, a great many theorists have challenged and revised the question of what constitutes a speech act. My use of the term captures the sense that speaking is a performance where a great deal of what is expressed exists beyond the 'mere' meaning of the words used: by such things as pitch and tone of voice, verbosity, one's body positioning to his or her addressee (and audience/witnesses) and so on. Austin's classic example 'I dare you' involves such paralinguistic elements. As performance, this kind of speech act also necessarily interpellates others outside of the singular first and singular second person of the utterance, who are forced to act as witnesses. Austin would term this an 'illocutionary' speech act.

by the father–son relationship. This is the pattern of triangulation discussed in Chapter Four of this book, with Freadman acknowledging the ease of his relationship with his maternal grandfather in comparison to that with his father. The pattern is repeated again in Robert Gray's autobiography, as we will discover in the following chapter. The proliferation of this pattern raises a number of questions: What factors and attendant complications precipitate such a choice? Can one simply choose a patrimonial heritage, and what risks are involved in such a venture?

'Heir to Both His Fathers'

Interestingly, this courting of the more exotic (and the dismissal of the less exotic) side of the Hughes's heritage is a pattern established by the father, who 'was falling in love with his future father-in-law' (*The Idea* 80) long before Hughes was born, and who 'became a member of the family long before he married my mother' (90). Importantly, the site of this first 'falling in love' is the pub in Cessnock where the author's grandfather would go to drink and play his accordion:

> Like my father, I thought of my grandfather as larger than life. But perhaps this largeness had less to do with his actual size and character than seeing him through this other lens. He loved the Cessnock pubs, they were Australia to him, and he 'performed' in them [...] It wasn't just the accordion; my grandfather 'performed' simply by going to the pub every afternoon before returning home from work. He loved beer and he loved the company of men who shared this routine. (80)

John-Paul's largeness is attributed primarily to his foreignness. As a new migrant who 'imitates the surfaces, that is, the culture of our display', his 'performance' of Australian culture nonetheless 'reveals, in heightened form, what, either through blindness or excessive familiarity, we have not seen' (80). His is a performance of a learned masculinity, one both familiar to this foreigner for it aligns with the drinking culture of his hometown of Kiev, and simultaneously 'put on', an acting out of the cultural surfaces he encounters in Australian pubs.

Of course, the behaviour of the locals in such establishments is no less theatrical. Hughes recalls waiting on the streets outside the pub as a boy whilst he observed his father, assisted by alcohol, perform within:

> They are loud and they are clumsy and they are generous – and they are not how I know them anywhere else. They are in their element. I look

at my father and he seems at home in a way he does not seem at home outside – comfortable, light somehow, at ease. In the pub the world of men feels close to me, as if together we are all children again. (81)

It is interesting that this 'world of men' is accessible to the author, even though he must stay outside of this world, watching it from the street; an audience to the performance on the pub-as-stage. This scene accords with the one observed from the outside by Gray's mother of his father performing in country-town pubs: 'After she met my father, my mother would sometimes hear his "plummy" voice, while passing one of the pubs in town, raised above those of the other men [...] He stood with his head in the air, overwhelmed all competition, and *acted* "the real I am"' (*The Land* 54–5, emphasis mine).

Hughes's father (and subsequently, Hughes himself) is perhaps attracted to his future father-in-law's 'performance' because it differs so much from his own, a contrast the author makes explicit. Here also, as with Freadman's and even Gaita's fathers, the patrimonial bind may in part be a problem of portrayal. In auto/biography, some subjects are simply more representable than others; or to put it another way, some masculinities elude representation. John-Paul is expansive, gregarious, and though elusive, appears to have offered himself up as the subject of the author's search for origins. Hughes's father is the opposite:

My grandfather was an actor and he loved to perform, but he was secretive too, and always holding back. I was drawn to his voice. In comparison, particularly when I was younger, my father seemed unglamorous, a clerk in a coal mine; quiet and self-effacing, reticent, I thought, because there was never much to say, a product of the town of which he was a perfectly blended part and so of little interest beyond his immediate position as my father. (99)

As Hughes alludes to here, familiarity and exoticism play their part. The author's father so comprehensively represents the culture from which he came that he is barely visible to a son brought up within that culture. Australian masculinity, in contrast to its more effusive Eastern European counterpart (the grandfather loves acting and draws in the author with his voice), is again laconic, wary of speech. But importantly, for the sake of the current discussion, masculinity is rendered here as primarily a speech act, even if, in the father's case, 'there was never much to say'. A further key to Hughes's representation of his father's masculinity, and so an Australian masculinity, is his reticence: the father is 'unglamorous', 'quiet and self-effacing' and blends effortlessly into the country town that has shaped him.

Reticence and familiarity make the masculine subject very difficult to represent auto/biographically. 'I'm looking for something simple here', writes Hughes with a sense of frustration almost half way through the essay about his father; 'It's elusiveness resides in its proximity. Perhaps I find it so difficult to write about my father simply because so many of his traits are already my own' (99). Yet in Hughes's description of his father's invisibility there is a sense of wilful elusiveness, as if the father has directed the son's attention away from himself. The author acknowledges a conscious choice in siding with the maternal side of his heritage, and hints at some residual guilt for this act:

> Is it inevitable that all families align more closely with one side than the other? The house in which my father grew up still remains in the family [...] It's full of my father's family history yet somehow it seems less accessible to me than my mother's life with her parents in Kiev. About Scotland and Wales, unlike the Ukraine, no stories were passed down to me. There must have seemed plenty of time, and anyway, I was too young then to be told these things [...] too young, finally, to have any sense that my father, too, was too young: that his father and then his mother died before he was ready to know them. I've never really thought about how this must have affected him. Just that the house in Neath was a stranger's house; my family there, strangers. (84)

There is a palpable sense of loss expressed here at the way that death closes off access to one's heritage and opens up gaps in family history. Yet the loss is compounded by the father's unwillingness to speak of his past; by the fact that 'no stories were passed down to me'. Malouf notes a similar reticence regarding his narrator's father: 'He was not much of a talker, our father. He seldom told us things unless we asked. Then he would answer our questions too carefully, as if he feared, with his own lack of schooling, that he might lead us wrong [...] And he never told us stories, as our mother did, of his family and youth' (129).

Regarding the absence of stories from Hughes's paternal family, Greg McLaren wonders: 'Is it something to do with the circumspection of miners and their culture? A resentment of the past?' ('Sounds' 94). Hughes hints at this influence, picturing such a culture as strongly bonded by the shared struggle for miner's rights, though it is one to which he has no access:

> There is no other way to explain the closeness of the community into which [my father] was born, a closeness about which I know nothing, which might be glimpsed through the open doors of a pub, intimacies passed on like property from father to son, friendships inherited in the same way, deep legacies, whose ties are underground. (86)

Interestingly, however, Hughes attributes this rupture directly to his father, demonstrating how the pattern of choosing one's heritage began before he was born.

Further problematising the picture of the author's patrimony, we discover that this admiration the father and son share for John-Paul's version of masculinity operates both ways. The author complicates his observations about culture by stating that, 'what we think of as exotic may in fact experience what we regard as ordinary as equally exotic in return' (79). Hughes does not remember his paternal grandfather, who died when he was a young boy, and his father's unwillingness to speak of the past forces him to search for other sources:

> My grandfather found Cessnock exotic but I have difficulty explaining what this means. He told me once that my father's father was a strong man, restrained and courteous. I think he was drawn to this reticence, or 'dignity' as he called it, as he was drawn to all that he wasn't. The quietness of the town, its smallness and isolation. (105)

This reticence, rendered by John-Paul as dignity, is again associated with lack of speech, with the quietness of the town. It may be problematic to argue for this reserve as a uniquely *Australian* masculinity, for Hughes's paternal grandfather was Scottish (though he migrated to Australia as a 10-year-old). Perhaps the distinction could more accurately be characterised as being between an Anglo-Saxon masculinity and an Eastern European one. It is into these contrasting ancestries that the author is born, and must choose – with all of the attending guilt such choices carry. Though, as stated earlier, the author's choice to side with his maternal legacy was made by his father before him:

> he could feel himself slipping, away from his father, away from Neath, away from the culture that was dying anyway as the mines closed one by one. He needed to justify this crossing, if not to his father, then at least to himself, the attraction of something outside himself, something wonderfully exotic, but he knew that it was already there, the otherness was inside *him*: that he was, and could be so easily, heir to both his fathers. (103, emphasis in the original)

The need to justify one's decision to break away from a patrimonial legacy, so significant for the writer-son, seems in many cases to be preceded (and so justified?) by their own fathers having acted out the role of son-betrayers. The paternal grandfather of *12 Edmondstone Street*, who 'remained unknowable' to the narrator 'since I could not speak to him' (5), is pictured as an aggrieved 'exiled ruler of a minority kingdom' (6). He is abandoned by his daughters, who convert from the Maronite church to Catholicism, and by the narrator's father, who discards his Lebanese heritage, though not for the exotic but in this case for the familiar: 'My father too had betrayed him; or had, in his quiet way, adapted himself so completely to this new place that there was no link between them. But then, my father was born here, had grown up "Australian" in the rough South Brisbane "pushes" before the Great War' (7). Whatever the father's justification, his actions lead to a relational rupture of the patrimonial line just one generation later: though 'close, even companionable' at times, Malouf's grandfather remains 'a mystery' (5), his connection to the narrator's father barely glimpsed. 'What, I wonder now, was [my father's] relationship with the old man?' Malouf asks later, before admitting that, 'I can't speak for his feelings. He never expressed them. He never showed them either' (7). In *The Idea of Home*, Hughes echoes Malouf's experience, expressing this rupture in the following way: 'About my father's father I remember nothing […] I don't refer to him as my grandfather. He is always my father's father, as if the connection stops with my father' (84).

Choosing a Masculine Performance through Literary Influence

Hughes's sense of his ancestry affects both his evaluation and his own performances of masculinity in unique ways. Comparisons may be drawn between Hughes and Robert Rose who, until the car accident that renders him a quadriplegic, embodied the ideal of Australian masculinity. A heavy drinker and risk taker, Robert performed effortlessly within the male domains of the pub and sporting arena. Brother Peter, on the other hand, declares, 'I never thought I was bullet-proof' (285). Hughes connects his risk-taking behaviour as a young man directly to performing masculinity, though it is worth noting that his performances often take on a decidedly literary form:

> I have always had a tendency towards self-destruction. As a teenager I'd often ride on my best friend's motorbike with no lights, drunk and late at night […] I once drove a car through a guardrail on Mount View, drunk again, the car rolling three times before it stopped against a tree. In part, no doubt, this recklessness was no more than the cultivation of an image, the Romantic hero once again (Lord Byron of Hospital Hill, or the misunderstood visionary of Coleridge's opium addiction, doomed to a life of banality because of the accident of his birthplace). But it was also the only way I sensed of breaking free. (152–3)

Though here Hughes imagines himself within an Anglo-Saxon poetic tradition, his intertexts are most often taken from his preferred literary ancestry – that of his grandfather's Eastern European heritage. In the latter stages of *The Idea of Home*, following descriptions of the father and grandfather's performances in pubs, Hughes describes his own ease within this cultural space, though with a typically complicating twist. For it is not an Australian masculinity that the author enacts, but one borrowed from Russian literature:

> I saw myself in all that I read. My drinking, for instance. It wasn't that I thought of the Newcastle pubs as literal equivalents of the Gentleman's Clubs of Moscow and St Petersburg, but drinking in them, and talking with other students, I had a sense of myself as Pierre or Andrei Bolkonsky, a young man, full of the invincibility of youth, with my life before me and the world at my feet [...] and this talk about books, and politics and ideas like a rehearsal for this greatness. (178)

Imagining himself as one of Tolstoy's heroes is once again an act of choosing patrimony; Hughes explicitly frames himself within an Eastern European literary lineage rather than an Australian one or one drawn from his father's British ancestry. The author maps his process of choosing patrimony directly onto his reading life by means of citation chains – great novels that lead him to other great novelists that inevitably leads him to his adopted heartland of world literature. One such citation chain begins with Beckett's *Murphy*:

> With a logic that seemed perfectly clear at the time, I moved from Beckett to Kafka to Borges, and then, via Gogal's *Dead Souls*, to *Crime and Punishment*, *The Brothers Karamazov*, *Anna Karenin*, and finally to the two greatest novels of the nineteenth century, *The Idiot* and *War and Peace*. When I think about this list now it strikes me that Beckett is the only English writer there, and he was Irish and wrote most of his work in French. The literature I love has always been a literature of translation [...] It's Russia again – Russia is about as close as I can get to my ancestral homeland. (174)

Of course this is not entirely true. As Sonia Mycak has recently demonstrated, there is a rich tradition of Ukrainian literature even within Australia into which Hughes could have chosen to write himself. While it seems problematic that Hughes effaces his heritage in this way, such a manoeuvre is yet again an act of choosing patrimony – in this case, a literary one that allows the author to figure himself as an heir to the giants of Russian literature.

Such choices continue to manifest in the present: the philosophers referenced in *The Idea of Home* are predominantly continental – Bachelard, Benjamin, Wittgenstein – while his 'intellectual autobiography' *Someone Else*, marketed as a kind of sequel to *The Idea of Home*, honours largely European writers and thinkers. So Dostoyevsky is figured as a taxi driver in East Sydney, who argues with God in the kitchen of his Stanley Street terrace in Kings Cross, while in a stunning textual conceit, Max Brod is portrayed in conversation with a young John Hughes at a beachside café in an unnamed Australian seaside town. By discovering himself in Brod's posthumously published diaries in the preface to *Someone Else*, Hughes literally writes himself into world literary space, uncannily reversing the notion of influence.

When asked about the significance of his chosen literary heritage, Hughes stated:

> I think there are obviously many writers who think of themselves within a national literary frame – I'm not one of them. I happen to have been born and to live in this place, but books don't have the same reverence for borders, and what I read and what I love, comes from other places, though it speaks to me powerfully *in this place at this time*. (In Mansfield, 'Beating' 102, emphasis in the original)

The Idea of Home demonstrates, surprisingly unselfconsciously, how the great Russian novels of the nineteenth century spoke to a working-class boy from Cessnock in the 1970s and 80s. Having failed to recreate his grandfather's fabled journey through Eastern Europe, Hughes spends much of his closing essay mapping the novels of Tolstoy and Dostoyevsky onto his hometown of Newcastle, demonstrating the process by which world literature can be provincialised and travel inward: 'Reading Dostoyevsky and Tolstoy was like looking into a fairground mirror – the distorted shapes they threw back at me were living and my own. (Dostoyevsky understood Newcastle!)' (191).

Performing Masculinity in the Garage, on the Verandah and in the Workplace

Before returning to the other major site of performing masculinity – the sporting field – there are three further key sites where Hughes investigates his patrimony, and in each of these there can be discerned a tension between father and son, as well as between the laconic and the erudite voice. The first of these is the garage to which Hughes's father retreats every Sunday morning 'to prepare the lawnmower' (*Idea of Home* 93). In contrast to his romanticisation of the pub, here the author adopts an astringent tone:

> As I grew older I started thinking of the garage as a kind of bedroom, of the countless men who spent so much of their lives beneath their cars, and built cupboards and drawers and tool racks around them. If the house

was a body, I thought, the garage would be its dick. This is probably spite more than anything else, a reaction to a feeling of exclusion from a world of fascination to which I felt I should belong. (94)

Hughes's experience is not unique. Gray expresses a similar sense of segregation from this world, yet it is not his father's domain but his maternal grandfather's: 'I was allowed to sit in there with him and watch him at his craft, in the hope I suppose that I might be lured into practicality, away from so much time "off with the fairies"' (*The Land* 131). For Malouf, the father's toolshed under the house is a place to observe the father, 'a world of silence [...] that belonged to his deep communication with measurements, and tools, and dove-tail joints' where words are hardly spoken (129). Such imagery recalls Gaita's depiction of his father's silent communion with his tools (97). For the sophisticated, intellectual author-sons represented, the garage or toolshed may be a source of fascination, but it remains a somewhat inaccessible world.

In most of the texts discussed, the authors represent the family home as a feminine domain. In *The Watcher*, Porter famously gives elaborate and detailed descriptions of the interior of the family home, including a 'Utrecht velvet suite' and 'a be-bobbed mantel-drape of magenta plush' (14). The images are deliberately ornamental, and while Porter attempts to shift responsibility for this onto his father, 'marking him down as an indubitable Australian, one of a nation of men willing to live in a feminised house' (13), the impression created by these descriptions is that of an autobiographer committed to constructing an image of the world *through* his mother. While Hughes's mother is by no means as central in his work, his portrayal of her domain in 'My Mother's House' contains some of the same elements of nostalgia as Porter's memorable portrait. One room that is unambiguously a maternal space is the kitchen. The author watches his mother and grandmother cooking and talking in the kitchen, enjoying the scene from which he is excluded, primarily by language, but also by gender: 'I don't mind the exclusion. Nor does my father. We're used to it. We enjoy the space it gives us, the privilege of our proximity to what feels like a secret intimacy' (56). Later, Hughes describes how (despite his grandfather's wish for him to speak only English), 'like my father I did learn another language, though it wasn't Russian; a language learnt in the kitchen, bound up with its rituals, and not ruled by precision or certainty or the need for perfect comprehension; a language of half knowing' (92). A less fond recollection involves the way Hughes's mother would act as a kind of gatekeeper between the outside world and the home within: 'When we were children we had to wash our feet in the laundry tub before coming into the house, even if we'd been wearing shoes and socks [...] She had a better eye for dirt than we did and if we didn't pass inspection (a regular occurrence) she would send us out to do them again. Even my father was not immune' (61).

The space in the house that the men of Hughes's family do occupy (though not without certain discomforts and problems of communication) is the verandah, a space that is tellingly both a part of the house and outside of it. Malouf, Australia's pre-eminent topographical mapper of the family home, describes the verandah as a 'no-man's land' (20), caught between the unknown world outside and the domestic realm within. In Hughes's rendering, this borderland (which for his grandfather includes the garden) becomes a space both for male solitude and communion:

> My mother is inside, talking to my grandmother and watching American soap operas on the television, but my father likes to be on his own. He will spend most of the day on the verandah, reading Wilbur Smith and James Michener in the big plastic hardcovers he has borrowed from Cessnock Library. (100)

It is worth noting that the books Hughes's father reads are in clear contrast with the literary work the author writes. Hughes's observation of his father's tastes lacks the derogatory tone given by Porter, whose father reads only 'the "relaxing" rubbish of Westerns and thrillers' (93). Yet this can be identified as a kind of meta-site for the performing of a laconic masculinity that contrasts with the erudite version of these literary sons, and must surely problematise the notion of these fathers ascribing value to the literary achievements of their sons.

The verandah Hughes pictures his father reading on is the same one the author earlier describes as the space his father and grandfather would retreat to after dinner when his parents were courting:

> My father stayed later and later. And my grandfather bought him a fold-out bed. Because he loved the conversations too, the reserve of the young man who sat opposite him and whose stillness and quiet resolve seemed to speak of a place and a culture where he might at last be secure. (89–90)

Perhaps the strength of this father resides in his stillness, in his near-muteness, for in it John-Paul finds an openness, a hospitality towards the other that brings about a sense of place, of home. Yet again, as with Gaita's and Freadman's Sons' Books, this father's self-effacement makes his unique form of decency difficult to adequately represent in writing.

In the current scene the grandfather has died and the father occupies his seat, with the adult author taking his father's place as the quiet observer: 'It seems I have been listening here all my life, to my grandfather, and now to my father. We talk of small things mainly, of sport and sometimes politics. My father rarely speaks about himself. Yet as he grows old the past intrudes' (100). Again alcohol plays a role in the performance, allowing this normally reticent man to become vocal in his reminiscence: 'While my father talks I say nothing. The beer has made us close' (101). Yet even this ease does not last long, and the author captures the awkwardness between the two men:

> My father is quiet now, guilty almost, as if he has said too much. He is waiting for me to speak and I will, though it won't be what he wants me to say. The inhibition I used to feel whenever I had to talk to him about myself is still there, though I am now forty-two years old; my cowardice; my inability, ever, to speak much of the truth; the clumsy uneasiness of my affection. And the betrayal. I remember, sitting as we are sitting in the chairs that don't quite face, an earlier time when my grandfather was still alive and I would sit with him in this same place at the start of the holidays and watch my father's car back out of the drive. (102)

'The chairs that don't quite face' is a vivid image of the difficulty of communication for the laconic, reticent Australian father and son, and demonstrates that the erudite writer-son is not immune to the problems of speech that befall the father. There is deep longing here, but also a seemingly insurmountable impasse. 'We were shy of one another', Malouf's narrator states of the father, and later he describes a scene of supreme ambivalence: 'We walked together in silence, but with a strong sense on my part at least, of our being together and at one. I liked my father. I wished he would talk to me and tell me things. I didn't know him. He puzzled me' (130). Echoing this sentiment, Hughes, in interview, describes his essay on his father as 'a conversation, but a conversation with someone who can't talk, so I have to play both roles: son and father'. He also clarifies his father's reserve as being particular to his relationship with his son: 'His reticence, after all, was as much to do with me as him (things I didn't ask him, didn't want him to talk about, didn't want him to ask me, etc.) – he certainly wasn't reticent with his friends' (in Mansfield, 'Beating' 102). Calvino similarly links the struggle to communicate as father and son with one's body positioning, anticipating Hughes's 'chairs that don't quite face': 'Talking to each other was difficult. Both verbose by nature, possessed of an ocean of words, in each other's presence we became mute, would walk in silence side by side along the road to San Giovanni' (10).

Hughes's memory of sitting on the verandah and watching his father back out the driveway is another telling image, for it alludes to another site of masculine performance to which the son is excluded – the father's male-dominated workplace. 'It is hard to imagine what others do with their day', the author states, describing the routine of his father's workday as a clerk in a nearby coalmine, beginning at 6AM and finishing at 4:30PM. 'I know almost nothing about what he did in the office at Bloomfield (he never talked about it and never brought work home)' (107). Malouf concurs with this experience, stating that, 'My father's world was foreign to me. He disappeared into it at six o'clock, before my sister and I were up, and came back again at tea time, not long before we were packed off to bed' (129). Hughes's only role in his father's daily routine was, along with his brother, to be woken early on winter mornings to help their father push-start his VW Beetle: 'he'd come into the bedroom and nudge my brother and me awake and we'd dress quickly and push the car down the street with him until it kicked and started and we'd walk back inside the clouds of our breath' (107). Calvino likewise recalls his father as an impediment to sleep. This father would wake Calvino and his brother 'with gruff shouts and shoulder-shaking' so they could assist him in carrying vegetables (14).[4] His manner lacks any of the gentleness implied by Hughes's father's 'nudge', which may help to account for his more sympathetic representation in *The Idea of Home.*

Hughes's lack of knowledge of his father's world is brought home to him at his father's retirement party, when the guest of honour gives a speech and the image of his competence in this public domain makes him seem like a stranger:

> For the first time in my life I was struck by my father as a man apart from me, a man I did not know. I had always been conscious of how much I had kept from him but I had never thought of him as any more than my own. It was a strange sensation; exhilarating, but also isolating […] He spoke calmly and with the assurance of one used to such occasions. He made everyone listen. He didn't like wearing a suit and yet he seemed as comfortable as in his own skin. He spoke for twenty minutes without notes, with the fluency and timing of a natural *performer*, and it occurred to me that this kind of public world, though he gave nothing of this away at home, was as natural to him as the world of the pub – the world of a Soccer Club Committee Room, union meetings, and the large, formal public occasions that are a regular part of work, the serious world of

---

4   Fascinatingly, while both Hughes and Calvino refer offhandedly to their brothers, they write almost compulsively as only children. Neither includes a disclaimer about this in the mode of Freadman's preface. Gray, who has two brothers and a sister, writes in his autobiography that, 'the one in the family who is going to be a writer is always an only child' (178). Such a pattern highlights the uniqueness of Rose's fraternal son–father auto/biography.

men. I heard the strong voice and I recognised it as my own but the man from whom it came was not my father: He had eluded me in the very instant he was relinquishing the world into which he had escaped. (106–7, emphasis mine)

Once more the scene is identified as both a performance and a speech act, the author drawing attention to the strength and familiarity of his father's voice, though this makes the occasion more perplexing, for this is not the father he knows. One gets a sense of the distance between father and son in this scene, the impasse of knowing or understanding the father who stands and enunciates before the son, but also the impossibility of ignoring him, recalling Calvino's paradoxical formulation of his father's 'noisy and distant presence' (15). Throughout Hughes's auto/biography the figure of the father remains thoroughly elusive for the author, someone he cannot adequately represent in his writing, someone who constantly evades representation or comprehension. Also telling in this scene is the notion of the workplace as a site of escape. Like the verandah and the pub, these male domains are places of temporary refuge from the domestic, sites where male performance is less constrained, though closely observed by the writer-son.

Sport and the Paternal Gaze

Frustrated by his failure to do his father justice in his reminiscences, Hughes searches out a more physical connection to his father and his family line, attempting to seek this heritage through the body and echoing the book's epigraph from Carlos Drummond De Andrade, 'The strange idea of family travelling through the flesh':

> One memory I forgot. [...] There was a time when I was growing up when I did not feel comfortable with the thought of touching him, when I did not feel comfortable, I suppose, with the thought of our two bodies. Now when I pull my shirt over my head or stand under the shower or lie in bed I smell myself and it is him. My father's scent when I was a child. It's an eerie kind of intimacy. It makes me wonder if he noticed the same with his father, and if so, if this scent of mine is the same. (112)

In struggling against his ambivalence toward the father, each son attempts to find, through writing, a way to pay his father his due, but in my reading of Hughes's auto/biographical strain to know and be authentically connected to his patrimony, I find an accord between ethics and truth-telling that is not found in any other Son's Book discussed. It is Hughes's bodily form of intimacy, what McLaren calls 'the silent transmission of a family line' ('Sounds' 94), that leads him ultimately to a kind of resolution of his competing patrimonies that lies beyond language. In searching for a way to describe the value imparted by his father, Hughes offers the following tribute:

> The impossibility of true succession is a form of jealousy (or failure) common to all sons; that the past is by its very nature exotic because it won't allow the present in. I watched my father as I grew. I learnt fairness and tolerance through the skin, as gestures and as ways of holding myself, and not as words or ideas; I learnt how not to judge, to see people positively, or more than that, to see them as they want to be seen. I was not taught and yet I learnt. (111–12)[5]

It is a strong evocation of an important notion for Hughes, borrowed from Proust (and repeated in *Someone Else*) that aptly expresses the author's understanding of inheritance. Towards the conclusion of *The Idea of Home* Hughes quotes from *The Remembrance of Things Past*: 'The dead annex the living who become their replicas and successors, the continuators of their interrupted life' (201). Expanding on this idea, Hughes writes that, 'We forget the dead [...] even as our bodies become the repositories of their memories; annexed by history, our gestures repeat, perhaps eternally, what cannot be forgotten' (201). This process is clearly at work in the author's embodiment of his father's heritage through a performance of masculinity, illuminating his understanding of how he carries on his father's legacy.

As the discussion of image and text in *Rose Boys* demonstrated, watching and monitoring the performance of masculinity between father and son is a two-way process: the watching son is at times keenly aware of himself being observed by the father. No similar pictorial representation of the father's gaze on the son is provided in *The Idea of Home*, the author explaining in interview that, 'It wasn't really a visual thing I was after [...] Including photographs of my father wouldn't have taken me any closer to representing those qualities I write about, that are so resistant to evocation' (in Mansfield, 'Beating' 260).[6] However, as the author details in his book, so great was his father's desire to

---

5 This echoes, but perfects, an earlier attempt at honouring the father: 'The things I learned from him you couldn't get from talking (how do you teach openness, responsibility, curiosity, loyalty, respect, integrity, attachment, temper?). They were inherited bodily, transferred like rubbings: his mannerisms, gestures, actions, values' (101).
6 In his poem 'Photographs' Hughes pictures a father figure who is difficult to represent photographically, and in fact eludes representation: 'My father didn't like photographs. / Standing in front of the camera / Made him feel like a stripper must, he said. / He loved standing behind' (38).

protect his sons from the dangers of rugby league that he became their soccer coach, so it is not difficult to imagine a young John Hughes practising his kicking under the father's watchful eye. Tellingly, in attempting to account for 'the sense of strength and security I felt in him', the author describes his father's gaze:

> He had this disarming habit of looking you squarely in the eyes whenever he spoke to you [...] I think [his sense of strength] was in the eyes, skin ferning from years of concentration, dark focused, searching – they gave nothing away but seemed to take everything in, opened like numbers on a page. (95)

The context that affords the physical proximity for such an intimate investigation of the father's eyes is unsurprisingly a sporting one, as father prepares son for a soccer game: 'I remember watching him lace my football boots, the sound of his concentrated breathing' (96). Hughes's attention to authenticity in such moments is astonishing: this is Australian relational auto/biography writ intimate. But when the son of this memory has grown up and stopped playing sport, can the paternal gaze be re-directed into his chosen world of literature? Evidence suggests that it is greatly desired. Hughes's wish for his father to repeat the patrimonial act of gazing by 'watching me as I write' (87) is of course difficult to actualise neatly. Rose comes close by describing his father watching him perform at the launch of his first book of poetry, and even alluded in interview to the tantalising image of father and son performing together at a writer's festival. Yet can these acts of writing or even performing literature be construed as performances of patrimony? Or is the Australian conception of idealised masculinity in the Son's Book antithetical with the image of the writer, even the heroic writer?

Conclusion: The Writer as Sportsman?

In his poem 'The Best Place...', Robert Gray compares the act of writing to soccer, the chosen sport of his youth: 'The desk lamp / curves its shadow across / all the shelved books, and they become / a crowd canopied in that vast South American football / stadium, / whose voices now, in the midst of play / you can no longer hear' (*Skylight* 24–5). As Alan Urquhart has observed: 'This extraordinary image of the poet losing himself in the play of writing, like a Pele or a Maradona, is betrayed only by this need for the imaginary applause of the "shelved books"' (57). The joy expressed in the poet's solitude is undercut by his desire for an audience to his performance. While the location of this unusual sporting metaphor is South America rather than

Australia, it is observably male-centric, recalling as it does Connell's depiction of such events as sites for the display of 'exemplary masculinities'. Yet could the scene to which it refers, the act of writing, be construed as a performance of masculinity?

Gray must content himself with his shelved books, for as we will discover, his autobiography reveals that his father refused to read his poetry, though the author does not express resentment at this repudiation (*The Land* 402). Hughes's father, on the other hand, *has* read and enjoyed his work, though tellingly there has been little interaction between them regarding the son's depiction of the father, nor has the author fretted much about how his father may feel about being the subject of his writing. As the author explains:

> It's funny (but not surprising) that unlike my mother, my father has never commented on my representation of him and I've never asked him about it. He says he likes the book, and I think he likes the fact that other people (and especially his surviving friends) like the book. And ironically, because he is so reticent, I never for a moment in the writing of 'Country Towns' worried what he might think of my representation of him. (In Mansfield, 'Beating' 102)

Hughes is roundly pessimistic about the possibility of writing as a performance of masculinity, making the extraordinary statement that, 'being a writer is about as low a form of masculine achievement as I can imagine in Australia' (in Mansfield, 'Beating' 100). As to the question of the writer-as-sportsman courting admiration from the father, Hughes's ambivalence, as with his representation of his father, seems palpable. Responding to a request to expand on the image of his father watching him as he writes, Hughes states:

> There was something quixotic, or at least whimsical, in my wish in that essay. The sense in which I didn't measure up in terms of my father's expectations, not so much on the sporting field (though that would have been good), but that I didn't study law or medicine and so succeed in a professional way, rise above my class background in a way that would make me a conventional kind of success. The thought that he might see success in writing as comparable to this, or at least a partial compensation, I could never take seriously, though I could hope. So there's a kind of irony here, I suppose – that he would never see writing in this way, anyway […] but even if he did, it would always be secondary to a son who had made it in medicine or the law. But with that said, as I write in the essay, the importance of sport to country towns (and to Australian culture generally) can't be underestimated. And as a writer, even a good writer, there was

no way I'd ever match the sporting stars. (Incidentally, a couple of years ago I was inaugurated into the newly established Cessnock Hall of Fame. It gave my father particular pleasure that this happened before Andrew Johns – a much more famous native son.) But in my own mind, there was a kind of proving going on (as there is always with the son) – that I can't help but see my writing in sporting terms, not as a competition, but as a test of character and a challenge to the self, and if I'm honest, a form of display. So not so much changing anything in terms of how my father saw me (changing anything in our relationship, that is), but certainly in terms of how I see myself, and how I see him seeing me in my imagination. (In Mansfield, 'Beating' 100)

The intense ambivalence towards the father expressed in *The Idea of Home* is echoed here – a desire for the father's approval and a simultaneous sense of resignation that 'I didn't measure up'. Hughes casts his father's attitude as typically Australian, one who enjoys seeing his son beat Andrew Johns into the Cessnock Hall of Fame, whilst acknowledging the provincial nature of such success and knowing that, ultimately, even the best writers in Australia will never match the sporting stars. Despite such acknowledgement, the desire remains, and so the writing performance continues to be cast in sporting terms, as a test of character, a challenge to the self, and most tellingly of all, as a form of display.

Though Hughes has, for the moment at least, left the autobiographical essay behind, a great many of *The Idea of Home*'s interests and obsessions are carried over into his first novel *The Remnants*, including the autobiographical persona – the name the author gives to the father of this text is John Hughes. As the author explains in interview, the novel is 'an exploration of how the son represents the father (and becomes that father!)' (in Mansfield, 'Beating' 100). This unusual textual metamorphosis has in fact already been enacted in autobiography, as we will now explore in Robert Gray's *The Land I Came Through Last*.

Chapter Seven

'NEITHER TO VINDICATE NOR TO VILIFY': BECOMING THE FATHER IN ROBERT GRAY'S *THE LAND I CAME THROUGH LAST*

> I might have loved him had I dared, and had we been able to talk to each other.
>
> —Patrick White, *Flaws in the Glass*

> If I think of you
> I'm horrified – I become obsessed
> with you. It is like
> love.
> I am filled with pity.
> I want to live.
>
> —Robert Gray, 'Poem to my Father'

> Gray has no centre to him. I cannot find, in this book, the man's heart, mind, spirit or gut.
>
> —Robert Adamson, 'Review of *Grass Script*'

Early in *The Land I Came Through Last*, Robert Gray's auto/biographical account of his parents' troubled relationship, the author offers the following description of his father:

> My father's expression, at first sight, mixed intelligence with arrogance, but that look was undermined, for me, as I grew aware of how underneath it there was a secretive discomfort. There was always about him, I felt, for all the authority of his talk, a subtle embarrassment, a consciousness of what would have been thought his moral weakness. (18)

The father's moral weakness – his alcoholism – is, as Gray's portrait makes clear, a red herring. While the book contains some astonishing descriptions of drunkenness and its destructive effects, Gray's account of his father is far more complex and penetrating than a simple lesson on the dangers of alcohol. Crucially, the passage given above, while remarkable as a demonstration of the author's ability to succinctly portray the instability of the father who is progressively revealed through the text, is also a strikingly apt description of the book itself. The authorial voice of this text is distinctly assured – Gray's memories of childhood are untentative and revealing, and he writes with a blunt and reflective honesty about a number of significant people in his life in a way that is rarely flattering but nonetheless demonstrates the impact they have had on him. Ego is an important theme in the work, and while it would be unfair to describe the author as merely arrogant, *The Land I Came Through Last* is narrated in a highly mannered register with seemingly incontestable self-assuredness, beginning in his preface with a claim to 'objectivity' (1). Yet there is something disconcerting about the autobiographical self portrayed by Gray. It may be the reader who experiences this 'secretive discomfort', but it stems from the uncertain status of the author in his autobiography. 'For all the authority of his talk', there is in Gray's self-consciously mannered voice something unsettlingly feigned. A defining feature of the text is the extent to which the author dissimulates his identity in his act of writing by employing all his powers as an accomplished poet.

Gray's description of his father's expression is revealing in another way. While it is the paternal influence that the author seems throughout his life to have most struggled against, to have desired the most distance from, *The Land I Came Through Last* ultimately demonstrates some uncanny resemblances between father and son. Despite the author's delineation and renunciation of his father's weaknesses and inadequacies, and despite an inclination to believe that more of the mother has survived within himself, Gray's text, in some surprising ways, reveals the way in which, *pace* Euripides, the 'flaws' of the father can be repeated in the son. This chapter investigates Gray's autobiography as a contemporary exemplar of the supremely ambivalent writer-son, demonstrating the way that, despite himself, Gray enacts a textual becoming of the father he disavows.

'Diptych' as Autobiography

Gray is one of Australia's most celebrated poets. Emerging out of the so-called 'Generation of 68', he in many ways defined himself against the poets of this era such as Robert Adamson and John Tranter. Rejecting the 'formalist' postmodern agenda of the Australian proponents of the American New

School, Gray was a vocal participant in the 'Poetry Wars', anthologising (along with Geoffrey Lehmann) the 'naturalist' or 'objectivist' poets against Tranter's 'abstractionist' anthologies, and becoming a kind of self-appointed defender of Les Murray against the 'self-conscious avant-gardism' of his detractors (in Williams 34). Gray has described his own poetry and literary position as 'a belief in the need to be dialectical: I value both aestheticism and human content [...] I believe in imagination and in reason' (Untitled 520), and has, interestingly, linked this dialectical impulse to his parents (in Williams 27). As Adamson has observed of Gray's poetry, 'One of Gray's great subjects is his parents' ('Like a Dog' 23), and one of our tasks here will be to compare how they fare in adaptation into the genre of autobiography. Gray published his first poetry collection *Creekwater Journal* in 1974, and has subsequently published seven further volumes, as well as numerous 'collected works'. He has received a number of awards, including the NSW Premier's Literary Award's Kenneth Slessor Prize for Poetry, and the Victorian Premier's Literary Award's C. J. Dennis Prize for Poetry, which he has won twice. Of relevance to the current discussion, he received the Patrick White Award in 1990.

Gray's first foray into prose autobiography has been widely and favourably reviewed since its release in 2008. Praise for the *The Land I Came Through Last* has primarily centred on the quality of its writing. Gray's one-time adversary Adamson describes it as 'luminous writing [that] contains many set pieces of exemplary prose' ('Like a Dog' 23). Andrew Riemer acclaims Gray's writing as 'evocative but unsentimental, illuminated here and there by delicate images of the natural world' (28). Geordie Williamson compares it to Wordsworth's *The Prelude*, stating that 'the best sections of share something of that great poem's combination of watchfulness and visionary access' (11), while Dianne Stubbings calls it 'both unique and haunting' (13). It won the 'NIB' CAL Waverly Library Award for Literature and the Alex Buzo Prize in 2009. Most reviewers have criticised the book for being overlong and note the author's elision of the self, desiring 'greater emphasis on what made Gray into the accomplished poet he is' (Riemer 29). The author's elisions will gain greater importance as my analysis progresses.

Gray's intention to write auto/biographically dates from at least 1993, originally conceived as a comparative biography of Gray's father and the author Patrick White. The book was to be titled 'Extreme People' (the name survives as the title of the penultimate chapter, dealing with the later lives and deaths of Gray's paternal aunts) and was to be structured in the following way: 'The first half is about my father and his family, all of whom were excessive in some way, and the second half is about Patrick White, who, you may agree with me, was also an extreme personality' ('Family Stories' 22). While this intended structure has not fully survived in the published book of

15 years later – the portion dealing with White, for example, reduced to one chapter – its skeleton remains upon the fleshed-out work of over four hundred pages. In fact, *The Land I Came Through Last* charts Gray's relationship with a series of father figures, including White, who are compared and contrasted with the father who ultimately dominates the work and is key in understanding the autobiographical self of the text.

While the author himself evidently did not much feature in his original plans, it is the autobiographical which asserted itself as the work developed, as the author acknowledges in his preface: 'At first, I thought I could treat my appearances in the book curtly, in the second person; autobiography seemed distasteful and too difficult. But that resistance was pushed aside in the midst of writing, as memories opened, "lighting one candle with another's flame"' (1).[1] In fact, significant portions of the work read as traditional autobiography rather than auto/biography, dealing almost exclusively with Gray's childhood memories of himself, including the recounting of the Romantic self's discovery of nature (122), his first sexual experiences (194, 267), and the poet's 'great revelation' of the transcendent power of language (201). A distinctive aspect of *The Land I Came Through Last* is the way the author writes of both a relational self (conceived of through portraits of his mother, father and other relatives) and simultaneously asserts an autonomous self, typified by what Gray describes as 'my self-sufficient nature' (122). Despite the author's stated desire to focus on his parents (1), the *autos* appears to have superseded the *bios*; although the 'I' of the text remains thoroughly elusive. Gray is capable of stunning moments of relationality; of demonstrating the way the other contributes to the conceptualisation of an author's identity. Yet the ambivalence of these relationships and his continual retreat to the language of self-construction highlight a split or incongruity in the autobiographical self offered.

The 'Toxic' Father

Gray's autobiography is a fitting place to conclude this study of patrimonial life narrative as it moves us to the opposite pole from the 'tribute' mode of texts such as *Romulus, My Father*. Whilst we have already explored a denunciatory representation in *The Watcher*, Porter's father was at worst a hapless paternal figure; an inadequate masculine model for his sensitive writer-son.

---

[1] The poet's aversion to the term autobiography echoes Vincent Buckley's disclaimer in the preface to *Cutting Green Hay* that 'I prefer, also, to be free of chronology, and of whatever bonds are entailed by autobiography or its trendy successor, the "memoir", new presbyter to its old priest: both of them too full of obligation and temptation' (xii). Gray's preface, like Buckley's, reads as a kind of pre-emptive strike against the critic, who might, through 'intellectual fashion' question the 'objectivity' of his autobiography (1).

Even Porter's most strident indictment of his father as 'a blind wrecker' (92) contains a sense that the damage caused to the family was unintentional; the result of ineffective fathering or incompatible temperaments rather than wilful destructiveness. Redman's delineation of 'the monstrous, "toxic" Father' (130) of the denunciatory mode could not be applied to any of the paternal figures explored so far.[2] Gray's portrait amply fills this gap; for here the father is sacrificed to his text, though this seems nothing less than he deserves.

The Land I Came Through Last portrays a man whose impact on his family is unremittingly destructive. An irresponsible and unrepentant alcoholic, Geoffrey Gray drinks and gambles away the family property, forcing his wife to work in a series of menial jobs in order to provide for her four children. Further, Gray's portrayal is of a man with a repellent personality; a narcissistic and self-destructive 'snob' with a sharp tongue who is a misogynist and a homophobe. Though never physically violent, Geoffrey uses verbal abuse and a sardonic wit to constantly demean his wife and sons; his sole 'cherished' daughter is the only family member spared his insults. So caustic is this father's tongue that Gray's paternal grandfather refuses to visit their home: 'He was too intimidated by my father's sarcasm' (128). As Adamson astutely concludes of Gray's father, 'I searched this book for redeeming qualities in him and found none. The more we discover about him the more awful he becomes' ('Like a Dog' 23).[3] However, for all its negativity, Gray's paternal portrait inexplicably stops short of denunciation. He claims to write 'neither to vindicate nor to vilify' the father, but to 'retain a sense of [him] as [he was]' (1). The following discussion attempts to puzzle out this incongruity. How does Gray manage such a feat? Is his 'dry eyed' yet sympathetic attempt not to judge his father a supremely ethical act? Is it disingenuous? Does it demonstrate autobiography's capacity for resolution through the act of writing? And how does it complicate, or how is it complicated by, the unsettling similarities between the figures of father and son in *The Land I Came Through Last*?

As Barbour finds, a key to not judging one's parents is to explore the 'traumas' of their pasts that may have incapacitated them for parenthood ('Judging' 75–6). That Gray desires to make sense of the man his father became is signalled in the text's opening line: 'My father was a remittance man in his own country' (3). Born into an upper-middle-class household in

---

2   Though not explored in any detail, the exceptions to this are the fathers of *Gatton Man*, *Desirelines* and *Sunshine and Shadow*.
3   Adamson's own autobiography of childhood *Inside Out* (2004) interestingly elides his father almost entirely, despite some of his most celebrated poems focussing around the author's patrimonial inheritance. For a Son's Denunciatory Poem of the Father, see Adamson's 'The Horse and Cart' in *Where I Come From* (Sydney: Big-Smoke Books, 1979), 15.

Vaucluse, as an adult Geoffrey becomes an embarrassment to his family due to his drinking and carousing and is banished from Sydney to the North Coast of NSW:[4] 'They bought him a plantation there [...] on the condition that he not return to the city' (3). Tellingly, in a reversal of the disavowal of one's paternal heritage witnessed in Chapter Six of this book, Geoffrey's repudiation of his first-born son Robert is preceded by rejection by his own father, who disowned his son and refused to see him even when on his deathbed (24). Told almost nothing of his paternal heritage by his father, Gray must rely on the testimony of others in order to tell this narrative of rejection, including his mother and his paternal aunts. His mother provides unflattering portraits of a paternal grandmother who was 'a caricature of vanity' and a patriarch whose 'decorum was entirely superficial. Everyone speaks of him as relentlessly jovial, hedonistic and rash' (26). In letters his paternal aunts give him, written between them and his father during Geoffrey's period of exile, Gray discovers, along with confirmation of his own disavowal, the extent of Geoffrey's 'self-pity and frustration' (6) at his banishment: 'I think my father wished that everyone he could possibly incriminate in his failure, however unreasonably, should know of and carry an apportioned blame' (5).

While it is Geoffrey's uncontrolled drinking that causes him to be sent away, the Grays of Vaucluse were far from teetotal. The author's depiction of his paternal grandfather's drinking escapades (including a memorable session with Jack London in which he 'outdrank the great writer' (27)) almost eclipse stories of the father's binges, while a photograph of his grandfather's hunting parties (34) establish him as a traditional masculine patriarch; an early twentieth century exemplar of hegemonic masculinity. In a telling passage, Gray explicitly links his father's and paternal grandfather's behaviour to parochial notions of male identity:

> Despite my mother's low opinion of him, my grandfather does seem to have been 'good value', for men at least. To both him and his son, what was important was how they stood in other men's eyes – how much bonhomie they asserted, how generous they were, how 'manly' in their drinking, how forceful as raconteurs. Such primitive command is most convincing if backed up by some physical accomplishment, and my father had his swimming, my grandfather his shooting, and evidently swimming, too. Male camaraderie of such an overt sort used often to be thought a particularly Australian trait, but surely the Greeks gathered on the beach at Ilium not just in the hope of loot, but in response to such an atavism. (47)

---

4   The location is obviously Coffs Harbour, though Gray never refers to his hometown by name, which stands as another odd concealment in the text.

While the Australian drinking (and sporting) culture has to date been an important site for performing (and proving) one's masculinity, here it takes on the force of family myth. Notwithstanding notions of class at play in the act of disavowing his son, the insight offered regarding the grandfather's 'hypocritical' reasoning highlights a peculiarity of how Australian manliness is often measured:

> My mother believed she understood the failure of my father's relationship with my grandfather [...] For him, it was a mystery that his father, so relentlessly drawn to a good time, was prepared to accept anyone else's riotous living, and be anyone's friend, but his own [...] She told me: 'Your father had really just one fault, in the old man's eyes – he couldn't hold his liquor. That's the thing those people won't forgive'. (45)

Though apportioning culpability in the opposite direction, Gray's aunt Olga confirms the extent of Geoffrey's refutation by his family, telling the young Robert that, 'It was all your father's fault, what happened to Dad: it was because he didn't really have a son' (48). For this 'prodigal son', as he is elsewhere described (24), there would be no chance of return, let alone redemption.

Gray again engages explicitly with Australian notions of masculinity and hero archetypes, positing his father as a kind of anti-hero who embodies a cultural shift from the bushman of early Australian literature. The author quotes from Paterson's 'The Man From Snowy River' – 'It was grand to see that mountain horseman ride' – before recounting a 'notorious story' of his father's drunken 'last ride', in which he drives his car off the road and plunges down an embankment before careering through a banana plantation, then emerging from the wreckage and bowing before a stunned farmer's wife (9–10). Gray previously recounted this event in 'Diptych', and has elsewhere drawn socio-historical significance from its comparison with Paterson's stockman, stating that 'I see lots of symbolism for the change that has come over men's lives in Australia' ('Family Stories' 22–3). Drawing a contrast between the two in his autobiography, Gray writes that

> my father's ride was the opposite of such a heroic one. It was bungling and inadvertent, risible, and quite useless – and yet it exemplified something about him that was more than just these things. It was a debacle, but one that he must try to redeem, with a gesture. (10)

Such a description may again be aptly ascribed to Gray's autobiography of childhood. The mannered or heroic gesture is a defining feature of Geoffrey's performance of masculinity, and subsequently of the author's own textual performance.

Gray stops short of exculpating his father's failings based solely on his experience of banishment, echoing his original assessment in 'Poem to My Father': 'What went wrong/ when you were young? It was nothing exceptional/ that I can find' (*Poems* 59–60).[5] The author's analysis of his father as a child demonstrates how his 'malicious' tendencies predated any later misfortune: 'In his boyhood [...] he continually provoked and discomforted the household, just as later on, with my mother and her children, he would do so again' (35). While Gray's anecdotes of his father's 'boyish pranks' – such as knocking a bucket of mop-water onto a maid, or filling female underwear on the line with mud – seem relatively harmless, the author asserts that 'there was always a colouring of cruelty to them' (35). The author's grandfather, somewhat more indulgently than in later years, believed that such incidents 'showed character in the boy' (38). In the family studio portrait reproduced in his text, Gray describes his father, the only boy, as 'full of self-confidence, and seems almost preening. One knows, without needing to have been told, that this was a family in which a son, whatever his faults, had a special standing' (36–7). One might wonder whether envy plays a role in such observations: Gray, the first-born of three sons, enjoyed no such 'special standing' in his father's estimations, this position occupied instead by the author's only sister.

Geoffrey's unsuitability for fatherhood is confirmed by his absence at Robert's birth, and by the fact that, when he finally arrives via a detour to the pub, 'he was, to my mother's shame, by far the most incapable person in the ward' (72). Later, when she goes into labour with her third child, Gray's mother insists that her two young sons 'should come with her in the ambulance, and not be looked after by our father. She probably thought he had more alcohol somewhere' (84). On separate trips to Sydney with his father, young Robert is abandoned for up to twenty-four hours due to his father's irresponsibility or bad judgement (114–16). Gray recounts few if any acts of fatherly attention or care, though his early memories of accompanying Geoffrey to work at his banana plantation hint ruefully of an experience of companionship between father and son: 'not for many years would I feel so close to him again' (92). Even with his cherished daughter Geoffrey proves an inadequate father, as evidenced when she scalds herself with boiling water and it is Robert who has the sense to properly treat her burns.

---

5   Adamson describes the poem as 'a passive-aggressive version of Sylvia Plath's *Daddy*' which 'has more compassion, in a twisted way, because there's no redemption' ('Like a Dog' 23).

In judging this father as deficient, the reader is asked to balance two competing narratives of his identity formation: certain episodes, such as those of Geoffrey's childhood, indicate a constancy to the father's wretchedness; while Gray's narrative at the same time charts a descent into wretchedness 'the worse things got for him' (62). Late in the text Gray goes to some length to explain and even excuse his father's neglect, though he is so thoroughly unconvincing that one must question his motives. How much does an auto/biographer stand to gain in portraying himself as the forgiving son? Whatever the case, by the time the author is a teenager, the father's presence is unremittingly 'toxic', as Gray's description of a typical domestic scene makes clear:

> At dinner times we washed our faces, combed our hair, and sat at the table in our places, with napkins, bread and butter plates, cut glass butter dish and a butter knife, and refrained from speaking – unless spoken to. We waited for our father to begin the meal, and to begin his monologue, poisoning the air. (184)

Though Geoffrey does not repeat his father's repudiation by banishing his own son, the result of his constant demeaning is the same. When Robert drops out of school and leaves home at the age of 17, the blame is slated home to his father: 'my mother agreed that I should use the remaining funds to get away from my father. Not only did I worsen his irritability, I now had a positive dislike for him, which she could see me struggling to suppress' (243).

'Ineffectual Love': Gray's Surrogate Fathers

In light of the father's supreme inadequacy, Gray's portrayal of the paternal figures to which he turns is instructive. Without venturing too far into psychoanalysis, it is worth noting that every significant male relationship Gray describes involves an older man.[6] In *Romulus, My Father* a figure such as Mitru served as a favourable comparison for the honoured father, highlighting Romulus's superior 'moral strength'. Gray's surrogate fathers have the reverse effect: their interest or care further tarnishes the image of the father. However, these substitute relationships are compensatory only up to a point, and this is a key factor in Gray's construction of relationality.

---

6 Two further examples of this pattern not discussed here are Gray's relationships with Bruce Chatwin (336–43) and Les Murray (339–41). Though Murray is only seven years Gray's senior, their public relationship has often been construed, much to Gray's chagrin, as one between teacher and disciple. See Gray's response to such a suggestion in his interview with Barbara Williams (37–8).

The first surrogate figure is the author's high school English teacher, who 'was an occasional drinking companion of my father; and became something of a friend to me' (222). His similarities with Gray's father are many: an opinionated alcoholic who liked to perform, he also shares the father's penchant for word-play and puns. However, unlike the father, this teacher 'awakens in [Gray] a furious autodidacticism' (Williamson 11),[7] encouraging and fostering his emerging interest in literature by introducing him to many classic writers. Their conversations are remembered fondly, prompting one of the few definitive tributes in the text: 'My gratitude to him is as ardent now as it was then, although I did not express it at the time. The relationship between pupil and teacher can be among the deepest one has' (227). Though there are no sexual overtones, Gray's portrait echoes Smith's description of his English teacher as 'neither father nor lover, yet something of both in his adolescent search for an intellectual security' (173). In a gesture typical of Gray's memorialisation of others, his tribute is driven in part by guilt: Robert failed to complete high school and so did not top the State in English as his teacher had hoped, foreshadowing the insufficiency of most surrogate relationships in *The Land I Came Through Last*: 'I repaid his interest in me with disappointment' (228).[8]

As with *The Idea of Home*, the maternal grandfather functions in this text as a contrasting masculine model to that offered by the father, providing an alternative patrimony for the writer-son. The pattern of triangulation described by Gray is a neat reversal of Hughes's explored in Chapter Six. Here Gray's grandfather is the reticent, laconic male who performs his masculinity in his toolshed and embodies the reserve of the country town from which the author comes, while Gray's father is the gregarious outsider. However, in this case Gray rejects (or in the father's case, attempts to reject) the masculine model offered by both men. In a chapter titled 'An Ineffectual Love' Gray charts the older man's well-meaning involvement in his childhood.

---

7   Williamson's language is telling. Despite his desire to recognise his 'teachers', essentially Gray shows that everything he has learnt he has taught himself.

8   This surrogate father is briefly replaced by another 'gentle, cultivated man' (276) in the editor of the local newspaper where Robert is employed upon leaving school. Gray credits this man with teaching him much about the art of writing for an audience (276). But the relationship is again cut short when this mentor is 'crudely' replaced with a more aggressive editor, prompting Gray's swift resignation from the paper. As Robert departs to pursue a journalistic career in Sydney, his mentor assures him that, 'He would watch for my by-line' (277). Robert's applications are rejected by the major Sydney newspapers, and while he works for a short period at *The Readers Digest*, his work is never published.

A dependable presence in Gray's earliest memories, he would do what he could to 'come to my mother's aid', though his deference meant that he 'must be careful not to interfere' (128). As he grows up, Robert increasingly seeks refuge at his maternal grandparents' house which, while it is a place almost devoid of communication, offers sanctuary from the father: 'What I liked was that "nobody picked on me" there, as I explained to my grandfather, when he asked why I had come visiting again' (137). Robert finds further companionship in the long hours spent in his grandfather's shed, reading the older man's collection of 'girly' magazines: 'I used politely to decline his offer of pieces of timber, a spare vice and a wood-plane. We would sit indoors together on sunny afternoons, a page turned by me, an outburst of mallet-hammering from him' (132).

Although his grandfather attempts to assist Robert in his interests and endeavours – making him soccer boots to practice 'for my future professional career' (134) and bicycles to aid him in delivering newspapers – what makes his support, like his companionship, ineffectual is that however well-intentioned, it disappoints. The boots and the bicycles break, leading to numerous 'narrow escapes' (138). The symbol of this failed relationship becomes the canoe his grandfather builds, his 'masterpiece' (140), which proves barely seaworthy. When Robert finds it at the creek one day, destroyed by vandals, the author states, 'I realised I felt relief. I knew I was probably going to go down with the boat sooner or later [...] I let my grandfather believe the canoe was safe at home' (144). Ten years later, after his grandfather has died, Gray returns to his hometown and, walking along the creek, discovers a part of the canoe floating amongst the detritus: 'The message seemed to be, "Know your place. Don't get above yourself"' (145). The event leads to one of the most devastating and revealing passages in the text, where, with typically imagistic prose, the author sets out the great limitations of his capacity for authentic relationships:

> The bulldozed earth on which I stood, with night almost completely lowered, smelled rankly. [...] I was filled with disgust, about something I could not limit or name – at the sordidness of everything. It included my own ingratitude. My grandfather was lying in the graveyard on a hillside nearby, and I stood holding the work of his hands, and of more than his hands. (145)

As we find expressed at the resting place of his final surrogate father, Patrick White, Gray's regret and desire for writing to redeem his ingratitude is tempered by his realisation of its impossibility. 'The work of Gray's hands', however significant in literary merit, cannot resolve these failed relationships.

'An Elusive Friendship': Gray's Father and Patrick White

This failure is no more explicitly demonstrated than by Gray's depiction of Patrick White. Of his intention to write about White, the author once claimed, 'I didn't have a chance to thank Patrick [for giving him the Patrick White Award, almost White's final act before death]. But it seems to me now appropriate to write about him in the same book as about my father, because of his long encouragement of my writing' ('Family Stories' 29). On many levels, this would appear an extraordinary statement when compared to the finished product. How does White's support of Gray's writing make it appropriate that he be written about in the author's Book of the Father? Gray records no support of his writing from either of his parents, and in fact his father's attitude is strikingly narcissistic:

> On one visit he said to me, 'I hear that you've published a book. I think it would be better if I didn't see it. You weren't intending to show me, I can tell. Very wise. If I liked it, I would be jealous and find fault, and if I didn't like it I would be even harder on you, so it's best that we pass over the matter entirely. (402)

Fascinatingly, Gray's own bizarre refusal to read White's novels until after his death (279) mirrors his father's behaviour, demonstrating again the uncanny resemblance of father and son. Gray's claim to have read White only after he died contradicts an earlier statement in his review of David Marr's biography that, 'I first read his books when young, as they came out' ('Smile' 11). It is unclear which of his statements is true or how changing his position serves his purpose of repaying his debt to White. While the quotation given regarding Gray's motivations for writing about his father and White is typically ambiguous, and while Gray makes no Gossian claim of his text as 'a monument to the father', it is difficult to find evidence in *The Land I Came Through Last* to support the notion that Gray has written in any sense to 'thank' or pay tribute to his father.

What then of Gray's portrait of White? Is the act of writing in this case an attempt to pay tribute? Gray's early recollections of White are positively scathing – he is described as 'self-dramatising', with 'the unpleasant air of a masochist', who 'did sadistic things to people with words' (353). Importantly, explicit comparisons are made between White and Gray's father, particularly the harm they did to others with language, though Gray insists on the latter's superior abilities:

> Their likeness I found in the practiced way both did sadistic things to people with words, out of what Patrick identified, for himself, as

'self-loathing'. (My father's cutting remarks could not compare in animus but were far more inventive than any I heard from the famous writer.) (353)

While Gray's portrayal is by no means the first unflattering biographical record of White, his is a starkly pessimistic vision of a famous friend. Admittedly, in his later anecdotes, particularly those that depict White's relationship with Manoly Lascaris, there is a distinct softening in tone (376–7). Then, following White's death and Gray's controversial receipt of the Patrick White Award, we find another declaration of guilt:

> Wanting to thank him, I found myself standing before an infinite silence, more adamant than any matter. I saw that my wariness had not been able to detract from the generosity of his nature. I realised the inadequate friend I had been, how misplaced all my suspicion and caution was. Thinking of him, I had overwhelmingly a sense of our loneliness. (379)

While Gray's portrayal of White could hardly be termed 'elegiac', it does ultimately convey some sense of the author's friendship with and admiration for his subject. Yet there is also the acknowledgement of the impossibility of atonement – what Gray describes as 'an infinite silence, more adamant than any matter'. Unfortunately for Gray, whose deconversion narrative demonstrates his disavowal of the existence of anything beyond 'matter', such finality is absolute and irredeemable.

'Mother and Son': Gray's Narrative of Deconversion

As with *The Boy Adeodatus*, the key figure in Gray's exploration of belief is his mother. Her presence in the narrative has the effect of softening the relentless flow of masculine self-regard, yet it also complicates the work. Crucially, the text's most striking moment of relationality is a maternal one. Much of Gray's early narrative is dominated by descriptions of solitary expeditions through the bushland of the northern coast of NSW, and of a corresponding interior life constructed through the passage of self-discovery, bearing out the author's claim that, 'I hardly had genuine contact with another person' (137). But following one such adventure, the author recalls standing on a hill above his childhood home and witnessing the figure of his mother:

> I waded through deep ferns, dragging my stick, and saw my mother come out onto our back porch and raise her face toward the hill, blindly, and call my name. I returned a single shout, which immediately released her posture and felt like a vibrant plasm between us. (182)

The passage again emphasises the importance of recognition in autobiography. The vital role of being named (and knowing one's name) is foregrounded as a key in identity formation. The author can see while his mother 'calls blindly', yet the connection is two-way, and it is, in fact, the seen self of the author who seems created out of the interaction, from the experience of being sought and known. The author emphasises the effect of his single shout, which released her posture and creates a connectedness, what the author terms a 'vibrant plasm between us'. It is a poignant moment in Gray's narrative, particularly considering the mother's subsequent disavowal of her son for his apostasy.

Gray charts what his mother refers to as her 'false starts' (56) in religious exploration, including being brought up 'an old-style Presbyterian' (54), and joining various sects such as British Israel, 'the Mormons and the Plymouth Brethren' (56). A common thread in these various faiths is their understated, un-Catholic style of worship: 'Christianity, for her, could only be authentic if experienced as a small meeting of "the meek of the Earth"; in the linoleum-floored sitting room of a working-class family, or on a folding chair at a rented, hollow municipal hall' (54). Though published one hundred years after *Father and Son*, and detailing a parent's spiritual quest half a world away from the one embarked on by Emily and Henry Gosse, we find in Gray's portrait of his mother an astonishing recurrence of the 'austere spirits' of the early 'Brethren' who were first brought together 'on terms of what may almost be called negation' (7). As we will discover, Gray's link to the apostate Edmund extends far beyond the oddly Victorian narrative voice adopted by the author.

In 'Diptych' Gray records his mother's maternal concern for all things, even and especially her ungrateful husband: 'Her care you could watch reappear like the edge of tidal water/in salt flats, about everything' (*Poems* 136). The image which opens the poem – that of the author's mother trying to stay awake to make sure his inebriated father finds his way home from the pub – is given detail and frequency in *The Land I Came Through Last*. Although Gray's mother takes a prohibition order against her husband in court to prevent him entering a hotel or club, the author describes witnessing him being bought drinks in the parking lot behind the town pub (102), and finding empty bottles scattered throughout their house and garden (103). Importantly, it is again the mother's 'care' which causes her to give in to her husband's self-destructiveness: 'She did not continue her part in the war of attrition on my father, she later said to me, because she decided it was too cruel for him not to have men to talk with' (102). As Son's Books typically make clear, masculine needs, including the need for male kinship, usually take precedence over the needs of the family.

A key aspect of his mother's character, which Gray seems at pains to point out, is her status as a long-suffering wife, to the extent that we do not condemn her when she turns violent against her husband. The author records many caustic arguments between his parents, who were both capable of verbal abuse, yet it is the father who has the advantage with regard to language, causing the mother to lash out:

> My mother said she was being 'driven to distraction', and numerous times made my father's nose bleed. I used to intervene with arms raised, and she would get a last blow in, in a style I particularly disliked, a stabbing gesture [...] My father never struck back, or even defended himself. (187)

These scenes of conflict are offset by moments of tenderness, rarely between husband and wife but typically between mother and son. With fondness, the author recalls being taught to read by his mother from the age of three: 'I followed her about for hours of the day, my finger under different sounds in a book, and she corrected and answered me, with what I felt even then was the life-supporting gift of her patience' (79). Gray quotes from Wordsworth's maternal tribute in *The Prelude* to demonstrate the 'connection between the emotional reliability of a parent in one's childhood and being at home in the world' (81). In the context of the majority of my authors' preferred model of the 'bardic poet-prophet', such an accolade is not bestowed lightly.

In 'The Church of the Midnight Cry' Gray deals in detail with his mother's conversion to the Jehovah's Witnesses and the author's own brief but intense indoctrination. In fact, this chapter could be described as *Father and Son* in miniature; the narrative of Gray's brief conversion and deconversion from a puritanical faith. Like Edmund Gosse, young Robert seems to have thrived in the church meetings of this old-style religion due to his as yet undiscovered talent with language and literature: 'I had performed well in the public speaking classes [...] and was commended by the visiting inspectors from national head office as a Bible student, so I was always given the difficult houses to call upon' (211). In a strikingly Gossian moment, which also recalls Carey's rewriting of *Father and Son* in *Oscar and Lucinda*, the young Gray is sent 'witnessing' to the clergy of his small country town: 'There was a fierce table tennis match of Biblical quotations, bandied back and forth, until I was ordered off the premises by someone I thought was a sore loser' (211).

In an echo of his father's 'unjust' banishment, Gray's deconversion that leads to his own familial expulsion is precipitated by what he sees as the unwarranted, even 'ungodly' excommunication of another boy in the church for minor rebellious behaviour: 'I could not accept that God was going to be called on in support of such a petty exclusion, in that sordid little fibro shed' (215). The author's suspicions of God's existence, like Gosse's before him, are caused in part by the manner in which his name is conjured by others for exclusionary ends, recalling the 'torment of postal inquisition' offered in the epilogue of *Father and Son* to justify Gosse's disavowal of his father (166). When Gray moves to Sydney as a young man, his mother writes to him weekly: 'hundreds upon hundreds of letters, in my adulthood, all of them affectionate, all quoting a biblical text, for my guidance and persuasion' (244). Unlike Gosse however, Gray cannot quote from these letters, explaining that, 'Even in writing this book, I have been unable to bring myself to open them' (244).

Fascinatingly, Gray's deconversion is confirmed by his discovery of Henry Gosse's scientific nemesis:

> When I broke with the Witnesses, I happened to notice in the newsagency a paperback copy of *On the Origin of Species*. Standing and browsing in this, a little each day, I was charmed by the clear, calm, observational approach of Darwin to questions about nature [...] Buying this book was a celebration of my liberty. The world lay all before me... (217)

In another clear echo of Gosse, Gray's declaration of liberty and embracement of the world recalls the former's celebratory act of throwing off 'the yoke of his dedication' to 'fashion his inner life for himself'. Similarly, Darwin's 'calm, clear observational approach', an obvious forerunner to the 'positive position' of 'empiricism' in the work of David Hume, which is later singled out by Gray for praise (349), has led the author to his current embracement of a humanist materialist logic. Or, as the author has stated in interview, 'There can be no Essence, in anything, or anywhere. There is no self, no soul, no God' (Williams 30), a stance that neatly actualises Gosse's pronouncement that 'The Lord will never come' (165). Both authors' desire for and claim to have attained such 'objectivity' in the prefaces to their autobiographies (Gosse 3; Gray 1) testifies to the fact that, despite the destabilising of both truth and the author in the past 50 years of autobiographical theory, for some autobiographers, 'The world is' still 'as it reliably appears' (Gray, *The Land* 349).

As with Gosse's break from his father, Gray's deconversion does carry a relational cost, in this case with his mother: 'Only gradually did I come to realise how much I had been cut out of her confidence, how subtly she had distanced me' (216). The 'vibrant plasm between' mother and son is broken, reaching its lowest point when she refuses to let him sit beside her at his father's funeral, stating: 'I want only my believing sons with me' (412). It is a poignant experience of banishment, softened only by the later passages of reconciliation during his mother's late life, when her interest in religion seems to have abated somewhat.

'Determined to Believe or Not Believe by Temperament Alone': Gray's Apostasy

However, as with Gray's exploration of his father's identity formation, an odd disjunction occurs in his narrative of deconversion. Much of the text is written from the perspective of the adult narrator looking back, with Gray's narration dominated by an at times didactic tone. Yet at various instances the narrator moves much closer to the autobiographical subject of his younger self, and the narrative is driven instead by vividly recounted memories with little extraneous comment or critique. This creates a tension between narrative and narrator, a conflict regarding when things seem to have occurred and the authorial claims about the importance of events. This is particularly true of Gray's exploration of religion, where an incongruity exists between the autobiographical subject's spiritual journey to unbelief and the narrator's assessment of his subject's journey.

Gray gives an early indication of what may be described the current state-of-play with regards to religion:

> My mother was that very person to whom, in an earlier incarnation, the Christian ideas were first preached – one of the 'meek', the 'poor in spirit', the spiritually 'heavy-laden'. It is understandable that in a later world, still insecure in much the same ways, such a person would again be attracted by a plain form of what seem to me *entirely compensatory beliefs*. (60, emphasis added)

However, as Gray's narrative continues, the question of when these beliefs became entirely compensatory for the author is a difficult one to answer, for a gulf develops between narrated experience and the narrator's critique. Gray himself voices this disjunction in describing the event of his dog being run over by a truck when he was six years old, an incident he calls 'my baptism in reality', the moment when he realised that 'this was just the empty way of things' (87). However, the childhood self remains silent, Robert stating, 'I know I must never hint to my mother about such feelings'. In a gesture that will be repeated in later moments of epiphany, Gray's first moment of deconversion is accompanied by a heightened sense of the natural world, opening up a dialectic between the physical and spiritual, where nature functions independently of any metaphysical self: 'I thought the dew on the grass more brilliant than ever' (87). Again, one finds an echo of Gosse's renunciation of God and discovery of the natural world (165). Gray remains within his child's mind for a few moments more, before abruptly reverting to an authorial mode in the final sentence:

> She was talking to us, at that moment, of a heaven for dogs, but I could not imagine it; it did not fit with what had just happened. The two concepts grated in my head. What about rabbits, in that dog's heaven? It seems to me now that I never believed in my mother's consolations, and that one is determined to believe or not believe by temperament alone. (87)

The notion of belief being determined by temperament recalls the subtitle of Gosse's autobiography, and is one Gray revisits throughout his autobiography. Gray insists that as a child, 'The private living quarters within me were firmly closed against [religion], although no one suspected' (203). The author identifies a second moment of deconversion as his maternal grandmother declines into death. Here the realm of the physical negates for Gray any possibility of a spiritual world: 'From that time, I gave up all those indulgent fantasies of mine, and the world became for me completely physical. There was only this. Things were as they showed themselves to be' (151–2). Echoing notions of objectivity in his preface, the author offers what Kevin Hart calls his 'counter-*credo*' (24): 'Things were as they showed themselves to be'. While his final rejection of his mother's religion is still to come, the author overrides his narrative of progress with a statement that negates the need for any such narrative.

Interestingly, despite his pronouncements to the contrary, this narrative of deconversion is not Gray's final association with religion. Pages after his break from the Jehovah's Witnesses, Gray details a brief yet intense exploration of Theosophism (300–305). In fact, the deconversion narrative detailed in *The Land I Came Through Last* is perhaps only a precursor to the major spiritual journey charted in Gray's poetry. In his study of the integration of Buddhist ideas in Gray's poetry, Greg McLaren chronicles – if not Gray's 'deconversion' from Buddhism – a clear progression from his attempts to embody Buddhist principles of non-attachment and 'no-self' in his early- to mid-period poetry to an abandonment of these principles in favour of 'attachment to nature' and 'materialist philosophies' in his later work (*Translations* 18): 'it seems Gray's early determination to integrate his Buddhist practice with his poetics and place eventually succumbs to the strength of his attachment to his rationalist and materialist leanings' (149). Whilst Gray would perhaps oppose categorising this movement a 'deconversion', arguing elsewhere that 'I was interested in Buddhism because, basically, it's atheistic, it doesn't require faith' (cited in McLaren 177), McLaren's demonstration of 'a major set of tensions' (18) in Gray's poetry, between what he desires to achieve and what is actually shown, highlights again the ambiguity of the autobiographical self of Robert Gray.

Interestingly, what would seem to have been a major thread of Gray's poetic oeuvre rates barely more than a mention in his autobiography: 'I was attracted to Buddhism, which claimed it had no problem with science' (218). This is the extent of Gray's comment on his Buddhist period, which contrasts with his comments in interviews about centrality of Buddhism to his poetry. Gray's elision of aspects of his life that he formerly attributed deep significance to further problematises the stability of the self offered in his text.

The disjunction between what Gray says and does in his poetry is evident in his narrative of deconversion in *The Land I Came Through Last*. Ultimately, Gray is an effective demonstration of the fact that one may dispense with the metaphysical and seek 'the clear, calm daylight of the rational mind', but the residuals of belief, or the opposing inclination to believe, is not always that easily thrown off. The author at one stage aptly labels his stance as 'fascinated disbelief' (231). Ambiguous to the end, Gray's verb formulation in the final lines of his autobiography (following the death of his mother) hints at a kind of divine intercession: 'That night, from the train, I was shown a farmhouse window, in a dark, surging mountain; and, at daybreak, a dangling river, more crystalline than a chandelier' (435). This ambiguity accords with Gray's pronouncement that 'Things were as they showed themselves to be' (152). One might ask: showed themselves to whom?

Gray's Elegies: Death and the Impossibility of Redemption

The final chapters of Gray's autobiography are structured around death. As the author explains: 'At a certain stage of our lives, the people we know who are older than we are all begin to die, with an insistent, staccato rhythm. I thought for a while I ought to call this book *Gray's Elegies*' (384). Yet how strong is the elegiac impulse in Gray? With his largely negative portraits of family members and his focus on flawed and difficult personalities, surely none of his portrayals could be termed elegiac. It is difficult to imagine Gray's deceased relatives being flattered by the way they are represented, or to believe any portion of the text could function as a funeral address in the mode of *Romulus, My Father* or *Rose Boys*.

Gray's didactic determination that 'Only physical things exist. There are no qualities apart from mass' (350) finds focus in his pragmatic attitude towards the remains of the deceased. As we see in the twin scenes of scattering his parents' ashes, the author's lack of sentimentality in handling the remains of a loved one punctuates the text. Standing next to the pond where Patrick White's ashes were scattered, Gray gives an inventory of the detritus floating in it (382). When his wife gives birth to a stillborn son Robert names him (the name is not recorded in the text) and has him cremated 'at once, without ceremony' before she has an opportunity to hold the baby or decide upon the manner of his burial. 'I thought this would be best for my wife, but now I understand it was utterly wrong', Gray unconvincingly castigates himself, almost as an aside (322). The marriage ended soon after. In a narrative that turns so much on parental neglect and inadequacy, Gray's one-paragraph treatment of his own brief experience of fatherhood may stand as the supreme elision of the text.[9]

Gray's unsentimental mode is sustained throughout his depiction of memorialisation. At Olga's funeral the eulogy is given by a minister, who describes 'a person none of us could recognise' (387). When Olga's sister Margaret becomes agitated, making loud complaints about the minister's 'sentimentality' (387), the author is prodded from behind by another mourner upset by Margaret's display, but he refuses to stop her, stating, 'I thought she had a right' (387). In contrast to the sentimentality of the priest, the author then states bluntly: 'Even a fictional character, encountered at length, is not credible without some redeeming trait, but I have trouble remembering what Olga's was. I would like to speak well of my aunt, yet she remains in memory, as she was in life, a skirted, uncomfortable presence' (387). Unlike other autobiographers, for whom death may transform and soften memories of loved ones, creating a sense of debt which may be repaid by a more positive or 'nostalgic' rendering in the autobiographical act, Gray appears to feel desire but no obligation to 'speak well' of the dead. A more pressing obligation for Gray is his 'need for objectivity' (1), which amounts to the autobiographer's adage of 'being true' to one's past as experienced, even at the risk of appearing ungrateful. Tellingly, Gray's search for a 'redeeming' trait is driven by textual concerns, such as the desire for one's narrative to appear 'credible'.

Surprisingly, the author has spoken elsewhere about how death may affect the way someone is represented. In accounting for the softening in tone between his two poems dealing with his father, the author has stated that, 'After someone dies, you are no longer their victim – disturbingly, they become yours. You can say anything about them. The realization that he was now contained in my hand, as it were, tempered any bitterness' (Williams 29). How true is this sentiment of 'Gray's Elegies' in *The Land I Came Through Last*? Does he write without bitterness? One might expect, through the passing of time and the accumulated deaths of loved ones, to find a further tempering of Gray's tone towards his father in his autobiography, demonstrating the genre's great capacity to resolve the past. Certainly Geoffrey's final years

---

9   Gray alludes to a second experience of fatherhood, becoming a kind of stepfather to his long-time partner Dee's daughter Harriet (334–5). A photograph provided of the author with a young Harriet suggests a successful paternal relationship may have been later achieved (333).

afforded a kind of reconciliation between father and son – the older man's frailty stirring mixed emotions that again recalls Roth's *Patrimony* – though in Gray's rendering the father appears no less monstrous than previously. Of Gray's patience and persistence in the face of his father's continued belittlement, Adamson asks, 'I kept wondering why he went back time and again for more. Maybe for some basic approval?' (*The Land* 23). That it is never forthcoming should cause us to admire Gray's forbearance. But even here things do not feel right, as if something is missing in the emotional tone the author adopts.

The deaths of Gray's parents, set in stark opposition, conclude his narrative:

> My mother died quite differently from my father. Her life evaporated in the night, with no one noticing. She was typically gentle, isolated, self-effacing. My father died while making yet another attempt at escape; there was a crashing noise from his room at about one in the morning. He should have been asleep, but they found him fully dressed in his day clothes, except for the tie that he had been putting on. He died before a full-length mirror fitted on the inside of his wardrobe door. Life exceeds art: in his heart attack, he fell forward, and was left kneeling, his forehead propped against his broken image. (435)

'Life Exceeds Art' would have made an apt title for *The Land I Came Through Last*. Gray implies both that his parents died as they had lived, and that their deaths, like much of Gray's life, were appropriately novelistic. Gray's father in particular seems never to have been properly prepared for life, a disjunction between the gentlemanly way he purported himself and the extremity of his alcoholism: 'My father informed me once he could never be called a drunkard while ever his shoes were clean' (17). Yet the last sentence is apt in another way: for in his 'art' of autobiography, Gray becomes a mirror of his father.

'A Distinction I Did Not Want': Resembling the Father

These contrasting deaths echo the structure of Gray's poem 'Diptych', which sets contrasting portraits of Gray's parents alongside each other. As Gray comments of the poem: 'In a way, I was fortunate that they were so different: I was able to see the inadequacies of both their extreme temperaments' (in Williams 27). Yet while 'Diptych' achieves a synergy in its consideration of these two opposing characters, this balance seems somewhat lacking in *The Land I Came Through Last*. Gray's claim of his father that, 'I can imagine no one/with a manner more easily, and coolly, precise' (*Poems* 137), seems oddly appropriate when applied to the 'formal, Victorian register' of his autobiography.[10] In seeking to avoid the 'inadequacies of both of their extreme temperaments' (and of others such as White and Gray's aunts), Gray manages to convey very little authentic emotion in his autobiography. Any genuine 'self' seems so embedded within his self-consciously mannered style as to be virtually irretrievable. For Gray as autobiographer, as he claims of his father, 'manner' seems to have 'subsumed all of feeling' (*Poems* 137).

A corollary to this is the fact that despite seeming ultimately to eschew the influence of his father in favour of his mother, it is the father who, despite his best intentions, seems reflected in Gray himself. Perhaps the closest Gray comes to unqualified tribute in his autobiography is late in his text:

> Since she died, I have noticed that it is mostly my mother's nature that survives in me, and only with her descendants, among whom it will randomly reappear, will it really end. I can feel her warmth, as a person, possess me [...] the feeling that if we could only get things just right, in our beliefs, we would be transformed; her sense of *vanitas*. (434, emphasis original)

It is an appealing sentiment – that despite the obvious differences in their religious convictions and the gap this created between them, the positive aspects of the mother live on in the son – that his inheritance is the preservation of her searching nature. Yet the statement rings false. Gray has disparaged his mother's consolations and compensatory beliefs with too much frequency and vigour for one to accept, as the text draws to a close, that the author has inherited from his mother 'the feeling that if we could only get things just right, in our beliefs, we would be transformed'. From the little Gray reveals about his siblings, it is easier to imagine that in them the mother's nature may 'randomly appear'. Notwithstanding the author's seeming desire for it to be otherwise, what is demonstrated in *The Land I Came Through Last* is the aptness of this phrase in relation to the father's nature.

Considering the difficult and at times fractured relationship between father and son, it is hardly surprising that the author would at times explicitly draw distinctions between his father and himself. As a defining characteristic of the father is his drinking, Gray is prompted often to remind us of his moderation in this regard (284). During his short stint at an advertising agency in Sydney,

---

10 Gray spoke at the launch of *The Land I Came Through Last* of his need for different registers to portray the various people and periods in his life. He described requiring a 'formal, Victorian register' for 'those kind of people', meaning Gray's father and Patrick White in particular. (Unpublished launch speech, 12 September 2008.)

Gray records his first experience of drunkenness – one he finds distinctly unpleasant: 'I wondered if that could have been how my father felt, on the occasions when he staggered by the roadside, and fell down. How could it have not created an aversion?' (316). The contrast is drawn more explicitly when the author encounters other substances: 'It felt to me that because they were mechanical, drugs turned you into an object for yourself; more than ever divided, wrenched about like a gear stick' (318). In almost every aspect of his life, Gray's father seems to have been 'an object for himself', though the second of Gray's descriptions, relating to self-division, is apt not for father but for son, despite Gray's aversion to drugs.

Another point of contrast between father and son is their literary allegiances. Literature plays a fascinating role in Gray's relationship with his father. Early in the text, Gray describes his father as 'formidably well-read. This seems the right word for such a jealously possessed distinction' (11). Despite their shared love of reading, books become a point of conflict, a subject of brinkmanship, and ultimately a tool for the son to assert his independence. As Gray explains:

> When it appeared that I had some ability in English, he began challenging me to identify quotations. His manner was, as usual, disparaging. I learned that these lines were nearly all from Kipling, Longfellow, or Browning, and very soon I could outwit him, just on the 'feel' of the quotation. He gave that away. None of those are poets that I can stand. (In Williams 28)

As in interview, rarely does the topic of the father's taste in literature come up in *The Land I Came Through Last* without Gray pointing out what little interest these authors are to him. This is true also of White's literary recommendations, such as Dostoyevsky, whom Gray 'detested' (364). Interestingly, Gray leaves the reader in no doubt as to his own 'superior' taste in literature, dedicating many passages of his autobiography to detailing his life of reading (176–8, 230, 289, 326–7, 344–5, 364–5).

The pivotal contrast Gray draws between his father and himself regards success. In a telling exchange between Gray and a nurse at his father's nursing home, Gray responds to her assertion of his love for his father by explaining: 'I wouldn't say I love him [...] I'm bothered by him. His life has been such a waste' (408). Waste is a recurrent notion in relation to the author's father, implying as it does both an achievement-based assessment of worth and a firmly held sense that the father could have been much more than the 'failure' he became, though unlike Freadman's *Shadow of Doubt*, here we find no attempt to redeem the father's life by writing of it. In drawing comparison between White and his father, Gray highlights the chasm between their accomplishments: 'The difference between Patrick and my father was, of course, extreme: that of a Nobel Prize winner on the one side, an all-round failure on the other' (352). The comparison is also relevant – and more fraught – between father and son:

> I sometimes imagine I lived the sort of life that my father might have wanted, although his love of evocation with words and of precision in language was not nearly as strong as mine. I usually end up admitting he would not have had the resolve for such a life. (343–4)

Even here, it is as if the author cannot resist the urge to place himself above his father, to draw distinction not only between their achievements, but between their talents. To give him credit, the author concedes further similarities with his father amongst the many contrasts, although by no means unreservedly: 'I realise I have been as self-absorbed as he was, as indifferent to other people's opinion, in the pursuit of my enthusiasm, and almost equally as irresponsible, in some eyes. There has been, though, no self-destructiveness' (344). Gray's qualification 'in some eyes' seems again an echo of the father's victim-mentality. Tellingly, the key difference between father and son, according to Gray, is the harm Geoffrey inflicted on himself rather than his treatment of others. While it would certainly be unjust to claim that this son has been as toxic a presence on those around him as the father, the distinction Gray seems most proud of is that he did not drink himself to death.

Late in the text the author quotes from a notebook written in 1974 to establish an epiphany he had about his father's drinking. It is again revealing with regard to his mixed feelings about his father's selfishness: 'He was a functional alcoholic, not a binge drinker. His only problem was our objection. His relentless conceit, self-centeredness. A determined wastrel. Almost admirable, in his independence' (404). Gray's language incenses Adamson: 'A wastrel? What a lame word to use. Gray is a wily poet, so what is this exactly? Bravado, or possibly anti-hero worship? Was Gray reading his father's copy of Somerset Maugham's *The Moon and Sixpence* at the time? Maybe love really is blind' ('Like a Dog' 23). Rather than disposing us favourably towards him for cutting his father 'some slack', Gray's empathy and admiration for Geoffrey's 'independence' draws him ever closer to the relational ineptitude of his patrimonial heritage.

An interesting way the father and son intersect is in the manner that Gray fixates on Geoffrey's use of puns and allusions. A telling exchange in the text occurs when the son disparages the father's use of puns as 'the lowest form of humour' and the father agrees: 'Strangely, it was this small, passing comment about puns which first made me conscious of my father's deep pessimism towards himself – I seemed to catch a glimpse of his self-distaste, beneath what

I had taken to be invulnerable conceit' (22). Again, there seems something instructive in this description of the father when applied to the book itself. Gray's own self-assurance is destabilised by an undercurrent of inauthenticity in the work, a self set against itself or somehow disassembled beneath the surface of the 'invulnerable conceit' of his writing.

Yet despite this early disdain of his father's 'narcissistic' humour (18), the author proceeds to record his most memorable puns with exasperating frequency throughout his text, regardless of their racist or homophobic overtones (19–22, 201, 236–7, 403, 411). One of the more disquieting moments in the book comes when Gray records his own flirtatious pun in an exchange with his father's nurse: 'My name's Richard, but I don't mind if you abbreviate it [...] I suppose you're going to tell me your name's Virginia' (408). Perhaps our discomfort is caused in part by Australians' innate dislike of those who recount demonstrations of their own sharp-wittedness, a cultural aversion Gray himself notes in recounting a conversation with David Malouf about Bruce Chatwin's showy anecdotes. Despite Gray's self-deprecating aside: 'I'm afraid so. Nothing too rarefied, I had decided', the scene feels disconcertingly showy, an excuse to exhibit the author's easy charm. In short, it feels like something his father would do.[11]

Ego and conceit seem another shared trait of father and son, and one which, when recognised in the other, further problematises their relationship. Though undercut by his 'secretive discomfort', the father's 'invulnerable conceit' is regularly remarked upon by the author. In turn, the father's growing displeasure with his oldest son is linked to the author's capacity for self-regard: 'I had many conflicts with my father, my part almost invariably reactive. His mockery fastened on my "narcissism", as he called it, an air of self-involvement I had, [...] on my "getting about myself"' (179). In describing a visit Gray's partner Dee makes to a Zen Centre monastery in San Francisco, the author comments that, 'There was a freshness about the experience, which she identified as a lack of egotism' (373). It is an otherwise seemingly innocuous aside, yet the line is jarring in an autobiography that seems overburdened with ego. What makes the book such an uncomfortable reading experience is the way it posits so many extreme, 'larger-than-life' figures (and didactically expressed opinions)

---

11 No less disquieting is the pun-based exchange between father and son regarding White's sexuality: 'He's one of those petulant people, isn't he? The ones who get excited about each other's waste-disposal apparatus' (404). Though Gray cannot match his father's puerility, he nonetheless retorts 'irritably, I haven't told him, "get behind me Satan"'. As Adamson remarks, rather than taking umbrage at his father's remark, 'Gray interprets this as a father's inept concern for the son's morals', and most extraordinary of all, 'what most disappoints Gray is that his father doesn't even smile at this attempt to match his wordplay' ('Like a Dog' 23).

alongside each other, at times vying for attention. The author's valorisation of David Hume and rational thought (348–50), his defense of Murray against 'the leftist literati' (339–43), and his towering portrait of White contribute to the book's suffocating sense of male reputation and self-regard.

To what extent does an awareness of ego in the other contribute to self-awareness with regard to Gray and his father? Their relational self-conceptualisation is strangely complex. On the one hand, the author is capable of insights such as this: 'I knew, although it stung at the time, that my mother had been right about my egotism. My father saw into my vanity, too. He was always ready to discomfort me with it, though even I understood it was compensatory' (124). Yet on the other, the author's dichotomised, confused mixture of recognition of and differentiation from his father make any notion of a relational self in his autobiography difficult to identify. In his preface the author states that, though he tries for an 'objective' representation of others, 'A writer can only hope to create a sense of his subjects by accumulating their gestures; he has to trust that within his encircling imagery, if it is insistent enough, the dead will appear for a moment, like a glimmer on the waves' (2). The author indeed captures an astounding performance of masculinity by accumulating his father's mannered gestures. But what of the self? Gray's coup in *The Land I Came Through Last* may be that though he succeeds in being revelatory in his representation of others, he ironically reveals no tangible or stable self. The author's description of 'encircling imagery', with its implications of containment, seems telling in this regard. What is he trying to hold back? Though the work is unfailingly honest and confessional in nature, disclosing many unflattering self-revelations, one is left to wonder what has been omitted.

There are numerous instances of Gray's doubling with his father. As Ian Templeman notes, 'flicking backwards and forwards between the photographs, one recognises a strong physical resemblance between father and son' (33), though it is much more than this. When he realises that his aunts are favouring him due to 'having being singled out from photographs as "a Gray"', the author states starkly that it was 'a distinction I did not want' (154). One indeed sees, in the heavily grained image of the author as a boy (178) a resemblance with the photograph of the father as a child (37) that is more than merely physical: Gray, too, fairly 'preens'. Likewise, the image of his father in uniform (61), in which 'he appears to have just swaggered into his pose' (60) finds some accord with the ethereal and glamorous photographs the author provides of himself as a man (290, 314, 318). Though coming from different eras stylistically, these are evidently men for whom 'style' and poise are vitally important. The author describes his father's appearance as unusual 'for the care that he took with it' (17) and asserts that, 'despite his looks, my father was vain' (18). Of himself, the author remarks, 'It was my good luck, given my temperament and physique, to have come of age in a decade in which a more nuanced type of male was the most acceptable to women, or fashionable to them' (318). Though only one image is given of Gray's paternal grandfather, it would not be stretching things to propose a certain continuity to this patrimonial line; despite their inclination to disown each other, being a male Gray involves a certain interest in style.

'The Gentleman Possessing a Coded Manner': Gray's Preoccupation with Style

Having successfully pitched the idea of a biography of Gray's father and White to his publishers, mostly due to public interest in the latter, the author was paid 'a generous advance' which by late 1993 'I have now spent, and the book is only a quarter done. I am probably writing it fuelled only by honour, now, and an interest in the problems of style. I hope these will get me to the finish' (23). Gray's interest in the problems of style feels informative here in relation to the time it took to finally publish the work, and also to its highly mannered prose, which contributes to the book's lack of immediacy: an important characteristic of his poetry. Another description of Gray's father seems pertinent in relation to his book. In explaining the father's conception of a gentleman, Gray writes, 'The gentleman as someone considerate to others was not his concern, however; it was only the gentleman as possessing a certain coded manner; a style, which preoccupied him' (7). Likewise, in Gray's performance of autobiography, 'the problems of style' dominate over ethical questions of representation, or even of being considerate to others.

This is no more apparent than in Gray's descriptions of scattering of his parents' ashes. Though these events take place 30 years apart, they are paralleled closely in the text, occurring as they do at the same location, and in the narrative follow on from an inadequate funeral service. The morning after his father's funeral, Gray and his brother rise early the next morning and drive to the top of a hill overlooking the ocean. In prying open his father's urn with a pocket-knife, Gray slips and cuts his thumb deeply, stating:

> I sighed with pain, yet felt instantly this was right. With the dripping hand I scooped up the ashes and strewed them, although I glimpsed my brother's distaste. In a vast relinquishment, I felt the pity of it all. The dark hours of my father's life were done, and I saw how we rise and are consumed, infinite particles, driven before the light. A phrase came unexpectedly into mind, from Heinrich Heine. 'You, proud heart, you have what you desired.' (413)

One senses the author's desire for language, including his striking imagery, to somehow do the work of tribute that cannot be done directly, knowing that no one else will succeed if the great poet fails.

The author returns to the same spot following his mother's death, because 'nowhere else seemed possible' (435). It again follows an 'austere, unemotive' Jehovah's Witness memorial service. In typically imagistic prose, the author sets the scene: 'The day looked thwarted and metallic. It was chill out on the hillslope, amid the wide sluice of silver grass. The grey sea, stiff as mud, barely stirred' (435). As he scatters his mother's ashes, the author states, 'I could not overcome my disgust that rattling dice should decide what one's single experience of life would be. Both of us made, with its brutal irony, an open, immemorial gesture' (435). It is an oddly prosaic description in a work remarkable for its clarity of description, implying perhaps the author's desire to shield this very private moment from full exposure. Then again, Gray is fond of the grand immemorial gesture. One senses again in the author's crafted prose an attempt to redeem his childhood or his mother's life, even if it is only through the gesture of his exceptional writing. But what we are left with, once again, is little more than poetic display.

Conclusion: His Father's Son

Critics of Gray's poetry have often highlighted a curious disjunction in his use of imagery to reveal 'objective nature'. In 1979 Robert Adamson noted that, 'In almost every poem Gray discovers an object [...] then immediately looks about to see if it is like something else. Everything in Gray's work is something other than it is' (67), asserts Adamson, which is roughly the opposite of Gray's formulation that 'the world is as it reliably appears'. Angus Nicholls writes that, 'Through Gray's use of the simile, we are not given "objective nature"; rather we see nature as it appears to Gray subjectively' (106). In other words, the poet's near-reflex tendency to allow almost nothing to simply be itself seems to contradict his ostensible project to record nature in the most objective form possible. Charting a gradual movement away from a stance of 'objectivity' in his poetry, Alan Urquhart notes in Gray's later work a 'realisation by the poet that such objectivity can never be objectively "objective", but simply another mask or pose' (54). This disjunction has led critics to wonder what is being repressed. Urquhart calls it 'the concealment of the darker side of the poet's personality' (48). Adamson states simply that, 'It *is* fair to ask the question, where's Gray?' ('Review' 69, emphasis in the original). Gray's curious construal of his subject matter in poetry, one compounded by a stance that denies any such act of interpretation is taking place, is mirrored by his claim to 'objectivity' in an autobiography so curiously mannered and elusive. What ultimately stands out in *The Land I Came Through Last* is the remarkable level of dissimulation, which, whether conscious or not, makes it difficult to feel with any assurance that this is an encounter with an authentic autobiographical self.

While its many echoes of *Father and Son* serve to prove my contention regarding the ongoing relevance of this paradigm case in an Australian context, one may excuse Gosse many of his excessive pronouncements and stylistic immoderation, writing as he did as one of the last bastions of high Victorianism. Writing exactly 100 years later, Gray's autobiographical pose appears utterly strange in the context of contemporary son–father auto/biographies. From where does such a performance of autobiography originate? Upon consideration of the father of Gray's text, the precedent becomes clear. Although Gray portrays a 'toxic' father who is thoroughly irredeemable, his construction of relationality is such that no figure of his auto/biography is afforded an elegiac representation. Therefore, while it is as far from hagiography as one could imagine an autobiography being, *The Land I Came Through Last* ultimately serves to convince us that Robert Gray, despite himself, is indeed his father's son.

Conclusion

THE TURN TO THE FATHER IN AUTOBIOGRAPHY

God the father, land of our fathers, forefathers, founding fathers all refer to an origin or source, to what generated us, to an authority. We fall into the paternal line. Patronymic as identity.
—Siri Hustvedt, 'My Father Myself'

Between states of belonging and alienation, you try to keep afloat [...] You lose your father and the city you love. You bring both back to life, summon both to a distant country your children know as home. You discover or create this longing for your dead father, and reconstruct a lost city for him and you to inhabit. In between, the city and your father have become so abstract that you panic and try to pin them down in words; but when they visit you in dreams, their corporeality, their aliveness startle you. [...] So begins your impossible project.
—Kim Cheng Boey, *Between Stations*

He goes with his father to Newlands because sport – rugby in winter, cricket in summer – is the strongest surviving bond between them, and because it went through his heart like a knife, the first Saturday after his return to the country, to see his father put on his coat and without a word go off to Newlands like a lonely child. [...] So he is cast back on his father, as his father is cast back on him. As they live together, so on Saturdays they take their pleasure together. That is the law of the family.
—J. M. Coetzee, *Summertime*

While son–father auto/biographies have been written for at least the past 100 years, investigations of patrimony seem presently to be gathering pace to the point where one might propose that they constitute a verifiable movement. Of course, the impulse to write the father exists within the larger field of relational auto/biography that has developed apace for the past two decades. Autobiographies that focus on parents now constitute an eminently marketable branch of life writing for which the reading public's appetite appears insatiable. Despite significant sociological shifts in the structure of the family since the Second World War, the desire to write of one's parents seems impervious to (and in part driven by) changes to the traditional family unit, demonstrated by the number of works detailing the search for lost or unaccountable fathers.

In tracking a 'turn to the father' in auto/biography by male authors, I do not necessarily imply a consequent 'turn from the mother', although this book has detailed individual examples of such a pattern. Rather, this focus on a patrimonial frame should be read within a series of broader trends in literary and cultural studies. The first of these is that feminist theory and gender studies have rendered masculinity 'visible', revealing the extent to which it functioned previously as a kind of 'normative' gender. Secondly, feminist criticism has made the patrimonial political, so that any representation of masculinity is a challenge to other representations and simultaneously available to be disputed itself. This has led to masculinity being a contested subject position, meaning that there are competing ways of 'being male'. An increasing interest in the father in autobiography and his influence on a writer-son's masculinity is therefore a result of this shift.

In his recent book *Postcolonial Life Writing*, Bart Moore Gilbert argues that feminism and a turn to women's writing in the recent past has had an important but potentially distorting influence on the field of autobiography studies (xvi–xxi). As Gillian Whitlock has noted, Moore Gilbert seems to indicate not only that autobiographical writing by women has occasionally been emphasised at the expense of good writing by men, but also that feminist-inflected criticism has been hegemonic.[1] The attention to writing by men and to discourses of patrimony as a shaping field of intertextual autobiographical narrative in this book seems timely.

Nevertheless, the practice of studying the father–son relationship seems not without its risks, reframing attention as it does on distinctly 'male' notions of personhood that were, up until recently, the dominant mode of conceptualising culture and identity. Does a study such as mine re-privilege 'male matters', whilst forcing the feminine, or indeed any other category of gender, to the margins once again? Craig Howes' observation that 'the topic of ethics and life writing seemed patriarchal almost by definition' (247) appears to carry through in this book: the overwhelming majority of theorists and critics addressed here are male and write about notions of identity in a way that, despite their ostensible focus on patrimony, do not always sufficiently acknowledge assumptions regarding essentialist notions of selfhood. As a 'privileged' white male critic, I too am implicated in this trend.

---

1 Personal correspondence with Whitlock, January 2010.

A brief anecdote illustrates the contested space of gender in autobiographical criticism. Of the forty-odd participants at a recent conference on autobiography and therapy in Australia, only two were male. Many of the presenters engaged explicitly with feminist theories, a number of who discussed their process of writing their own memoirs. During the question time following my paper on *Rose Boys*, a number of participants questioned my approach of analysing the text as a narrative of patrimony, expressing concern that 'reading for the father' might re-inscribe masculinity as the normative gender in literature and once again render the feminine invisible in such texts. In my interview with Rose following my paper, the author himself appeared to echo this sentiment to a degree, explaining that, 'There is another way of reading the memoir. Some readers have formed a tremendous affection and admiration for the portrait of my mother [...] They respond to her endless, systemic compassion' (in Mansfield, 'Cathartic' 28). Though I have impugned my authors for tentativeness at various points, I must admit to residual anxieties about my project.

Tracking the Turn to the Father

This increased focus on the father is by no means restricted to an Australian literary context. Roger J. Porter's recent study *Bureau of Missing Persons* explores what he terms 'The Child's Book of Parental Deception' in such countries as Britain, Australia and the United States, with a focus on sons and daughters who write of discovering in middle age that their fathers led secret lives. Porter charts the ethics of exposing the father's concealment, and develops his exploration of autobiographers as 'sleuths of selfhood'. Two separate works on the subject by G. Thomas Couser are simultaneously in progress: a book-length study of patriographies in North America, currently titled *Our Fathers*, and a memoir of the author's own father ('Closet' 890). For Couser, as for Freadman and Eakin, the father has proved autobiographically inevitable.

In part, such studies are driven by the fact that Books of the Father continue to be written and published. Two very recent examples from expatriate writers in Australia are Kim Cheng Boey's collection of autobiographical essays *Between Stations* (2009) and J. M. Coetzee's 'fictional biography' *Summertime* (2009). Equal parts travel writing, intellectual autobiography and a memoir of childhood, *Between Stations* is a paean to the lost Singapore of Boey's memories, and a related attempt to understand his father, who abandoned his family when the author was a young boy and who has remained a shadowy presence in the son's life even after his premature death. Importantly, it was the act of emigrating to Australia with his young family and becoming an Australian citizen that triggers Boey's impulse to the write the father/fatherland, demonstrating not only that patriography is typically entwined with nationhood, but also that

Australian patriography is not bounded by national borders. As he reflects on his own experience of fatherhood, Boey's text becomes a profound meditation on the relationship between sons and fathers. A poet and lecturer in creative writing at Newcastle University, Boey observes:

> Fathers dead or alive are a recurrent theme in writing workshops. We talk about the errant ones, the absent and the prodigal, the tyrannical patriarchs, the silent and impenetrable ones who lead hidden lives. Mostly the fathers that appear in the poems and stories are safely dead and the dead have no means of answering back, correcting our skewed versions, our half-fictions we tell ourselves in order to make sense of what happened, to make amends. [...] memoir is a way of getting right in writing what went wrong in real life. It is a second chance, a way of rewriting the script to save yourself. Not the dead. They don't need that. (260)

Summertime, Coetzee's third volume of his 'fictionalised memoir' series, finds the author continuing to write of the self tangentially, eschewing any notion of author biography. *Summertime* poses as the notes and interviews for a posthumous biography of John Coetzee, compiled by a young academic named Vincent. Though set largely in South Africa, the novel was written after the author became an Australian citizen, in 2006. Throughout the many unflattering accounts of the famous author given by friends and ex-lovers in *Summertime*, the father remains a disquieting presence in the text. With John's mother having passed away, Coetzee senior and junior appear as a hapless couple, uncomfortably inhabiting the same house in a kind of domestic negation. The final lines of the text finally slip back into the first person, and as the father declines into death the diarist ends at the point of disavowal:

> He is going to have to abandon some of his personal projects and be a nurse. Alternatively, if he will not be a nurse, he must announce to his father: *I cannot face the prospect of ministering to you day and night. I am going to abandon you. Goodbye.* One or the other: there is no third way. (265–6, emphasis in the original)

One senses that the next wave of Australian patriography will broaden (and further complicate) the emerging picture of father–son relations in this country, and will include many expatriate writers and post–World War II second-generation migrants from Singapore, South Africa and elsewhere.

Reading for Ambivalence

Based on the texts analysed in this book, the dominant mode of the Australian Son's Book is the ambivalent representation of the father, though this is not to situate this mode as an in-between point on the elegiac-denunciatory spectrum. I concur with Redman that 'The "presence" of ambivalence can only be a starting point for interpretation. We need to inquire whether in a given case ambivalence is manifestly present and, if so, how it is constructed and expressed' (130). Freadman's ambivalence is of a different order to Gray's, for example. Whilst the former sets out to pay tribute to the father, Paul Freadman's textual elusiveness and the ongoing effects of his 'failed' life on the son cause the contradictory desire to triumph over the legacy of the father, as the author himself acknowledges. Gray sets out 'neither to vindicate nor to vilify' his father and his resulting ambivalence contributes to his inadvertent textual resemblance to the 'toxic' patrimony he portrays. Gray's confused and oscillating emotions towards the father were aptly expressed in his first poem on the subject, which is quoted as an epigraph for Chapter Seven.

Of the ambivalent representations of patrimony discussed here, I find Hughes's *The Idea of Home* to be the most ethical, or perhaps the most 'constructive' construction of this relationship.[2] Why? In part, this is due to his text being a kind of working through of his ambivalence, resulting in a satisfactory resolution of his anxieties about the father–son relationship and a fitting tribute. In Hughes's autobiographical strain to know and be authentically connected to his patrimony, he strikes an equipoise between ethics and truth-telling that is not found in any other Son's Book explored. He is aided by his chosen genre of the autobiographical essay form: partially freed from the constraints of narrative, the author's writing process becomes an attempt to understand – or a 'groping for' – the father, even whilst acknowledging his ultimate unknowability.

Due to the overwhelming presence of ambivalence, Freadman's term The Son's Book of the Father is strikingly apt. The capitalisation confers an ambiguous weight to the genre, recalling Edmund Gosse's paradoxical, and possibly even specious, claim of *Father and Son* as 'a monument' to the father. Many authors (including Freadman) conceive of their work as a kind of 'gift' to the father or to the family, whilst at the same time embracing a candour and revealing an ambivalence that may cause us to wonder about the appropriateness of such a term. In the gospel of Matthew, Jesus uses the assumption of fatherly care as an exemplar for God's love, asking: 'Which of you, if his son asks for bread, will give him a stone? Or if he asks for a fish, will give him a snake?' (Matthew 7:9–10, NIV). We might ask the same of the

---

2 I have excluded *Rose Boys* from this determination, though some of the complexities of patrimonial ambivalence identified here befall Rose's construction of the fraternal frame.

son's 'gift' to the father. One imagines that a Son's Book may often appear to the father as more a stone or a snake. On first reading, one takes Freadman's *of* in similarly positive terms, perhaps glossing a preposition such as *for* or *to* in its place, raising expectations that the genre will unequivocally celebrate the father. However, on further consideration, *of* is usefully invested with ambiguity regarding what kind of portrait such a text will contain.

The limitation of Freadman's term, however, exists in the word 'father'. As my analysis demonstrates, these texts often conceive of patrimonial relationships beyond the strict 'father–son' dyad. Three key authors – Freadman, Hughes and Gray – frame their maternal grandfathers as offering an alternative version of masculinity, and even patrimony, to that offered by the father. They identify a pattern of triangulation where, as Freadman observed, each person's relation with one of the others is mediated by his relation with the third. In Rose's Brothers' Book of the Father, this triangulated pattern involves competing performances of sonship by male siblings. Others, such as Gaita and Gray, cast the patrimonial net even wider to include proximate males outside of the biological family. These men act as surrogate father figures in competition with the father for influence, and ultimately, for which patrimonial inheritance a writer-son chooses. For this reason, I favour my term 'patrimonial life narratives' for such texts.

My term has further advantages, focussing attention as it does on the narratological aspects of the genre. As discussed, particularly in chapters three and four, the demands of narrative and other aspects of autobiography as a literary form means a Son's Book must negotiate the conventions and limitations inherent in the act of representing patrimony within this frame. As relational auto/biography about male intersubjectivity, the Son's Book exists in an uneasy tension with its literary predecessors – slung awkwardly between canonical or traditional autobiography that privileges Romantic Selfhood, autonomy and an ethics of assertion, and relational life writing, which emphasises connectedness and an ethics of renunciation. As a result, some masculinities and patrimonies pose particular obstacles to being portrayed in such narratives. Added to this is the elusiveness of the dominant model of the father in the Australian context – the reticent-laconic – who in various ways resists representation.

Accounting for the Turn

What has caused this turn to the father in autobiography? Couser marks the increasing emergence of 'father memoirs' by both male and female authors from 1985 in the North American context, and has suggested at least two reasons for their prevalence. First, Couser notes the demographic influence of the 'North American baby boomer generation', which has largely taken up the project of writing the father, and sees as crucial the occasion of this generation's parents reaching old age and facing death: 'As the parents of this large and influential cohort age, become ill or disabled, and die, baby boomers ponder their parents' lives and, not incidentally, their own mortality' ('Presenting' 638).[3] The second is that the economic necessities of the modern, that is, post-war nuclear family, 'which was often categorized by an absent bread-winning father and an available stay-at home mother', have paradoxically resulted in the autobiographer's desire to seek the unknown in their writing and largely ignore the known. As the typically distant, absent or elusive parent, the father invites life writers to search them out in the act of writing: 'Unfair it may be, but in memoir the available parent tends to get taken for granted while the memoirist pursues the elusive one' (644).

Couser's first observation resonates with the Australian baby boomers discussed here. Gaita's and Freadman's (and to a lesser extent Gray's) experiences of watching their fathers decline into death inevitably colour and propel their works. Similarly, the inequitable decision of American life writers to search out and write the lesser-known parent holds in the Australian context. What I have termed the absent-present, reticent-laconic Aussie father pervades this entire study, troubling their sons with their unrepresentability. However, it is worth noting that none of the fathers discussed here would qualify for Roger Porter's study of the 'missing person' who led a secret life, at least to the extent that their sons are willing to bear witness.[4] Nor did any, with the exception of the mysterious Charlie of *The Boy Adeodatus*, abdicate their father-role by abandoning the family.

Born in 1961, Hughes is the only author who comes close to falling outside of the period designated to the baby boomer generation (typically 1946–64). Hughes's mode of 'ethical ambivalence' could cause us to speculate that the next generation of son–father auto/biographers will construct a less fraught, more settled relationship with their patrimonial inheritances. Further, this next generation of fathers' increasing involvement in the task of child-rearing must surely have an influence on how they are represented by their author-children.

What other factors may have caused such a concentrated focus on the father in contemporary Australian life writing? At the risk of standing on the

---

3   Couser notes that the majority of 'dementia narratives' are written by daughters, who typically become the designated caregiver.
4   Perhaps Merv Lilley's *Gatton Man* would qualify for Porter's sub-genre, though in this case the author only *accuses* his father of triple homicide, without the requisite evidence demanded by Porter's sleuths of selfhood.

same set of shoulders once too often, I quote the observation from Freadman that inspired the present study:

> Australian autobiography has produced a disproportionate number of examples of the Son's Book of the Father – an indication that this culture has rendered father–son relationships complex, perhaps even problematical. Various strands of cultural influence are at work here: the British 'stiff upper lip' ethos of emotional diffidence and inhibition; the bush ethos with its insistence on masculine self-sufficiency, stoicism, physical endurance, loyal but incurious styles of mateship; the bifurcation of parenting gender roles, both in the city and the country, where emotional closeness with children tends to be seen as the mother's prerogative; an edgy mistrust of self-analysis; the relative lack of an aristocratic class that condones and fosters less 'manly' styles of male conduct, identification with the arts and other non-sporting modes of self-expression; a 'knockabout' laconism that secures emotional ease at the cost of an openness to the inner life. (*Shadow of Doubt* 178)

Any impulse to dismiss the influence of 'the bush ethos' in a modern Australian context should be resisted here. Of the key authors here, only Freadman describes an urban upbringing. Likewise Freadman's insistence on the 'edgy mistrust of self-analysis' in Australia feels apt. He is the only author to engage explicitly with psychoanalysis in his text. A clear majority of the remaining writer-sons, while at times dismissive of their own fathers' lack of an inner life, fall somewhat short in their own propensity for systematic self-probing.

One might add two further reasons for the prevalence of the patrimonial frame, and to believe that the turn to the father will continue to form an ongoing examination of competing forms of masculinity in this country. The first, alluded to by Freadman, is the lasting currency and influence of the ANZAC tradition and its accompanying valorisation of the myths of mateship, demonstrated by the enduring popularity of texts like A. B. Facey's *A Fortunate Life*. The fact that the last of those who served in the two world wars will not be alive much beyond the next decade may likely escalate the focus on what these generations of fathers have bequeathed to us. The second is the accompanying strain of hyper-nationalism that has become prominent in the past decade, which often manifests as an aggressive or 'traditional' masculinity. While none of the contemporary texts explored here are consciously political in their constructions of masculinity, one may detect in Rose's or Hughes' portrayal, for example, the implicit wish to hold up a model of Australian fatherhood that defies certain stereotypes of the 'Aussie bloke'.

Whatever the case, considering such contested space, one may speculate that the next generation of son–father auto/biographers will continue to engage with the valorisation and vilification of competing versions of masculinity. My sense is that this turn to the father has not yet reached its full calibration, and that author-sons will continue to create monuments and tributes to, mount searches and performances for, elucidate defences and denouncements of, and seek dialogue and resolution with their patrimonial inheritances through the act of writing autobiographically.

BIBLIOGRAPHY

Adamson, Jane, Richard Freadman and David Parker (eds). *Renegotiating Ethics in Literature, Philosophy and Theory* Cambridge: Cambridge University Press, 1998
Adamson, Robert. 'Review of *Grass Script*'. *New Poetry* 27.4 (1979): 67–70
———. 'Like a Dog Pointing'. *Australian Literary Review* (December 2008): 23
Allen, Peter. 'Sir Edmund Gosse and his Modern Readers: The Continued Appeal of *Father and Son*'. *ELH* 55.2 (Summer 1988): 487–503
Anderson, Linda. *Autobiography: The New Critical Idiom*. London: Routledge, 2001
Arnade, Charles W. 'A Teacher's Search for His Immigrant Family's Memories'. *Antipodes* 19.2 (December 2005): 229–30
Ashcroft, Bill. *On Post-colonial Futures: Transformations of Colonial Cultures*. London: Continuum, 2001
Attridge, Derek. *The Singularity of Literature*. London: Routledge, 2004
Augustine, Saint, Bishop of Hippo. *Confessions of Saint Augustine*, trans. W. Watts. London: Heinemann, 1946
Avildsen, John G. (dir.) *Rocky*. Moore Park: Twentieth Century Fox, 2007
Baier, Annette. 'Trust and Antitrust'. *Ethics* 96.2 (January 1986): 231–60
Barry, Elaine. *Robert Frost on Writing*. New Brunswick: Rutgers University Press, 1973
Barbour, John D. *Versions of Deconversion: Autobiography and the Loss of Faith*. Charlottesville: University of Virginia Press, 2004
———. 'Judging and Not Judging Parents'. *The Ethics of Life Writing* Ithaca, NY: Cornell University Press, 2004: 73–99
Benstock, Shari. *The Private Self*. London: Routledge, 1988
Boey, Kim Cheng. *Between Stations*. Artarmon: Giramondo Publishing, 2009
Bollen, Jonathan, Bruce Parr and Adrian Kiernander. *Men at Play: Masculinities in Australian Theatre since the 1950s*. Amsterdam: Rodopi, 2008
Booth, Wayne. *The Company We Keep*. Berkeley. University of California Press, 1988
Brooks-Davies, Douglas. *Fielding, Dickens, Gosse, Iris Murdoch and Oedipal Hamlet*. Basingstoke: Macmillan, 1989
Brown, Peter. *Augustine of Hippo*. Berkeley: University of California Press, 1967
Brown, Ruth. 'English Heritage and Australian Culture: The Church and Literature in England in *Oscar and Lucinda*'. *Australian Literary Studies* 17.2 (1995): 135–40
Buchbinder, David. *Performance Anxieties: Re-producing Masculinity*. St Leonards: Allen & Unwin, 1998
Buckley, Jerome H. *The Turning Key: Autobiography and the Subjective Impulse Since 1800*. Cambridge, MA: Harvard University Press, 1984
Buckley, Vincent. *Cutting Green Hay: Friendships, Movements and Cultural Conflicts in Australia's Great Decades*. Melbourne: Allen Lane, 1983

Burns, D. R. '*The Watcher on the Cast-Iron Balcony*: Hal Porter's Triumph of Creative Contradiction'. *Australian Literary Studies* 12.3 (May 1986): 359–66
Butler, Judith. 'Burning Acts: Injurious Speech'. In Andrew Parker and Eve Kosofsky Sedgwick (eds), *Performativity and Performance*. New York: Routledge: 1995: 197–227
Byrne, Mark Levon. *Myths of Manhood: The Hero in Jungian Literature*. Sydney: RLA Press, 2001
Callahan, David. 'Peter Carey's *Oscar and Lucinda* and the Subversion of Subversion'. *Australian Studies* 4 (December 1990): 20–26
Carey, Peter. *Oscar and Lucinda*. St Lucia: University of Queensland Press, 1988
Calvino, Italo. *The Road to San Giovanni*. London: Vintage Press, 1994
Charteris, Evan. *The Life and Letters of Sir Edmund Gosse*. London: William Heinemann, 1931
Coe, Richard N. 'The Mother of Narcissus'. *Island Magazine* 18/19 (Autumn/Winter 1984): 66–72
Coetzee, J. M. *Summertime: Scenes From a Provincial Life*. North Sydney: Random House, 2009
Colmer, Dorothy and John Colmer (eds). *The Penguin Book of Australian Autobiography*. Ringwood: Penguin, 1987
Colmer, John. *Australian Autobiography: The Personal Quest*. Melbourne: Oxford University Press, 1989
Connell, R. W. *Gender*. Cambridge: Polity Press, 2002
———. 'Australian Masculinities'. In Stephen Tomson and Mike Donaldson (eds), *Male Trouble: Looking at Australian Masculinities*. North Melbourne: Pluto Press, 2003
Connell, R. W. and James W. Messerschmidt. 'Hegemonic Masculinity: Rethinking the Concept'. *Gender and Society* 19.6 (2005): 829–59
Crosswell, Brent. 'This Unsporting Life'. In Peter Craven, *Best Australian Essays 2002*. Melbourne: Black Inc., 2002
Couser, G. Thomas. *Vulnerable Subjects*. Ithaca, NY: Cornell University Press, 2004
———. 'Genre Matters: Form, Force, Filiation'. *Life Writing* 2.2 (2005): 123–40
———. 'Presenting Absent Fathers in Contemporary Memoir'. *Southwest Review* 90.4 (2005): 634–48
———. 'In My Father's Closet: Reflections of a Critic Turned Life Writer' *Literary Compass* 8.12 (2011): 890–99
Cowen, Zelman. *A Public Life: The Memoirs of Sir Zelman Cowen*. Carlton: Melbourne University Press, 2006
Dack, Peter and Stephen Dack, with Larry Writer. *Sunshine and Shadow: A Brother's Story*. Millers Point: Pier 9, 2010
Dalziell, Rosamund. *Shameful Autobiographies*. South Carlton: Melbourne University Press, 1999
Davis, G. Rocio. 'Writing Fathers: Auto/biography and Unfulfilled Vocation in Sara Suleri Goodyear's *Boys Will be Boys* and Hanif Kureishi's *My Ear and his Heart*'. *Life Writing* 6.2 (2009): 229–41
Dalbey, Gordon. *Father and Son: The Wound, the Healing, the Call to Manhood*. Nashville: Thomas Nelson, 1992
Dalziell, Rosamund. *Shameful Autobiographies*. South Carlton: Melbourne University Press, 1999
de Man, Paul. *The Rhetoric of Romanticism* New York: Columbia University Press, 1984
Derrida, Jacques. *Of Grammatology*, trans. G. Spivak. Baltimore: Johns Hopkins University Press, 1976

———. *The Ear of the Other: Otobiography, Transference, Translation: Texts and Discussions with Jacques Derrida*, trans. Peggy Kamuf, ed. Christie McDonald. New York: Schocken Books, 1985
———. 'Circumfession'. In Jacques Derrida with Geoffrey Bennington, *Jacques Derrida*. Chicago: University of Chicago Press, 1993
———. *Adieu to Emmanuel Levinas*. Stanford: Stanford University Press, 1999
Dow Adams, Timothy. *Light Writing and Life Writing: Photography in Autobiography*. Chapel Hill: University of North Carolina Press, 2000
Dudley, David L. *My Father's Shadow: Intergenerational Conflict in African American Men's Autobiography*. Philadelphia: University of Pennsylvania Press, 1991
During, Simon. 'Literary Subjectivity'. In Association for the Study of Australian Literature, *Current Tensions: Proceedings of the 18th Annual Conference: 6–11 July 1996*, ed. Sharyn Pearce and Philip Neilsen. Brisbane: Queensland University of Technology, 1996: 1–12
Egan, Susanna and Gabrielle Helms. 'Editorial: Auto/biography? Yes. But Canadian?' *Canadian Literature* 172 (Spring 2002): 5–16
Eakin, John Paul. *Touching the World*. Princeton: Princeton University Press, 1992
———. *How Our Lives Become Stories*. New York: Cornwell University Press, 1999
———. *The Ethics of Life Writing* Ithaca, NY: Cornell University Press, 2004
———. *Living Autobiographically: How We Create Identity in Narrative*. Ithaca, NY: Cornell University Press, 2008
Featherstone, Don. *Beautiful Lies: A Film about Peter Carey*. Videorecording. Sydney: AFI Distribution, 1987
Fitzgerald, Ross. 'Eulogy to a Mad Father'. *Sydney Morning Herald* (Spectrum), 7 February 1998
Flanagan, Richard. 'Review of *Romulus, My Father*'. *Sunday Age*, October 1998
Fleishman, Avrom. *Figures of Autobiography: The Language of Self-Writing in Victorian and Modern England*. Berkeley: University of California Press, 1983
Freadman, Richard. *Threads of Life: Autobiography and the Will*. Chicago: Chicago University Press, 2001
———. 'Close Yet Incongruous'. *Australian Book Review* 235 (October 2001): 23–4
———. *Shadow of Doubt: My Father and Myself*. Northcote: Bystander Press, 2003
———. 'Decent and Indecent: Writing my Father's Life'. In John Paul Eakin (ed.), *The Ethics of Life Writing*. Ithaca, NY: Cornwell University Press, 2004
———. 'Recognition and Autobiography' *Partial Answers: The Journal of Literature and the History of Ideas* 3.1 (Winter 2005): 133–61
Freadman, Richard and Seamus Miller. *Re-thinking Theory*. Cambridge: Cambridge University Press, 1992
Gaita, Raimond. 'Romulus Gaita: Turnings of Attention'. *Quadrant* 40.7/8 (July–August 1996): 22–5
———. *Romulus, My Father*. Melbourne: Text Publishing, 1998
———. '*Romulus, My Father*: A Reply'. *Critical Review* 41 (2001): 54–66. Online: http://search.informit.com.au.ezproxy1.library.usyd.edu.au/fullText;dn=200207173;res=APAFT> (accessed 20 April 2008).
———. '*Romulus, My Father*: From Book to Screenplay to Film'. In Nick Drake, *Romulus, My Father: Screenplay*. Sydney: Currency Press, 2007
———. *After Romulus*. Melbourne: Text Publishing, 2011
Garner, Helen. 'From Frogmore, Victoria'. In Drusilla Modejeska (ed.), *Best Australian Essays 2007*. Melbourne: Black Inc., 2007: 17–25

Geering, R. G. 'Hal Porter's Autobiography'. *Southerly* 36.2 (1976): 123–33
Giffin, Michael. 'Freedom and Necessity in the Culture of Interpretation'. *Literature and Theology* 9.3 (September 1995): 307–20. Online: http://litthe.oxfordjournals.org.ezproxy1.library.usyd.edu.au/content/9/3/307.full.pdf+html (accessed 15 October 2007)
Gilmore, Leigh. *The Limits of Autobiography: Trauma and Testimony*. Ithaca, NY: Cornell University Press, 2001
Goldsworthy, Peter. 'The Watcher with the Cast-Iron Alibi'. *Quadrant* 45.7/8 (July–August 2001): 76–9
Gosse, Edmund. *Father and Son: A Study of Two Temperaments*, ed. James Hepburn. London: Oxford University Press, 1974
———. *Father and Son: A Study of Two Temperaments*, ed. Michael Newton. Oxford: Oxford University Press, 2004
Gosse, Fayette. *William Gosse Hay*. Melbourne: Landsdowne Press, 1965
———. *The Gosses: An Anglo-Australian Family*. Canberra: Brian Clouston, 1981
Gray, Robert. (Untitled) in *Meanjin* 39.4 (Summer 1980): 520
———. *Skylight*. Sydney: Angus & Robinson, 1984
———. 'A Smile as Bleak as Moonlight'. *Sydney Review*, November 1991
———. 'Family Stories: The Problem for the Biographer'. *Sydney Papers* (Autumn 1994): 20–29
———. *New and Selected Poems*. Port Melbourne: Heinemann, 1995
———. *The Land I Came Through Last*. Artarmon: Giramondo Publishing, 2008
Grenville, Kate and Sue Woolfe. *Making Stories: How Ten Australian Novels Were Written*. Crows Nest: Allen & Unwin, 1993
Gusdorf, Georges. 'Conditions and Limits of Autobiography'. In James Olney (ed.), *Autobiography: Essays Theoretical and Critical*. Princeton: Princeton University Press, 1980
Hall, Sandra. 'Review of *Romulus, My Father*'. Online: www.smh.com.au/.../film-reviews/romulus-my father/.../1179601639605.html (accessed 18 August 2009)
Harley, Alexis S. C. *The Word of Life: Victorian Apostasy and Autobiography*. PhD thesis. Sydney: Sydney University, 2005
Hart, Kevin. 'Only This: Reading Robert Gray'. *Southerly* 69.2 (2009): 19–49
Hawkins, Anne Hunsaker. *Archetypes of Conversion*. Lewisburg: Bucknell University Press, 1985
Henderson, Heather. *The Victorian Self: Autobiography and Biblical Narrative* Ithaca, NY: Cornell University Press, 1989
Heseltine, Harry P. *The Uncertain Self: Essays in Australian Literature and Criticism*. Melbourne: Oxford University Press, 1986
Hooton, Joy. *Stories of Herself When Young*. Melbourne: Oxford University Press, 1990
Howes, Craig. 'Afterword'. In *The Ethics of Life Writing*. Ithaca, NY: Cornell University Press, 2004: 244–63
Hughes, John. 'Photographs'. In *Mattoid* 41 (1991): 35–40
———. *The Idea of Home*. Sydney: Artarmon: Giramondo Publishing, 2004
———. *Someone Else: Fictional Essays*. Artarmon: Giramondo Publishing, 2007
———. 'The Book of Libraries'. In *HEAT* 18 (2008): 55–75
———. *The Remnants*. Unpublished manuscript, 2009 (quoted with the author's permission)
Hustvedt, Siri. 'My Father Myself'. *Granta* 104 (2008): 56–75
Johnson, Barbara. *A World of Difference*. Baltimore: Johns Hopkins University Press, 1987

Johnson, Edgar. *One Mighty Torrent: The Drama of Biography*. New York: Macmillan, 1955
Johnson, William. *The Earlier Poems of William Wordsworth*. London: Edward Moxon, 1857
Johnstone, Richard. 'Cults of the Past'. *Australian Book Review* 266 (November 2004): 31–2
Kekes, John. *Moral Tradition and Individuality*. Princeton: Princeton University Press, 1989
Kimmel, Michael S. 'Masculinity as Homophobia: Fear, Shame and Silence in the Construction of Gender Identity'. In Harry Broad and Michael Kaufman (eds), *Theorizing Masculinities*. Thousand Oaks: Sage Publications, 1994: 119–41
Kinsella, John. 'Why I Didn't Play Australian Rules Football'. *Overland* 166 (2002): 21–4
Lamb, Karen. *Peter Carey: The Genesis of Fame*. Pymble: HarperCollins, 1992
Lehmann, Geoffrey and Robert Gray. *The Younger Australian Poets*. Sydney: Hale and Iremonger, 1983
Lejeune, Philippe. *On Autobiography*. Minneapolis: University of Minnesota Press, 1989
Lilley, Merv. *Gatton Man*. Ringwood: McPhee Gribble, 1994
Lindemann, Hilde. 'Review of *Vulnerable Subjects*'. *Literature and Medicine* 23.2 (2004): 372–4. Online: http://muse.jhu.edu.ezproxy1.library.usyd.edu.au/journals/literature_and_medicine/v023/23.2lindemann.html (accessed 24 May 2007)
Loraux, Nicole. *The Invention of Athens*. Cambridge, MA: Harvard University Press, 1996
Lord, Mary (ed.) *Hal Porter*. St Lucia: University of Queensland Press, 1980
———. *Hal Porter: Man of Many Parts*. Sydney: Random House, 1993
Lowell, Robert. *Day By Day*. London: Faber & Faber, 1978
Machann, Clinton. *The Genre of Autobiography in Victorian Literature*. Michigan: University of Michigan Press, 1994
McCooey, David. *Artful Histories: Modern Australian Autobiography*. Cambridge: University of Cambridge Press, 1996
———. 'Going Public: A Decade of Australian Autobiography'. *Australian Book Review* 281 (May 2006): 25–31.
McLaren, Greg. 'Sounds of Silence'. *Meanjin* 64.3 (2005): 91–6
———. *Translations Under the Trees: Australian Poets' Integration of Buddhist Ideas and Images*. PhD thesis. Sydney: Sydney University, 2005
Malone, Cynthia Northcutt. 'The Struggle of *Father and Son*: Edmund Gosse's Polemical Autobiography'. *a/b: Auto/biography Studies* 8.1 (1993): 16–32
Malouf, David. *12 Edmondstone Street*. Ringwood: Penguin, 1986
Manne, Robert. 'Robert Manne's Speech at the Launch of Raimond Gaita's *Romulus, My Father*'. *Australian Book Review* 198 (February/March 1998): 10–11
Mansfield, Stephen. '"Was it Cathartic?": An Interview with Peter Rose'. *Life Writing* 9.1 (2012): 21–33
———. 'Beating Andrew Johns into the Cessnock Hall of Fame: An Interview with John Hughes'. *Antipodes* 26.2 (2012): 98–103
Marcus, Laura. *Auto/biographical Discourses*. Manchester: Manchester University Press, 1994
Marshall, Alan. *I Can Jump Puddles*. Melbourne: F. W. Cheshire, 1955
Miller, Nancy K. 'Representing Others: Gender and the Subjects of Autobiography'. *differences: A Journal of Feminist Cultural Studies* 6.1 (1994): 1–18. Accessed online 25 October 2008 (web address unavailable)
Milliss, Roger. *Serpent's Tooth: An Autobiographical Novel*. Ringwood: Penguin, 1984
Mitchell, Jim. 'Review of *Romulus, My Father*'. Online: www.romulusmyfather.com.au/images/Reviews/arena/Eric Bana Reviews.pdf (accessed 3 March 2009)

Mordue, Mark. 'The Pieces Fit as Failure Succeeds'. *Sydney Morning Herald* (Spectrum), 4–5 December 2004: 9

Murray, James. *The Paradise Tree: An Eccentric Childhood Remembered*. Sydney: Allen & Unwin, 1988

Mycak, Sonia. 'A Model of Multicultural Literary Production: The Ukrainian-Australian Literary Field'. In Sonia Mycak and Amit Sarwal (eds), *Australian Made: A Multicultural Reader*. Sydney: Sydney University Press, 2010.

Newton, Michael 'Introduction'. In Edmund Gosse, *Father and Son*. Oxford: Oxford University Press, 2004

Nicholls, Angus. 'Robert Gray and Robert Adamson – A Dialectical Study of Late Australian Romanticism'. *Antipodes* (December 1997): 103–10

Nicholls, C. J. '"Passage" and "Becoming" in *Rose Boys*, by Peter Rose'. In Charlotte Sturgess (ed.), *The Politics and Poetics of Passage in Canadian and Australian Culture and Fiction*. Nantes: Universite de Nantes, 2006: 159–73

Nicholson, Harold. *The Development of English Biography*. London: Hogarth, 1948

Newman, John Henry. *Parochial and Plains Sermons Vol. 1*. London: Rivingtons 1928

Orel, Harold. *Victorian Literary Critics*. London: Macmillan, 1984

Olubas, Brigitta. 'Truth, Writing and National Belonging in *Romulus, My Father*'. *Australian Humanities Review* 43 (December 2007): 1–12. Online: http://www.australianhumanitiesreview.org/archive/Issue-December-2007/Olubas.html (accessed 22 November 2008)

Parker, Andrew and Eve Kosofsky Sedgwick (eds). *Performativity and Performance*. New York: Routledge: 1995

Parker, David. 'Multiculturalism and Universalism in *Romulus, My Father*'. *Critical Review* 41 (2001): 44–53. Online: http://search.informit.com.au.ezproxy1.library.usyd.edu.au/fullText;dn=200207173;res=APAFT> (accessed 20 April 2008).

———. 'Narratives of Autonomy and Narratives of Relationality in Auto/Biography'. *a/b: Auto/Biography Studies* 19.1/2 (2004): 137–55

———. 'Life Writing as Narrative of the Good: *Father and Son* and the Ethics of Authenticity'. In *The Ethics of Life Writing*. Ithaca, NY: Cornell University Press, 2004: 53–72

———. *The Self in Moral Space*. Ithaca, NY and London: Cornell University Press, 2007

Petersen, Kirsten Holst. 'Gambling on Reality: A Reading of Peter Carey's *Oscar and Lucinda*'. In Giovanna Capone (ed.), *European Perspectives: Contemporary Essays on Australian Literature*. St Lucia: University of Queensland Press, 1991

Peterson, Linda H. *Victorian Autobiography: The Tradition of Self-Interpretation*. New Haven: Yale University Press, 1986

Plato. *Plato's Gorgias*, trans. W. C. Helmbold. New York: The Liberal Arts Press, 1952

Porter, Hal. *The Watcher on the Cast-Iron Balcony*. London: Faber and Faber, 1971

———. *The Extra*. Melbourne: Thomas Nelson, 1975

Porter, Roger J. 'Finding the Father: Autobiography as Bureau of Missing Persons'. *a/b: Auto/Biography Studies* 19.1/2 (2004): 100–117

———. *Bureau of Missing Persons: Writing the Secret Lives of Fathers*. Ithaca, NY and London: Cornell University Press, 2011

Redman, C. Martin. 'Sons Writing Fathers in Auto/ Biography'. *a/b Auto/Biography Studies* 19.1/2 (Summer and Winter 2004): 129–36

Riemer, A. P. 'Stanzas Missing in a Moving Portrait of a Fine Poet'. *Sydney Morning Herald*, 6–7 September 2008: 28–9

Rigg, Julie. 'Review of Romulus, My father' 'Movietime', ABC Radio National, 1 June 2007. Online: www.romulusmyfather.com.au/images/Reviews/arena/Eric Bana Reviews.pdf (accessed 3 March 2009)
Roach, Vicki. 'Review of Romulus, My Father' *The Advertiser*, 2 June 2007: 21. Online: www.romulusmyfather.com.au/images/Reviews/arena/Eric Bana Reviews.pdf (accessed 4 March 2009)
Rogers, Daniel. *Naaman the Syrian his Disease and Cure*. London: Th. Harper for Philip Nevil, 1642
Rollins, Brooke. 'The Ethics of Epideitic Rhetoric: Addressing the Problem of Presence though Derrida's Funeral Orations'. *Rhetoric Society Quarterly* 35.1 (Winter 2005): 5–23
Rose, Peter. *The House of Vitriol*. Sydney: Picador, 1990
———. *Rose Boys*. Crows Nest: Allen & Unwin, 2001
———. 'The Consolations of Biography'. *Eureka Street*, January–February 2003: 28–31
———. 'The Disappointed Man'. *Australian Book Review* 257 (December 2003/January 2004): 46–7
———. *Rattus, Rattus: New and Selected Poems*. Cambridge: Salt Publishing, 2005
———. 'Learning to Surf: A Dream Manual'. *Antipodes* 20.1 (June 2006): 71
———. 'Facing North'. *The Weekend Australian*, 5–6 January 2008: 13
Rosenfield, Lawrence W. 'The Practical Celebration of Epideictic'. In Eugene E. White (ed.), *Rhetoric in Transition*. University Park: Pennsylvania State University Press, 1980: 131–55.
Ruth, D. W. 'Exile: A Moving Wound'. *Auto/Biography* 14.30 (2006): 245–66
Rutherford, Jennifer. *The Gauche Intruder: Freud, Lacan and the White Australian Fantasy*. Melbourne: Melbourne University Press, 2000
Rowe, Noel. *Ethical Investigations*. Sydney: Vagabond Press, 2008
Rowe, Penelope and Jessica Rowe. *The Best of Times, The Worst of Times*. Crows Nest: Allen & Unwin, 2005
Rugg, Linda Haverty. *Picturing Ourselves: Photography and Autobiography*. Chicago: University of Chicago Press, 1997
Schwenger, Peter. 'The Masculine Mode'. In Elaine Showalter (ed.), *Speaking of Gender*. New York: Routledge 1989: 101–12
Segal, Alex. 'Speaking with Authority': Biographical and Ethical Reflection in the Work of Raimond Gaita'. *Auto/Biography* 10 (2002): 11–19
———. 'Work, Character and Invisible Virtue: Raimond Gaita's Romulus, My Father in the Context of his Philosophy'. *Meridian* 19.1 (2008): 19–38
Seremetakis, C. Nadia. *The Senses Still*. Chicago: University of Chicago Press, 1996
Singer, Brian (dir.) *Superman Returns*. Burbank: Warner Brothers, 2006
Simpson, David. *Romanticism, Nationalism and the Revolt against Theory*. Chicago: University of Chicago Press, 1993
Sontag, Susan. *On Photography*. London: Allen Lane, 1978
Smith, Bernard. *The Boy Adeodatus*. Ringwood: Penguin, 1984
Smith, Sidonie and Julia Watson. *Reading Autobiography: A Guide for Interpreting Life Narratives*. Minneapolis: University of Minnesota Press, 2001
Stanton, Domna C. *The Female Autograph: Theory and Practice of Autobiography from the Tenth to Twentieth Century*. Chicago: University of Chicago Press, 1984
Strauss, Jennifer. 'Empire, History and Other Grand Illusions in Peter Carey's *Oscar and Lucinda*'. L. Gunner (ed.), *Aspects of Commonwealth Literature*, vol. 1. London: University of London, Institute of Commonwealth Studies, 1990. 97–107

Steinberg, Warren. *Masculinity: Identity, Conflict and Transformation*. Boston: Shambhala, 1993
Stevens, Wallace *Collected Poems* London: Faber & Faber, 1955
Stubbings, Diane. 'Haunting Voice Speaks Out to Us'. *Canberra Times*, 13 September 2008: 13
Symonds, John Addington. *The Memoirs of John Addington Symonds*. London: Hutchinson, 1984
Templeman, Ian. 'Life in its Dailiness'. *Australian Book Review* 309 (March 2009): 33–4
Thomas, Calvin. *Male Matters: Masculinity, Anxiety and the Male Body on the Line*. Illinois: University of Illinois Press, 1996
Thwaite, Ann. *Edmund Gosse: A Literary Landscape*. Oxford: Oxford University Press, 1985
———. *Glimpses of the Wonderful: The Life of Philip Henry Gosse*. London: Faber & Faber, 2002
Tridgell, Susan. 'Communicative Clashes in Australian Culture and Autobiography'. *Auto/Biography* 14.4 (2006): 285–301
Turcotte, Gerry. *Writers in Action: The Writer's Choice Evenings*. Sydney: Currency Press, 1990
Urquhart, Alan. 'Objectivity and Other Stances in the Poetry of Robert Gray'. *Westerly* 33.3 (1988): 45–58
Van den Berg, Jacinta. 'An Interview with Brian Castro'. *Southerly* 69.1 (2009): 127–39
Wallace-Crabbe, Chris. 'Autobiography'. In Laurie Hergenhan, *The Penguin New Literary History of Australia*. Ringwood: Penguin, 1988
———. 'Wrestling with Shadows Cast by a Father'. *The Age*, 10 January 2004: 4
West-Pavlov, Russell. 'Exile as Origin: Definitions of Australian Identities in Malouf's *12 Edmondstone Street*'. *Anglia* 119.1 (2001): 77–92
Wherrett, Peter and Richard Werrett. *Desirelines: An Unusual Family Memoir*. Rydalmere: Hodder Headline, 1998
Williams, Barbara. 'An Interview with Robert Gray'. *Southerly* 50.1 (March 1990): 27–44
Williamson, Geordie. 'Pastoral Sympathy of a Son'. *Weekend Australian*, 20–21 September 2008: 10–11
Windsor, Gerard. *Family Lore*. Port Melbourne: William Heinemann, 1990

INDEX

12 Edmondstone Street: *see* Malouf, David

A

Ackerley J. A. 6, 89, 130
Adamson, Robert 162–3, 165, 181, 184, 188
After Romulus; *see* Gaita, Raimond
Augustine, Saint 27, 45–6, 98

B

baby boomer generation 11n7, 197
Beckett, Samuel 150
Between Stations: *see* Boey, Kim Cheng
biblical typology 22, 25, 27
Boey, Kim Cheng 193–4
Boy Adeodatus, The: *see* Smith, Bernard
Bunyan, John 22

C

Calvino, Italo 141, 154–5
Carey, Peter 30, 34–8, 56
Christianity 29–30, 52, 174
Coetzee, J. M. 193–4
Colmer, John 40, 45
Confessions: *see* Augustine, Saint
Connell, R. W. 7, 143
conversion narratives 22, 44–6, 54–5, 173–9; *see also* deconversion narratives
Couser, G. Thomas: and patriography 5, 90, 104, 133, 193, 196–7; *Vulnerable Subjects* 10, 133
Cowen, Zelman 94, 100–102, 108

D

Dalziell, Rosamund 45, 51

deconversion narratives 12, 19, 23, 44, 46, 52–3, 173–9; *see also* conversion narratives
de Man, Paul 132–3
Derrida, Jacques 50, 122, 137
Dostoyevsky, Fyodor 150–51, 193
Dow Adams, Timothy 107, 116, 118

E

Eakin, John Paul 3–4, 20–21, 63, 89–90, 101, 110, 193
Edwardianism 21, 26, 52
ethics: and autobiography 9–10, 133, 156, 192–3, 195–6; and *Shadow of Doubt* 92, 95, 105, 110–111; and *Romulus, My Father* 69–70, 74; *see also* Socratic ethics

F

Father and Son: *see* Gosse, Edmund
feminist theory 3–4, 9, 80, 192–3
Freadman, Richard: as critic 9, 120–21, 125, 133, 135; and *Shadow of Doubt* 13, 34, 61–4, 87–112; and The Son's Book of the Father 6, 196, 198; *see also* ethics

G

Gaita, Raimond: and *After Romulus* 34, 65, 73–6, 79–80, 82, 85; and *Romulus, My Father* 11, 61–86, 101, 103, 110–111, 196; *see also* ethics
Gaita, Romulus 64, 74, 83, 87, 93, 97
Gatton Man: *see* Lilley, Merv
Gosse, Edmund 6, 12–13, 17–38, 41–3, 54, 175
Gosse, Fayette 32–3

Gosse, Philip Henry 17, 22, 33, 43
Gray, Robert 11, 13, 142, 158–9, 161–89, 195–6; and Buddhism 178–9; and the Jehovah's Witnesses 175–6, 178, 188

H

Harley, Alexis 18, 25–7, 29–32
Henderson, Heather 22–3, 25, 27
Hooton, Joy 3, 78
Hughes, John 11, 13, 30, 131, 139–60, 196–8

I

I Can Jump Puddles: see Marshall, Alan
Idea of Home, The: see John Hughes
indigenous autobiography 11n7

K

Kinsella, John 124–5

L

Land I Came Through Last, The: see Gray, Robert
Lejeune, Philippe 5, 10, 21, 133
Lilley, Merv 37, 48, 127
Lord, Mary 41–2, 52–5

M

Malouf, David 12, 141, 147, 149, 152–5, 175
Marshall, Alan 12, 42–3
masculinity: 19, 23, 40, 64, 101, 134; Australian 7, 12, 32, 51–5, 124–5, 146–50, 192–3, 198; and autobiography 71–3, 80, 192–3; Gosse and 28–32; hegemonic 7, 52, 138, 143, 166; as performance 13, 29–30, 52, 119–25, 129–31, 140–53, 157–60, 167–70, 186
McLaren, Greg 147, 157, 178–9
McCooey, David 40, 44, 53, 123
Miller, Nancy K. 3, 10
mother in patriography, the: 5, 9, 34, 192–3; in *Father and Son* 31, 34, 55; in *The Watcher on the Cast-Iron Balcony* 39–44, 47, 49–51, 55; in *Romulus, My Father* 65, 67–79; in *The Idea of Home* 140–45, 152–3; in *The Land I Came Through Last* 162–9, 173, 177, 181–2
Murray, Les 163
My Father and Myself: see Ackerley, J. A.

O

Oedipus complex 26, 48, 51
Olubas, Briggitta 68, 77
Oscar and Lucinda: see Cary, Peter

P

Parker, David: and autobiographical theory 4, 9–10; and *Father and Son* 27–8; and *Romulus, My Father* 68–72, 78, 83
patrimonial life narrative 6, 196
Patrimony: see Philip Roth
patriography: Australian examples of 48, 66, 71, 77, 86, 101, 193–4; and the question of genre 5, 90, 118; *Father and Son* as the first example of 20, 24, 30; *see also* Couser, Thomas G.
Peterson, Linda 22, 27
photographs in autobiography 106–7, 116–19, 129, 132, 157, 186
Plymouth Brethren 31, 35, 45, 174
Porter, Hal 7, 12, 19, 29, 39–56, 144, 152, 164
Porter, Roger J. 7, 37, 87, 107, 193
Prelude, The: see Wordsworth, William

R

Redman, C. Martin 5, 8–9, 118, 130, 195
relational autobiography 3, 9, 50
Road to San Giovanni, The: see Calvino, Italo
Romulus, My Father: see Gaita, Raimond
Rose, Bob 43, 116, 119–120, 123, 126–8, 130
Rose Boys: see Rose, Peter
Rose, Peter: as critic 91, 99; in interview 124, 128–37, 193; and *Rose Boys* 6, 11, 13, 31, 115–38, 157–8
Rose, Robert 116, 119, 122–3, 132, 149
Roth, Philip 6, 89, 118
Rowe, Noel 41, 57

S

Segal, Alex 74, 81–2, 85
Shadow of Doubt: see Freadman, Richard

Smith, Bernard 7, 12, 19, 45, 51, 197
Socratic ethics 70, 82, 84, 92–3; *see also* ethics and *Romulus, My Father*
Son's Book of the Father, The 6–7, 18, 78, 89, 195, 198; *see also* Freadman, Richard
speech act theory 30, 132, 137, 142–6
spiritual autobiography 19, 22, 37, 45, 54
Stanton, Domna C. 3, 50
Steinberg, Warren 119, 127
Summertime: *see* Coetzee, J. M.

T

Thwaite, Ann 29–31, 33, 41–3, 56–7
Tolstoy, Leo 78, 150–51

V

Victorianism 18–19, 22–7, 29–30, 37, 189
Vulnerable Subjects: *see* Couser, G. Thomas

W

Watcher on the Cast-Iron Balcony, The: *see* Porter, Hal
Wherrett, Peter and Richard 118, 127
White, Patrick 41, 163–4, 171–3, 182–3, 186–7
Whitlock, Gillian 3, 192
Wordsworth, William 19, 27–8, 32, 52, 56

www.ingramcontent.com/pod-product-compliance
Lightning Source LLC
Chambersburg PA
CBHW021827300426
44114CB00009BA/349